Dear Teachers and Parents,

Welcome to Darakwon's *High Score iBT TOEFL Listening for Junior* series.

Today, many English textbooks focus on the same topics and follow similar study patterns. Students are able to learn basic conversation skills, but too often, that is about it. They are limited because many texts do not allow students the opportunity to take it to the next level. The *High Score iBT TOEFL Listening for Junior* series has been created to change the way students study English. This wonderful series focuses on teaching students English by introducing them to an exciting variety of topics. By studying fascinating subjects and topics, students will become more interested in the English language, enhance their English vocabulary, and broaden their overall knowledge.

The *High Score iBT TOEFL Listening for Junior* series is written as a junior iBT TOEFL textbook. The books in this series cover topics that appear on the actual iBT TOEFL test. The questions in the books are also phrased just like those that students will find on the iBT TOEFL test. This should help familiarize students with the iBT TOEFL test and prepare them for when they take it in the future. By learning as much as they can about the iBT TOEFL test prior to taking it, the students will ensure that they will have some knowledge of many of the topics on the test and will be comfortable with the style of the test and the questions on it. All of these factors should lead to higher scores for the students.

Students will be able to use this series as a kind of stepping-stone for the actual iBT TOEFL test. The lectures and the conversations have been written at a level they will be able to understand and follow. They are also filled with real-world situations and interesting facts and information. I believe that students will find the content stimulating, and it will help them become familiar and comfortable with what to expect on the actual iBT TOEFL test. Furthermore, I hope this series will ignite a passion for the English language, one which will remain with each student for a lifetime.

Henry William Link, VI

Table of CONTENTS

About the TOEFL 4

How to Use This Book 8

Chapter 1 Cave and Rock Art (Focusing on Content Words) 13

Chapter 2 Office Hours (Linking) 29

Chapter 3 Deserts and Extreme Environments
(Focusing on Structure Words) 45

Chapter 4 Service Encounters (Chunking) 61

Chapter 5 Office Hours (Pitch and Intonation) 77

Chapter 6 Infectious Diseases (Signal Words and Phrases) 93

Chapter 7 Photography (Distinguishing Consonants) 109

Chapter 8 Inventions (Listening for Numbers) 125

Actual Test 141

Dictation Exercises 155

About the TOEFL

The TOEFL iBT

TOEFL is the Test of English as a Foreign Language. It measures the test taker's ability in English. Foreign students often need to take the TOEFL to get into an American college or university. For that reason, the TOEFL exam is very important.

The TOEFL iBT is an Internet-based test (iBT). Students take the TOEFL iBT on a computer at one of the test centers.

The TOEFL iBT tests four language skills. These skills are reading, listening, speaking, and writing. There are many different kinds of passages, lectures, conversations, and questions. Many sections combine two or more of these skills. So students must be capable in several English skills to get high scores on the exam.

The Format of the TOEFL iBT

There are four sections on the TOEFL iBT. These sections are Reading, Listening, Speaking, and Writing.

The Reading section has two passages. These passages are around 700 words long with 10 questions per passage. The Reading section of the test takes 35 minutes.

The Listening section has two types of passages. They are lectures and conversations. Each Listening section has 3 lectures. The lectures are 3-5 minutes each with 6 questions per lecture. Each Listening section has 2 conversations. The conversations are 3 minutes each with 5 questions per conversation. The Listening section of the test takes 36 minutes.

The Speaking section has two types of questions. They are independent and integrated questions. There is 1 independent question. The independent question asks about your own ideas, opinions, and experiences. There are 3 integrated questions. The integrated questions consist of conversations, reading passages, lectures, or combinations of them, just as you would see in or out of a classroom. They ask questions based on the reading and listening passages. The Speaking section of the test takes 16 minutes.

The Writing section has two types of questions: 1 integrated task and 1 academic discussion task. The integrated task combines a short reading passage and a short lecture. The test taker must then write an essay about these two. The academic discussion task asks a question about a personal experience or opinion. The test taker must then write an essay about this question. The Writing section of the test takes 29 minutes.

The Test Format

Test Section	Number of Questions	Timing	Score
Reading	• 2 passages, 10 questions each	35 minutes	30
Listening	• 3 lectures, 6 questions each • 2 conversations, 5 questions each	36 minutes	30
Speaking	• 1 independent task • 3 integrated tasks	16 minutes	30
Writing	• 1 integrated task • 1 academic discussion task	29 minutes	30

The Listening Section

There are 8 different kinds of questions in the Listening section. Each question appears a different number of times.

The different kinds of questions are:

1 Gist-Content Questions
These ask about the main idea of the lecture.
There is one of these questions for each lecture.

2 Gist-Purpose Questions
These ask about the reason why the speakers are talking.
There is one of these questions for each conversation.

3 Detail Questions
These ask about the main facts in the lecture or conversation.
There are 0-2 of these questions in each lecture or conversation.

4 Understanding Function of What Is Said Questions
These ask about the reason why the speaker says or mentions something.
There are 0-1 of these questions in each lecture or conversation.

5 Understanding Speaker's Attitude Questions
These ask about the attitude of the speaker.
There are 0-1 of these questions in each lecture or conversation.

About the TOEFL

6 Understanding Organization Questions

These ask about the overall organization of the lecture.

There are 0-1 of these questions in each lecture.

7 Connecting Content Questions

These ask about the understanding of the relationships among ideas in a lecture.

There are 0-1 of these questions in each lecture.

8 Making Inferences Questions

These ask about the conclusion based on information.

There are 0-1 of these questions in each lecture or conversation.

How to Use This Book

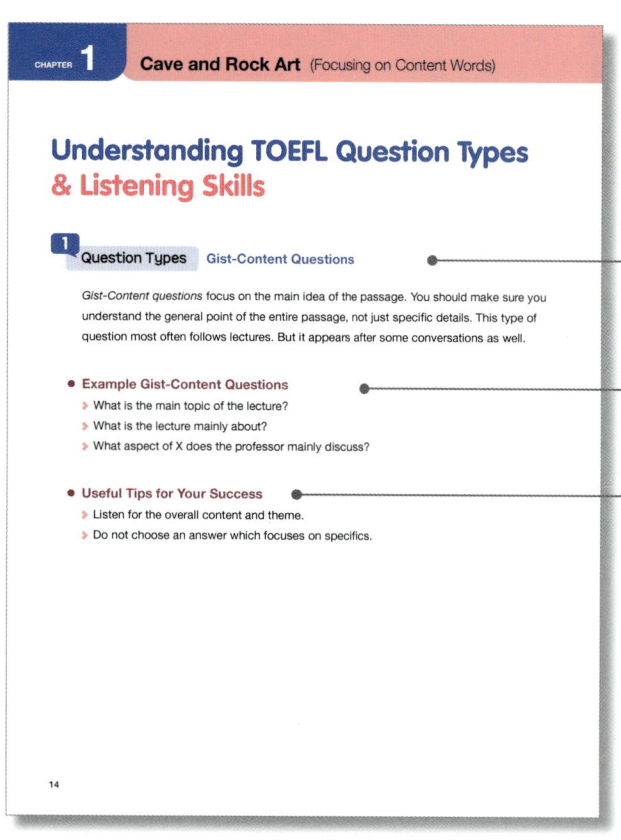

Question Types
This section describes the question or questions covered in the chapter. It provides an explanation of each question and how to try to answer it.

Example Questions
This section shows the different ways that the questions appear on the TOEFL test. Students can learn how to recognize the different types of questions in this section.

Useful Tips for Your Success
This section provides various tips on how to answer the questions properly. It also provides hints on the right and wrong approaches to answering each question.

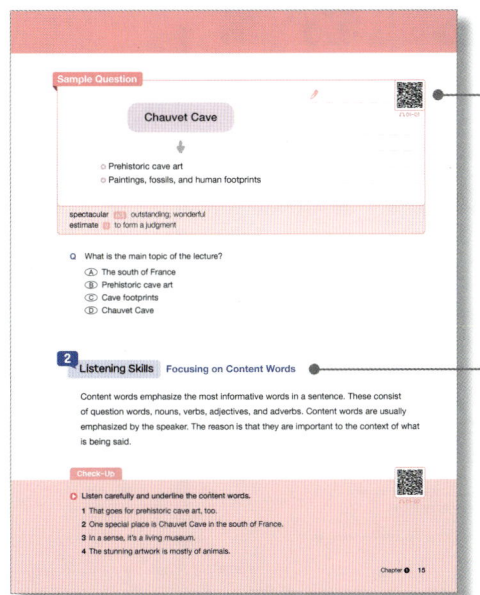

Sample Lecture or Conversation

This is a short 25-30 second lecture or conversation on one of the topics in the unit. It has one TOEFL question and one listening skills question.

Listening Skills

This is an explanation of the listening skill that the chapter covers.

Exercises

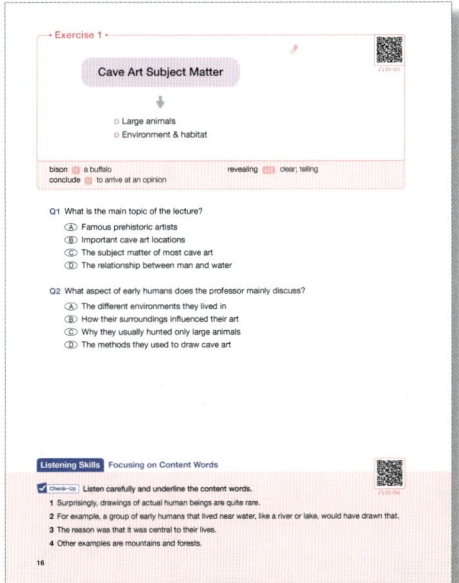

Long Lectures or Conversations

There are four long lectures or conversations. The conversations are between 80 and 100 seconds long. The lectures are 80 to 105 seconds. Each passage is on a topic that concerns the subject of the unit and has two TOEFL questions and one listening skills question.

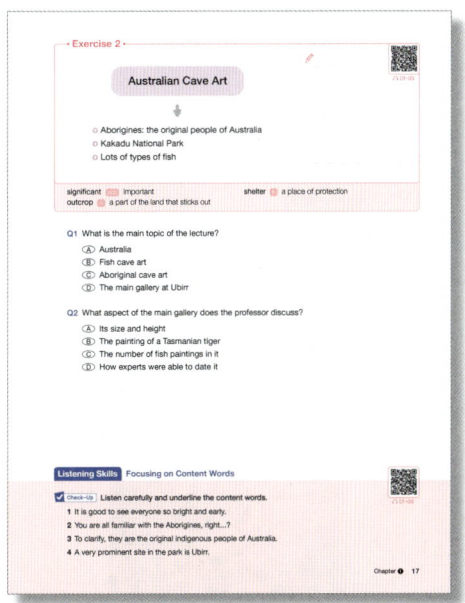

Longer Lectures or Conversations

There are four longer lectures or conversations. The conversations are between 110 and 125 seconds long. The lectures are 110 to 125 seconds. Each passage is on a topic that concerns the subject of the unit and has two TOEFL questions and one listening skills question.

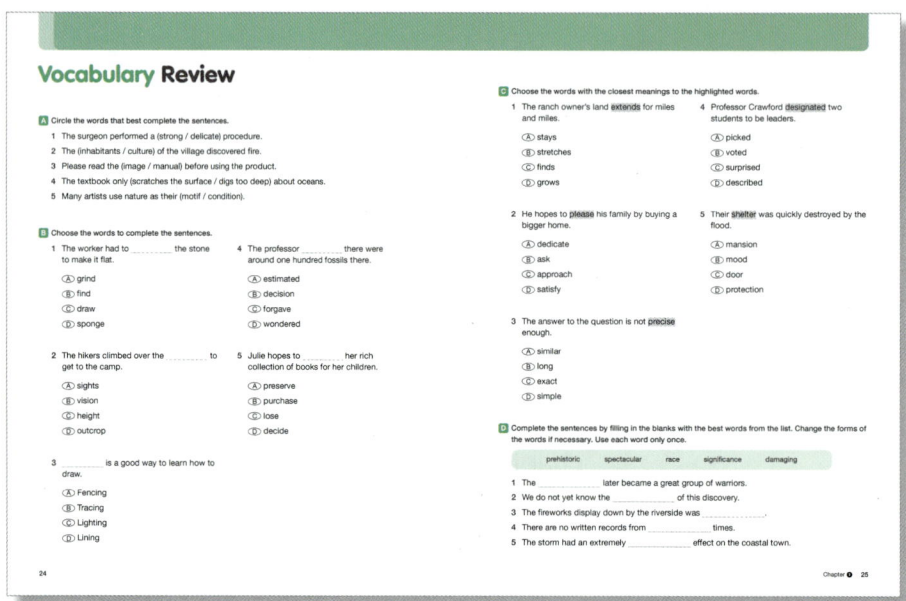

Vocabulary Review

This section provides a comprehensive review of the vocabulary found in the various passages in the unit. Each unit has twenty vocabulary review questions, and all of the answer choices are words that appear in the passages in the unit.

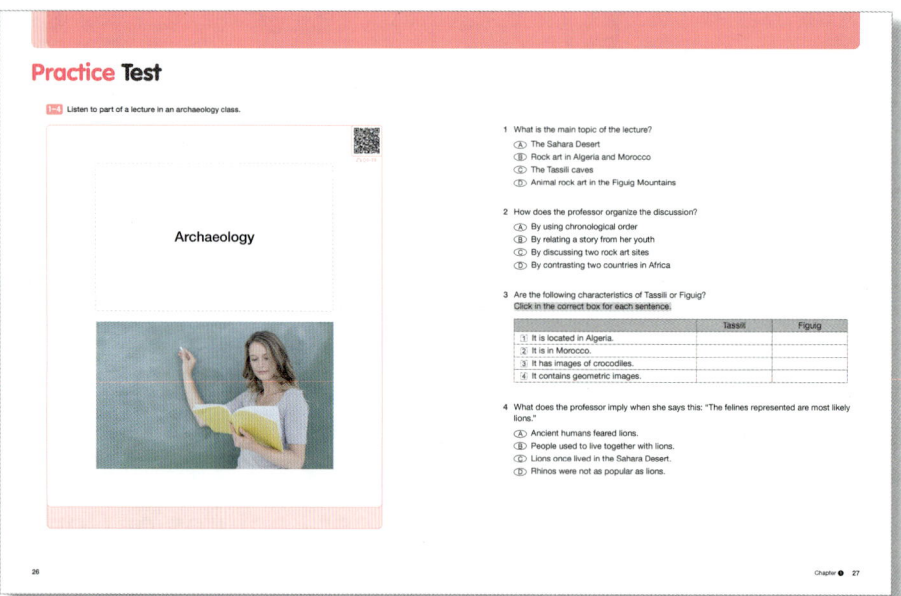

Practice Test

There is one lecture or conversation with 220-250 words. The lecture or conversation is on a topic that concerns the subject of the unit and has three or four TOEFL questions.

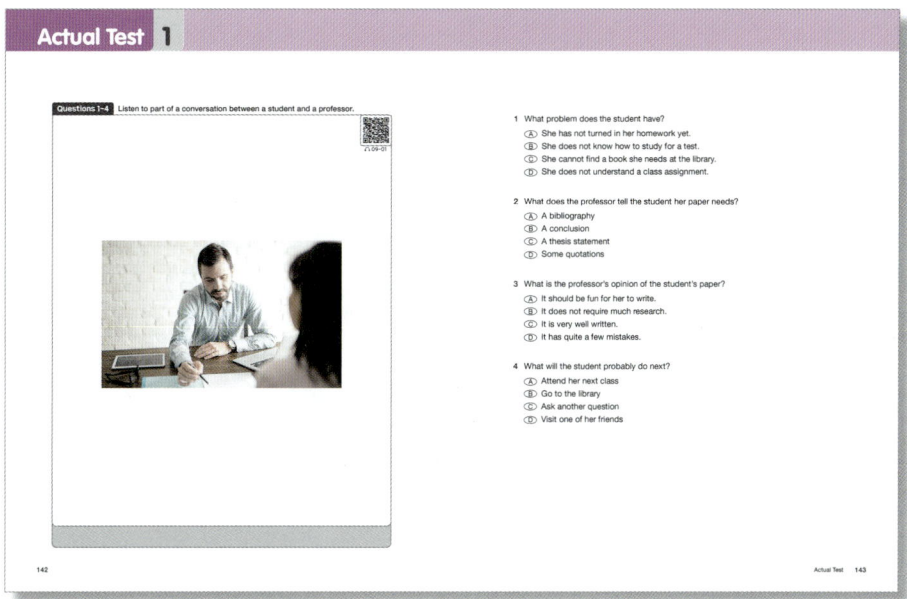

Actual Test

The actual test includes both lectures and conversations. The lectures are between 95 and 125 seconds long and include 5 questions each. The conversations are between 90 and 120 seconds long and include 4 questions each. There are different types of questions for each lecture or conversation. The questions are from all 8 types found in the Listening section. Additionally, the lectures are from topics that appear in the book while the conversations are new office hours or service encounters. These lectures and conversations as well as the questions are shorter versions of a typical TOEFL iBT Listening section.

CHAPTER

01

Cave and Rock Art

(Focusing on Content Words)

CHAPTER 1 **Cave and Rock Art** (Focusing on Content Words)

Understanding TOEFL Question Types & Listening Skills

1 Question Types — Gist-Content Questions

Gist-Content questions focus on the main idea of the passage. You should make sure you understand the general point of the entire passage, not just specific details. This type of question most often follows lectures. But it appears after some conversations as well.

- **Example Gist-Content Questions**
  - What is the main topic of the lecture?
  - What is the lecture mainly about?
  - What aspect of X does the professor mainly discuss?

- **Useful Tips for Your Success**
  - Listen for the overall content and theme.
  - Do not choose an answer which focuses on specifics.

Sample Question

Chauvet Cave
↓
- Prehistoric cave art
- Paintings, fossils, and human footprints

🎧 01-01

spectacular *adj* outstanding; wonderful
estimate *v* to form a judgment

Q What is the main topic of the lecture?
- Ⓐ The south of France
- Ⓑ Prehistoric cave art
- Ⓒ Cave footprints
- Ⓓ Chauvet Cave

2 Listening Skills — Focusing on Content Words

Content words emphasize the most informative words in a sentence. These consist of question words, nouns, verbs, adjectives, and adverbs. Content words are usually emphasized by the speaker. The reason is that they are important to the context of what is being said.

Check-Up

🎧 01-02

▶ Listen carefully and underline the content words.
1. That goes for prehistoric cave art, too.
2. One special place is Chauvet Cave in the south of France.
3. In a sense, it's a living museum.
4. The stunning artwork is mostly of animals.

• **Exercise 1** •

Cave Art Subject Matter

⬇

- Large animals
- Environment & habitat

bison n a buffalo
conclude v to arrive at an opinion
revealing adj clear; telling

Q1 What is the main topic of the lecture?
Ⓐ Famous prehistoric artists
Ⓑ Important cave art locations
Ⓒ The subject matter of most cave art
Ⓓ The relationship between man and water

Q2 What aspect of early humans does the professor mainly discuss?
Ⓐ The different environments they lived in
Ⓑ How their surroundings influenced their art
Ⓒ Why they usually hunted only large animals
Ⓓ The methods they used to draw cave art

Listening Skills Focusing on Content Words

✓ **Check-Up** Listen carefully and underline the content words.

1 Surprisingly, drawings of actual human beings are quite rare.
2 For example, a group of early humans that lived near water, like a river or lake, would have drawn that.
3 The reason was that it was central to their lives.
4 Other examples are mountains and forests.

• **Exercise 2** •

Australian Cave Art

⬇

- Aborigines: the original people of Australia
- Kakadu National Park
- Lots of types of fish

🎧 01-05

significant *adj* important
outcrop *n* a part of the land that sticks out

shelter *n* a place of protection

Q1 What is the main topic of the lecture?
- Ⓐ Australia
- Ⓑ Fish cave art
- Ⓒ Aboriginal cave art
- Ⓓ The main gallery at Ubirr

Q2 What aspect of the main gallery does the professor discuss?
- Ⓐ Its size and height
- Ⓑ The painting of a Tasmanian tiger
- Ⓒ The number of fish paintings in it
- Ⓓ How experts were able to date it

| Listening Skills | Focusing on Content Words |

🎧 01-06

✓ **Check-Up** Listen carefully and underline the content words.

1 It is good to see everyone so bright and early.
2 You are all familiar with the Aborigines, right . . . ?
3 To clarify, they are the original indigenous people of Australia.
4 A very prominent site in the park is Ubirr.

Chapter ❶ 17

Exercise 3

Rock Art: Two Main Types

- Petroglyphs: carvings in rock and stone
- Pictographs: involved the use of pigments

01-07

| scratch | v | to cut or carve | device | n | a tool with a certain purpose |
| grind | v | to reduce to small pieces; to crush | | | |

Q1 What is the lecture mainly about?
- Ⓐ Cave art
- Ⓑ Rock art
- Ⓒ Minerals
- Ⓓ Pictographs

Q2 What aspect of rock art does the professor mainly discuss?
- Ⓐ The two main types
- Ⓑ The differences between rock and stone
- Ⓒ The use of pigments
- Ⓓ The way handprints were made

Listening Skills Focusing on Content Words

01-08

✔  Listen carefully and underline the content words.

1 I'd like to move on to rock art, which is a very broad category.
2 On occasion, petroglyphs were even polished and painted.
3 Pigments are natural colored minerals used for rock art.
4 One of the most common pictographs discovered is the human hand.

• Exercise 4 •

Rock Art of Mexico

↓

- Baja Peninsula
- Paintings of giants
- A great variety

race n a specific group of people
designate v to choose

motif n a subject or theme

Q1 What is the main topic of the lecture?
- Ⓐ World Heritage Sites
- Ⓑ San Francisco
- Ⓒ Mexican rock paintings
- Ⓓ The Baja Peninsula

Q2 What aspect of Sierra de San Francisco does the professor mainly discuss?
- Ⓐ Why its rock art is unique
- Ⓑ Who created the paintings there
- Ⓒ How isolated that region is
- Ⓓ When the art there was done

Listening Skills Focusing on Content Words

✓ Check-Up Listen carefully and underline the content words.

1 Or so the legend goes.
2 Actually, it was designated as a World Heritage Site in the 1990s.
3 That is a huge size for a work of cave art.
4 The paintings at Sierra de San Francisco represent a great variety as well.

• Exercise 5 •

African Rock Art

- Apollo 11 cave
- One of the oldest on the Earth
- Tomb of slabs

scratch the surface *phr* merely to begin   **precise** *adj* correct; exact
slab *n* a broad, thick piece of stone

Q1 What is the lecture mainly about?
 Ⓐ Cave art around the world
 Ⓑ Some of the oldest known rock art
 Ⓒ Tombs in northern Africa
 Ⓓ 150,000-year-old rock art in Africa

Q2 What aspect of Apollo 11 does the professor discuss?
 Ⓐ The subjects of its paintings
 Ⓑ The age and the location of its art
 Ⓒ The discovery of the cave
 Ⓓ The dating process of its work

Listening Skills Focusing on Content Words

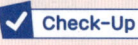 Listen carefully and underline the content words.

1 You can bet that some will never be found.
2 Dating has determined that it is around 30,000 years old.
3 Actually, the rock art exists on large slabs of rock brought from another location in Africa.
4 We'll discuss that some more during the next class.

Exercise 6

The Purpose of Cave Art

↓

- No written language
- Three theories

theory (n) an idea or notion about something
talented (adj) skilled
instruction manual (n) writing that explains how to do something

Q1 What is the main topic of the lecture?
- Ⓐ The way that people made cave art
- Ⓑ The religious importance of cave art
- Ⓒ The most popular types of cave art
- Ⓓ Reasons why people made cave art

Q2 What aspect of the cave at Lascaux does the professor mainly discuss?
- Ⓐ The ages of the paintings there
- Ⓑ The types of images on the walls
- Ⓒ The quality of the cave art there
- Ⓓ The paint used to make images

Listening Skills Focusing on Content Words

✓ **Check-Up** Listen carefully and underline the content words.
1 Why did prehistoric people make cave art?
2 First, some people believe prehistoric people were making art for art's sake.
3 The pictures were painted to make hunters familiar with the animals they would hunt.
4 Perhaps prehistoric people believed they could please their gods by painting pictures.

• **Exercise 7** •

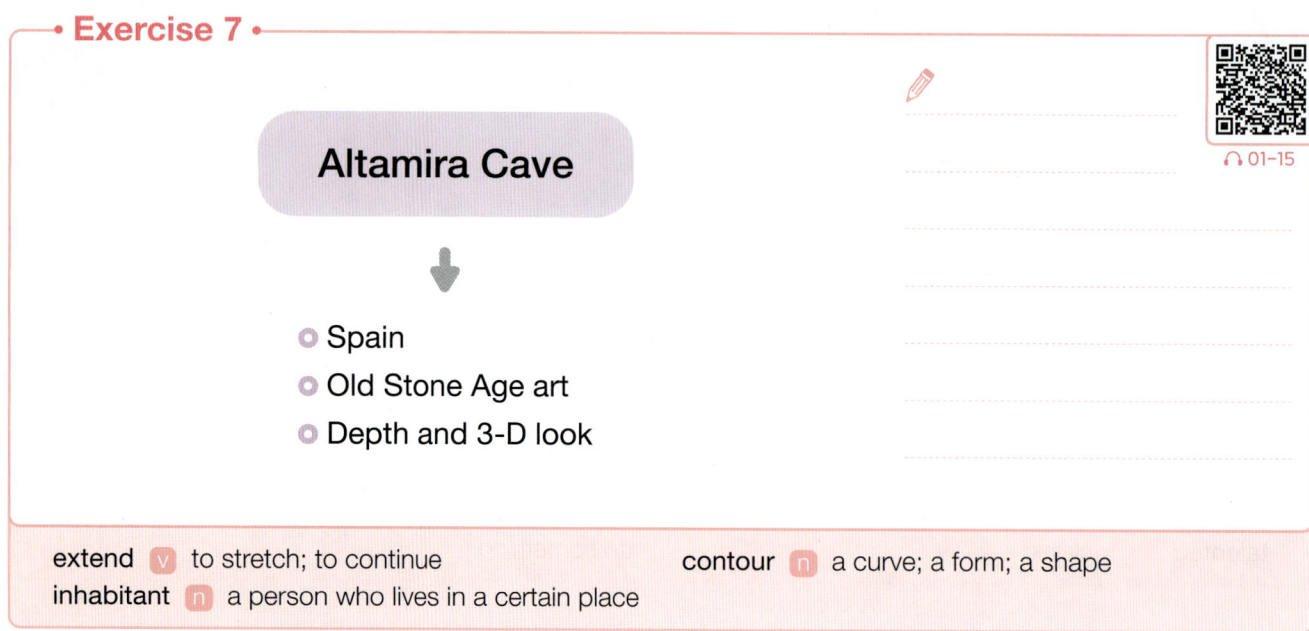

Altamira Cave

- Spain
- Old Stone Age art
- Depth and 3-D look

extend	v	to stretch; to continue
inhabitant	n	a person who lives in a certain place
contour	n	a curve; a form; a shape

Q1 What is the main topic of the lecture?

- Ⓐ The artifacts found in the Altamira cave
- Ⓑ The different ages of cave art in Altamira
- Ⓒ Some techniques used in the cave art of Altamira
- Ⓓ Why Altamira is a minor cave site

Q2 What aspect of the Altamira cave does the professor mainly discuss?

- Ⓐ The depth and the dimension of the artwork
- Ⓑ How it cannot be from the Paleolithic Age
- Ⓒ His trip to the cave when he was young
- Ⓓ The different shapes of the paintings and the sculptures

Listening Skills Focusing on Content Words

✓ Check-Up Listen carefully and underline the content words.

1. The dating of artifacts has established the cave art as being about 16,000 years old.
2. Now, listen closely to this.
3. First, the inhabitants used light and dark colors to add depth to their subjects.
4. They used them to give their pictures a 3-D look.

• **Exercise 8** •

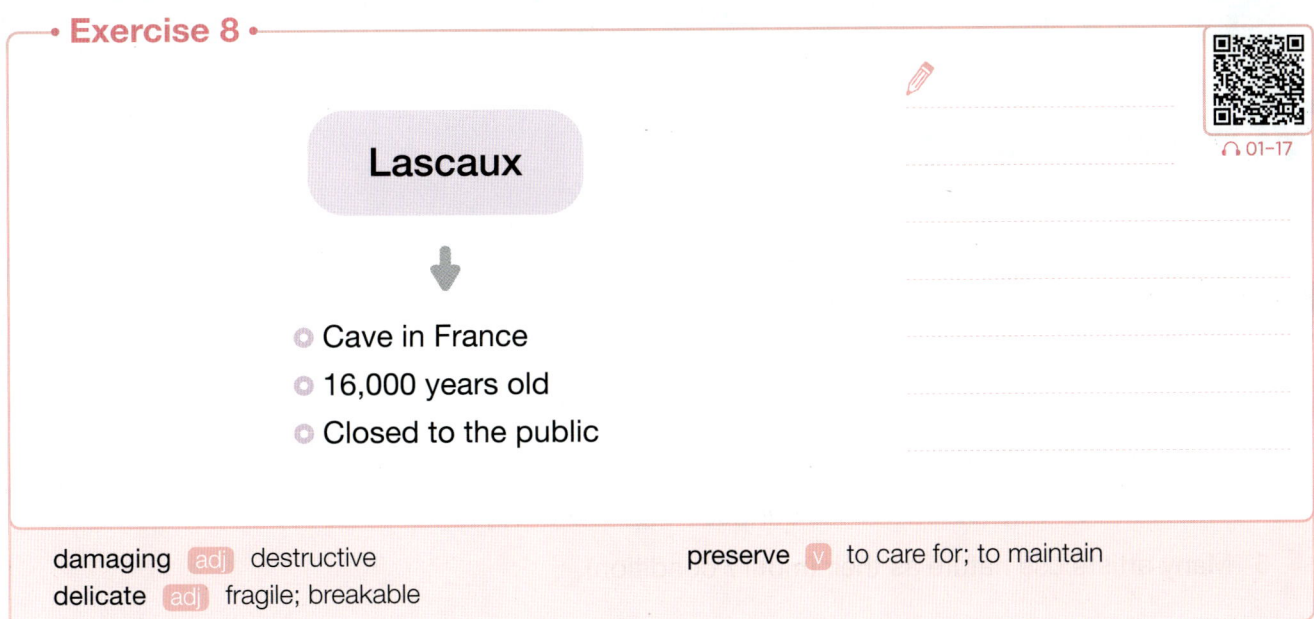

| damaging adj destructive | preserve v to care for; to maintain |
| delicate adj fragile; breakable | |

Q1 What is the main topic of the lecture?

Ⓐ How cave art is vulnerable
Ⓑ The new opening of Lascaux
Ⓒ How teenagers found the cave at Lascaux
Ⓓ Why the French need to protect cave art

Q2 What aspect of the Lascaux cave does the professor mainly discuss?

Ⓐ Why it was closed to the public
Ⓑ What it reveals about ancient Europeans
Ⓒ Why there are not any animal paintings
Ⓓ How carbon dioxide preserves the paintings there

Listening Skills Focusing on Content Words

 Listen carefully and underline the content words.

1 Lascaux is a very famous site.
2 It was actually discovered by some teenagers.
3 The French government closed the cave to the public to preserve the paintings.
4 That came as quite a surprise to my students and me.

Vocabulary Review

A Circle the words that best complete the sentences.

1 The surgeon performed a (strong / **delicate**) procedure.
2 The (**inhabitants** / culture) of the village discovered fire.
3 Please read the (image / **manual**) before using the product.
4 The textbook only (**scratches the surface** / digs too deep) about oceans.
5 Many artists use nature as their (**motif** / condition).

B Choose the words to complete the sentences.

1 The worker had to _____ the stone to make it flat.
   Ⓐ grind
   Ⓑ find
   Ⓒ draw
   Ⓓ sponge

2 The hikers climbed over the _____ to get to the camp.
   Ⓐ sights
   Ⓑ vision
   Ⓒ height
   Ⓓ outcrop

3 _____ is a good way to learn how to draw.
   Ⓐ Fencing
   Ⓑ Tracing
   Ⓒ Lighting
   Ⓓ Lining

4 The professor _____ there were around one hundred fossils there.
   Ⓐ estimated
   Ⓑ decision
   Ⓒ forgave
   Ⓓ wondered

5 Julie hopes to _____ her rich collection of books for her children.
   Ⓐ preserve
   Ⓑ purchase
   Ⓒ lose
   Ⓓ decide

C Choose the words with the closest meanings to the highlighted words.

1 The ranch owner's land extends for miles and miles.
   - Ⓐ stays
   - Ⓑ stretches
   - Ⓒ finds
   - Ⓓ grows

2 He hopes to please his family by buying a bigger home.
   - Ⓐ dedicate
   - Ⓑ ask
   - Ⓒ approach
   - Ⓓ satisfy

3 The answer to the question is not precise enough.
   - Ⓐ similar
   - Ⓑ long
   - Ⓒ exact
   - Ⓓ simple

4 Professor Crawford designated two students to be leaders.
   - Ⓐ picked
   - Ⓑ voted
   - Ⓒ surprised
   - Ⓓ described

5 Their shelter was quickly destroyed by the flood.
   - Ⓐ mansion
   - Ⓑ mood
   - Ⓒ door
   - Ⓓ protection

D Complete the sentences by filling in the blanks with the best words from the list. Change the forms of the words if necessary. Use each word only once.

| prehistoric | spectacular | race | significance | damaging |

1 The _____ later became a great group of warriors.
2 We do not yet know the _____ of this discovery.
3 The fireworks display down by the riverside was _____.
4 There are no written records from _____ times.
5 The storm had an extremely _____ effect on the coastal town.

Practice Test

1-4 Listen to part of a lecture in an archaeology class.

Archaeology

1 What is the main topic of the lecture?

  Ⓐ The Sahara Desert
  Ⓑ Rock art in Algeria and Morocco
  Ⓒ The Tassili caves
  Ⓓ Animal rock art in the Figuig Mountains

2 How does the professor organize the discussion?

  Ⓐ By using chronological order
  Ⓑ By relating a story from her youth
  Ⓒ By discussing two rock art sites
  Ⓓ By contrasting two countries in Africa

3 Are the following characteristics of Tassili or Figuig?
Click in the correct box for each sentence.

	Tassili	Figuig
1 It is located in Algeria.		
2 It is in Morocco.		
3 It has images of crocodiles.		
4 It contains geometric images.		

4 What does the professor imply when she says this: "The felines represented are most likely lions."

  Ⓐ Ancient humans feared lions.
  Ⓑ People used to live together with lions.
  Ⓒ Lions once lived in the Sahara Desert.
  Ⓓ Rhinos were not as popular as lions.

CHAPTER

02

Office Hours

(Linking)

CHAPTER 2   **Office Hours** (Linking)

Understanding TOEFL Question Types & Listening Skills

1 Question Types   Gist–Purpose Questions

Gist-Purpose questions ask about the reasons why people are having the conversation. Listen to the reasons why the student and the other person are meeting. The reason usually appears at the beginning of the conversation.

- **Example Gist-Purpose Questions**
  - Why does the student visit the professor?
  - Why did the professor ask to see the student?
  - Why does the professor explain X?

- **Useful Tips for Your Success**

  - Listen for
    - → the main theme of the conversation.
    - → the problem the student is trying to solve.
  - Don't
    - → focus on the facts of the conversation.
    - → ignore the beginning of the conversation.

Sample Question

Student → Wants to discuss a group project

Professor → Listens to the student's problem

🎧 02-01

detect (v) to sense; to notice
falling behind (phr) not doing enough

Q Why does the student visit the professor?

Ⓐ To tell her that his paper is going well
Ⓑ To ask her a question about a lecture
Ⓒ To speak to her about his group leader
Ⓓ To request extra time for a meeting

2 Listening Skills — Linking

Linking is joining the pronunciation of two words when speaking. This makes the words easier to speak. In addition, the words flow more smoothly. By using linking, you can speak more clearly and fluently. Learn to recognize linking when people use it. This will allow you to understand people much better.

Check-Up

▶ Listen carefully and write the words you hear.

1 _____
2 _____
3 _____
4 _____

🎧 02-02

• **Exercise 1** •

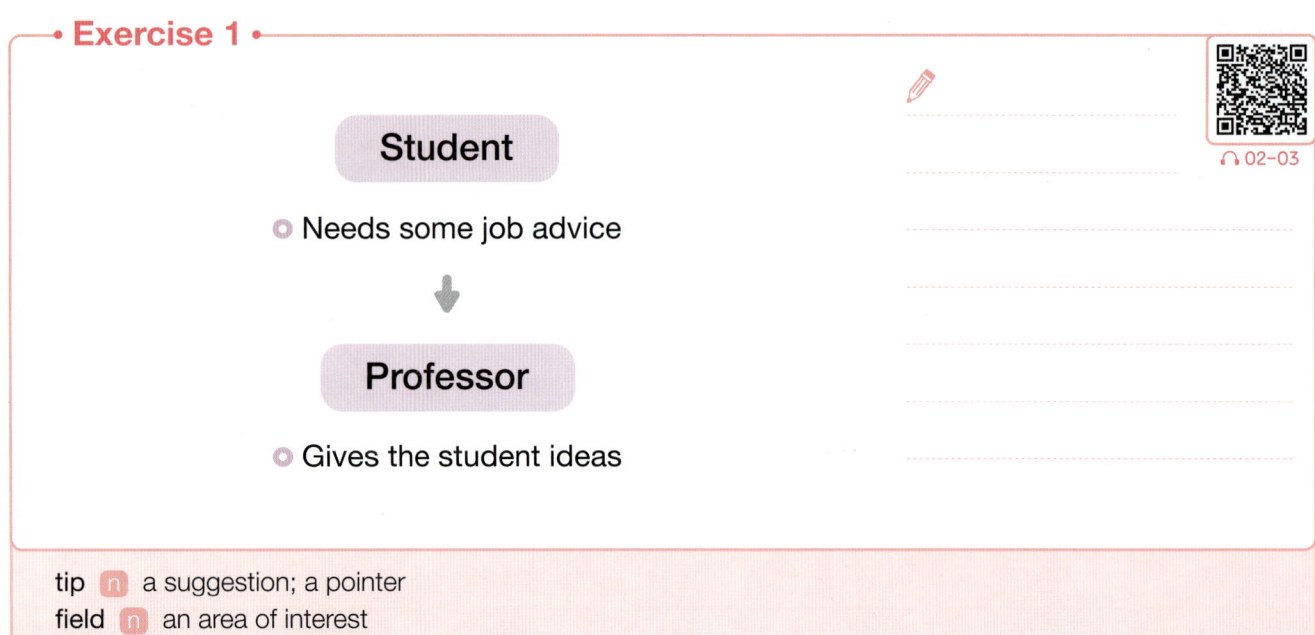

02-03

tip n a suggestion; a pointer
field n an area of interest

Q1 Why does the student visit the professor?

Ⓐ To invite him to graduation
Ⓑ To tell him about an important notice
Ⓒ To ask him about her job search
Ⓓ To seek his advice about a company

Q2 Why does the professor explain the notice on the bulletin board?

Ⓐ To give the student employment ideas
Ⓑ To explain a deadline to the student
Ⓒ To show the student some dates have changed
Ⓓ To point out that notices are not always correct

Listening Skills Linking

✓ **Check-Up** Listen carefully and write the words you hear.

02-04

1
2
3
4

• **Exercise 2** •

Student
- Did not perform well on the midterm

⬇

Professor
- Tells him about her grading policy

policy (n) a rule; a guideline
mark (n) a grade

Q1 Why did the professor ask to see the student?

- Ⓐ To go over a recent assignment
- Ⓑ To talk about an upcoming exam
- Ⓒ To tell him to join a study group
- Ⓓ To go over his midterm exam with him

Q2 Why does the professor explain her grading policy?

- Ⓐ To give the student hope for a high grade
- Ⓑ To say why the student cannot get an A
- Ⓒ To inform the student of the need to attend class
- Ⓓ To note that the student needs to work harder

Listening Skills Linking

✓ **Check-Up** Listen carefully and write the words you hear.

1 _____
2 _____
3 _____
4 _____

• Exercise 3 •

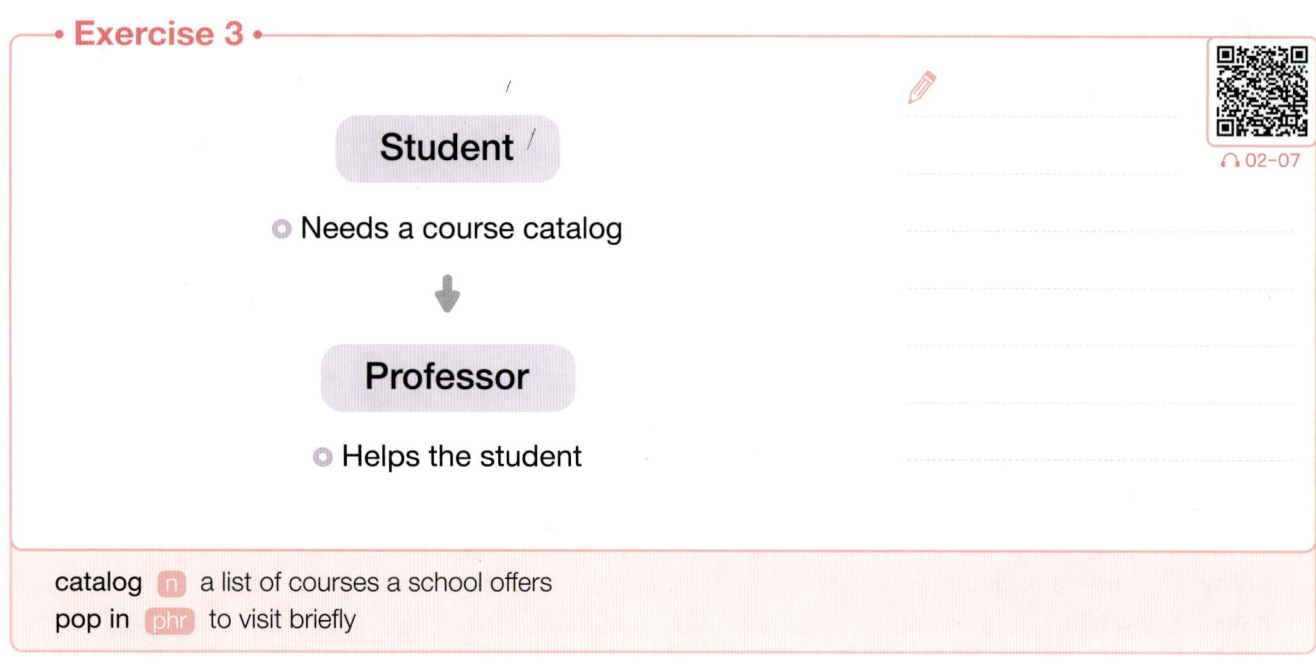

catalog n a list of courses a school offers
pop in phr to visit briefly

Q1 Why does the student visit the professor?
- Ⓐ To try to add his psychology class
- Ⓑ To find out a course number
- Ⓒ To give him a course catalog
- Ⓓ To find out where the Psychology Department is

Q2 Why does the professor explain where the Psychology Department is?
- Ⓐ To help the student locate her class
- Ⓑ To assist the student in dropping her class
- Ⓒ To tell the student where to get a course catalog
- Ⓓ To let the student know where the Registrar's office is

Listening Skills Linking

✓ Check-Up Listen carefully and write the words you hear.

1 _____
2 _____
3 _____
4 _____

• **Exercise 4** •

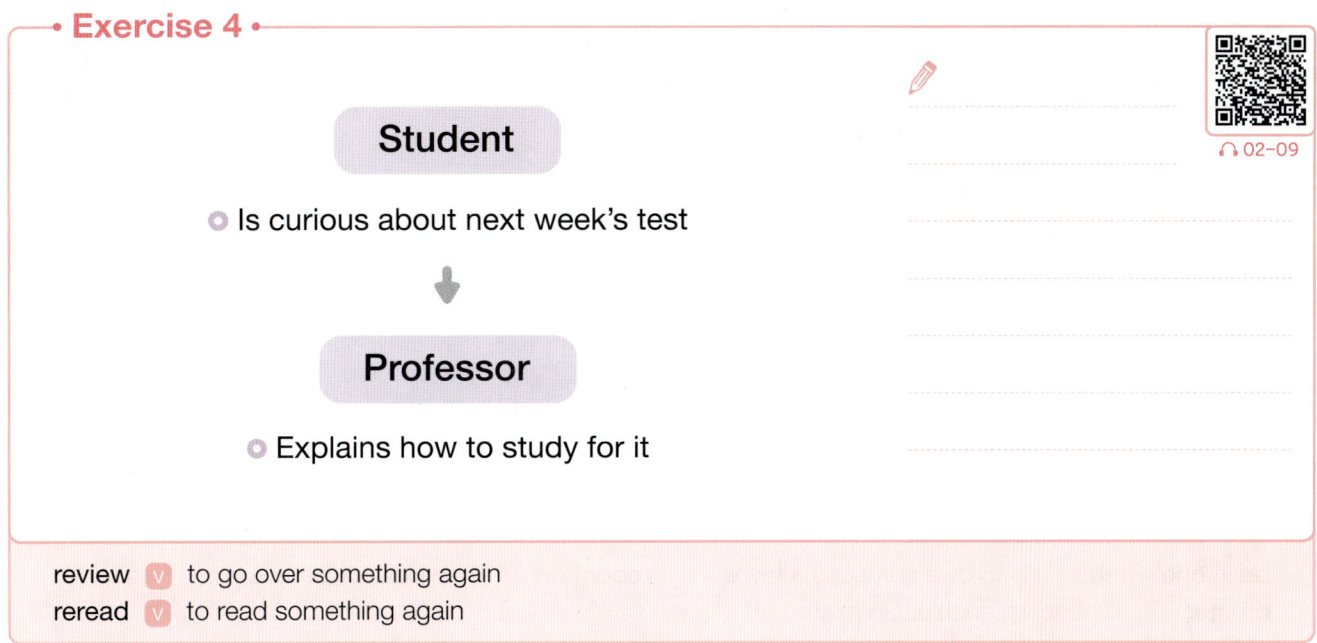

| review | v | to go over something again |
| reread | v | to read something again |

Q1 Why does the student visit the professor?

Ⓐ To ask about an upcoming test
Ⓑ To submit a homework assignment
Ⓒ To talk about the previous class
Ⓓ To discuss her class project

Q2 Why does the professor explain the importance of the book?

Ⓐ To get the student to buy the book
Ⓑ To provide the student with a study tip
Ⓒ To say the book is more important than notes
Ⓓ To make sure the student does her homework

Listening Skills Linking

Check-Up Listen carefully and write the words you hear.

1 _____
2 _____
3 _____
4 _____

• Exercise 5 •

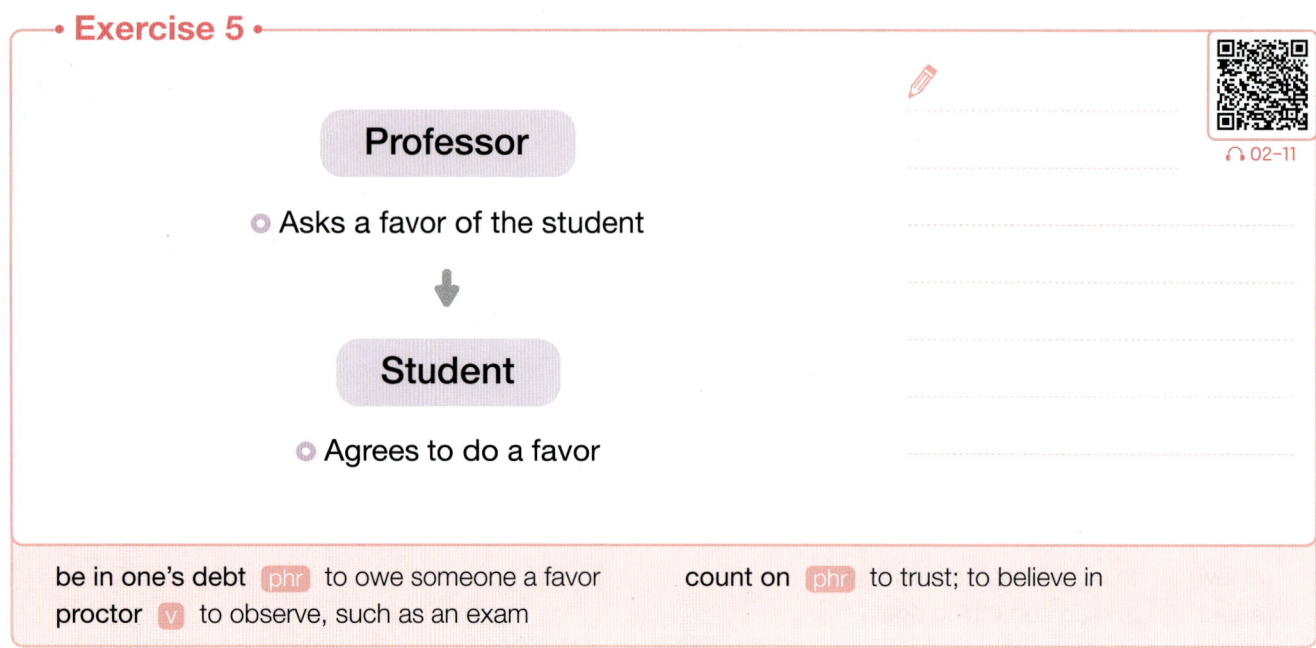

🎧 02-11

| be in one's debt phr to owe someone a favor | count on phr to trust; to believe in |
| proctor v to observe, such as an exam | |

Q1 Why did the professor ask to see the student?
  Ⓐ To see if he can oversee an exam
  Ⓑ To ask him about a chemistry lab report
  Ⓒ To check if he has finished her assignment
  Ⓓ To find out why he did poorly on a quiz

Q2 Why does the professor mention graduate assistants?
  Ⓐ She hopes the student will become one.
  Ⓑ She thinks they are not good proctors.
  Ⓒ She needs to find a substitute for one of them.
  Ⓓ She wants one to help the student study.

Listening Skills | Linking

🎧 02-12

✓ Check-Up Listen carefully and write the words you hear.

1 _____
2 _____
3 _____
4 _____

• **Exercise 6** •

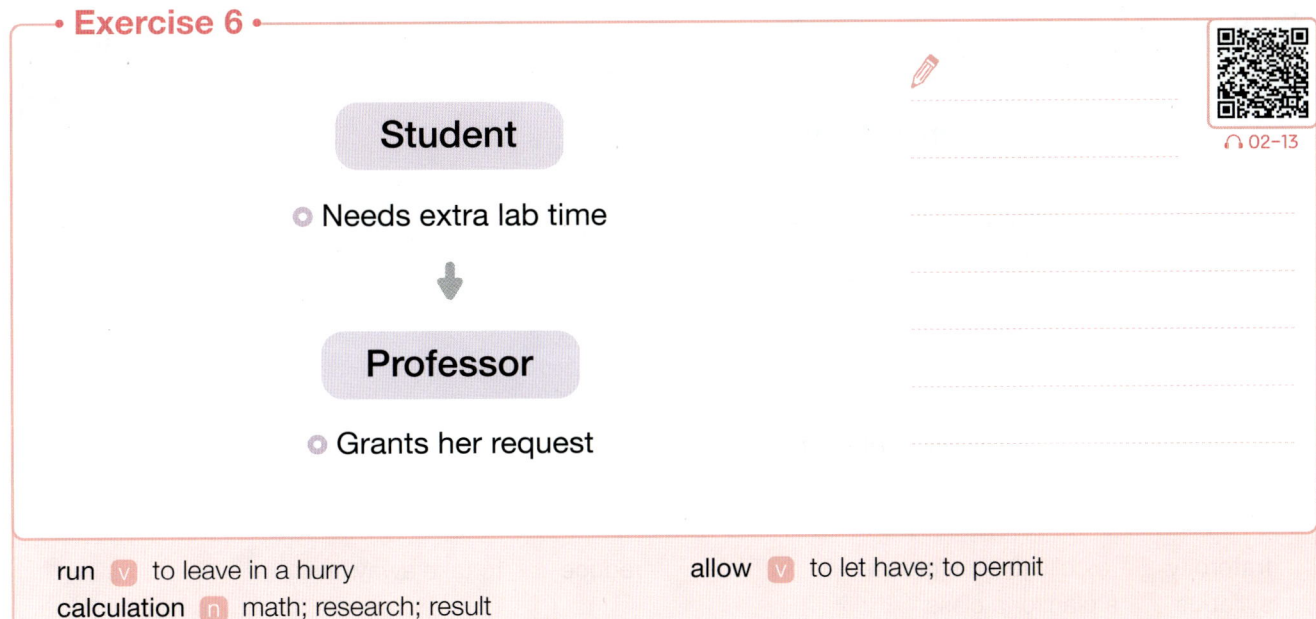

🎧 02-13

run v to leave in a hurry
calculation n math; research; result

allow v to let have; to permit

Q1 Why does the student visit the professor?
- Ⓐ She cannot attend a seminar.
- Ⓑ She needs him to edit an essay.
- Ⓒ She had an accident in the lab.
- Ⓓ She wants additional time in the lab.

Q2 Why does the professor talk about most students?
- Ⓐ They do not miss his classes.
- Ⓑ They do not visit his office.
- Ⓒ They avoid doing extra work.
- Ⓓ They think his class is exciting.

Listening Skills Linking

Check-Up Listen carefully and write the words you hear.

🎧 02-14

1 _____
2 _____
3 _____
4 _____

Exercise 7

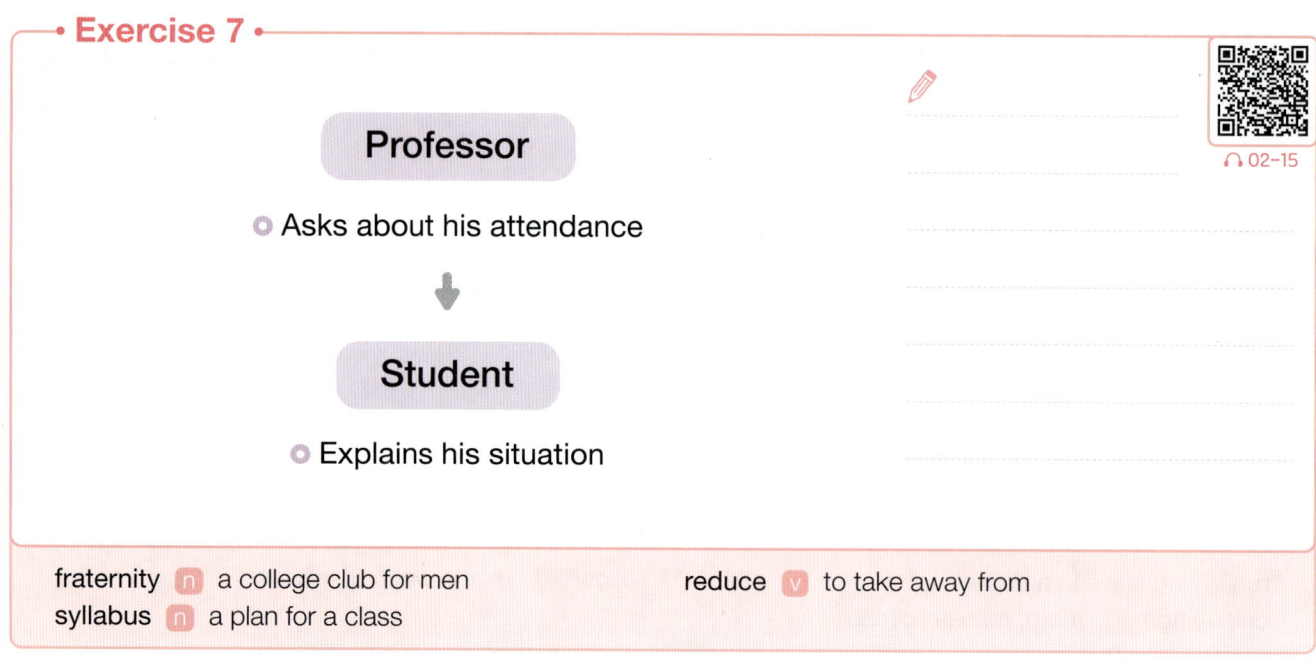

🎧 02-15

fraternity n a college club for men
syllabus n a plan for a class
reduce v to take away from

Q1 Why did the professor ask to see the student?

Ⓐ She wants him to retake an exam.
Ⓑ She wants an explanation for some missed classes.
Ⓒ She needs him to turn in his topic list.
Ⓓ She would like to congratulate him.

Q2 Why does the professor explain her class policy?

Ⓐ To state why she must give the student a C⁺
Ⓑ To make sure the student becomes the class leader
Ⓒ To warn the student about his grade falling
Ⓓ To explain why she cannot accept late papers

Listening Skills | Linking

✓ **Check-Up** Listen carefully and write the words you hear.

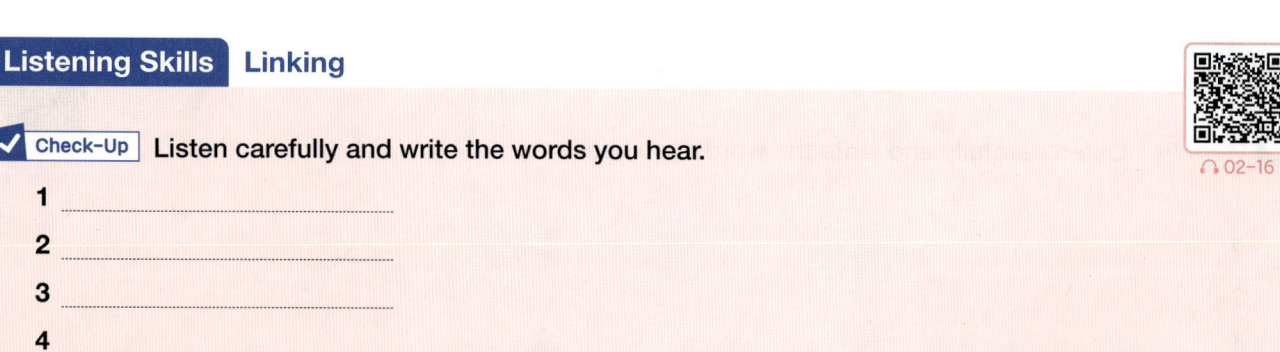

🎧 02-16

1 _____
2 _____
3 _____
4 _____

Exercise 8

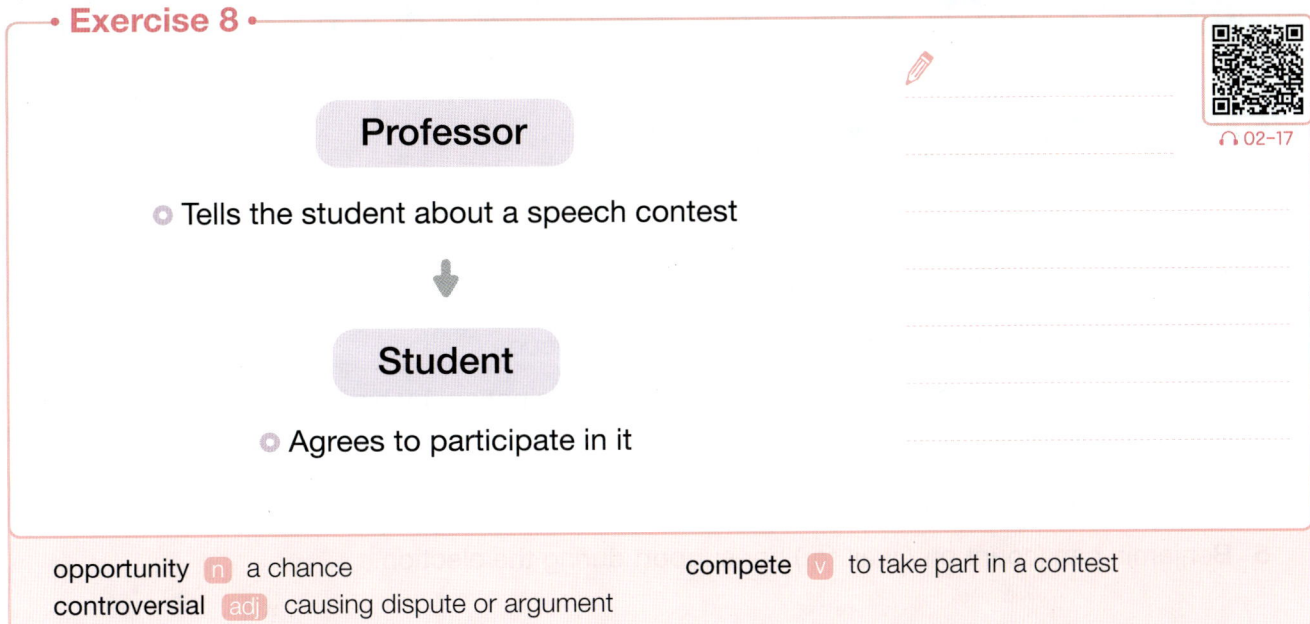

Professor
- Tells the student about a speech contest

↓

Student
- Agrees to participate in it

opportunity [n] a chance
controversial [adj] causing dispute or argument
compete [v] to take part in a contest

02-17

Q1 Why did the professor ask to see the student?
- Ⓐ To discuss a club activity
- Ⓑ To invite him to participate in a contest
- Ⓒ To tell him about an awards ceremony
- Ⓓ To discuss a job opportunity with him

Q2 Why does the professor talk about the topics?
- Ⓐ To point out how simple they are
- Ⓑ To respond to the student's question
- Ⓒ To explain what the student will speak about
- Ⓓ To encourage the student to prepare more

Listening Skills **Linking**

✓ **Check-Up** Listen carefully and write the words you hear.

1 _____
2 _____
3 _____
4 _____

02-18

Vocabulary Review

A Circle the words that best complete the sentences.

1. Her son does not know which (field / custom) to pursue.
2. The professor encourages class (presentation / participation) by his students.
3. The course (catalog / text) lists every class at the school.
4. Can you (suggest / sound) a solution to this problem?
5. Benjamin can (count on / wait for) her support during the election.

B Choose the words to complete the sentences.

1. We have to _____ very fast if we want to catch our flight.
   - A taxi
   - B run
   - C renew
   - D excuse

2. Cathy wants to _____ her weight by ten kilograms.
   - A reduce
   - B believe
   - C forget
   - D capture

3. You need to _____ her to take part in the contest.
   - A refuse
   - B remove
   - C convince
   - D accept

4. The company changed its _____ on employee vacations.
   - A policy
   - B money
   - C behavior
   - D open

5. The instructor always _____ the students to leave early on Fridays.
   - A hates
   - B restricts
   - C allows
   - D discovers

C Choose the words with the closest meanings to the highlighted words.

1 Graduate students sometimes proctor exams.
   - Ⓐ take
   - Ⓑ monitor
   - Ⓒ grade
   - Ⓓ complete

2 He wants to pop in on an old friend in New York.
   - Ⓐ look for
   - Ⓑ visit
   - Ⓒ consider
   - Ⓓ announce

3 They were looking for travel tips on the Internet.
   - Ⓐ advice
   - Ⓑ deals
   - Ⓒ discounts
   - Ⓓ times

4 Vince's calculations were proven correct by the expert.
   - Ⓐ support
   - Ⓑ research
   - Ⓒ trick
   - Ⓓ simplify

5 Fraternities are very popular on many school campuses.
   - Ⓐ Clubs
   - Ⓑ Parties
   - Ⓒ Friendship
   - Ⓓ Celebrities

D Complete the sentences by filling in the blanks with the best words from the list. Change the forms of the words if necessary. Use each word only once.

| review | stage | factor | falling behind | opportunity |

1 He likes to _____ his notes after class every day.
2 She has the _____ to find a good job after she graduates.
3 He is _____ in class because of his part-time job.
4 Please consider all of the _____ before making a decision.
5 Some people get nervous when they have to speak on _____.

Chapter ❷ 41

Practice Test

1-3 Listen to part of a conversation between a student and a professor.

02-19

1. Why does the student visit the professor?
   - Ⓐ To say she cannot attend class
   - Ⓑ To help organize a conference
   - Ⓒ To give the professor a paper
   - Ⓓ To pick up her test

2. What does the professor think of the academic conference?
   - Ⓐ It is a lot of extra work for him.
   - Ⓑ It should have more speakers.
   - Ⓒ It is one of the best in the country.
   - Ⓓ It should be limited to graduate students.

3. What does the professor imply when he says this: "The competition will be very stiff."
   - Ⓐ Not many people know about the conference.
   - Ⓑ It is difficult to have a paper accepted.
   - Ⓒ Last year's competition was more exciting.
   - Ⓓ It is tough for students to write conference papers.

CHAPTER

03

Deserts and Extreme Environments

(Focusing on Structure Words)

CHAPTER 3

Deserts and Extreme Environments
(Focusing on Structure Words)

Understanding TOEFL Question Types & Listening Skills

1 Question Types — Detail Questions

Detail questions test your understanding of details and facts from the passage. They often support the main idea of the listening passage. However, you may be asked about some details which are not related to the main topic.

● **Example Detail Questions**
  ❯ What is true about X?
  ❯ According to the professor, who is X?
  ❯ What is X?

● **Useful Tips for Your Success**
  ❯ Focus on the major points and check your notes to find the right answer.
  ❯ Never choose an answer just because it was mentioned in the conversation or lecture.

Sample Question

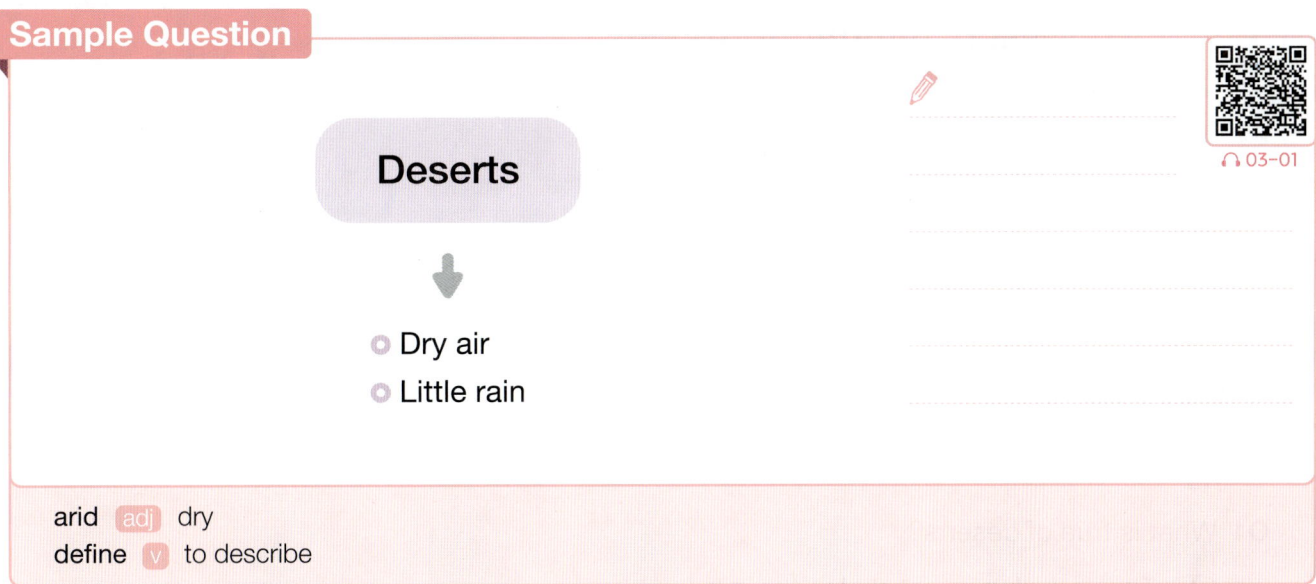

arid adj dry
define v to describe

Q According to the professor, what is the average annual rainfall in most deserts?
  Ⓐ One inch
  Ⓑ Five inches
  Ⓒ Ten inches
  Ⓓ Fifteen inches

2 Listening Skills — Focusing on Structure Words

Structure words are all of the words in a sentence other than the nouns, the verbs, the adjectives, and the adverbs. They are pronouns, prepositions, conjunctions, be-verbs, modal verbs, and articles. They mostly indicate grammatical relations.

Check-Up

▶ Listen carefully and underline the structure words.
1 They are very dry places.
2 Just because an area is arid, does that make it a desert?
3 Scientists have come up with a formula that defines what deserts are.
4 Some areas get more rain than that, but scientists still call them deserts.

Chapter ❸ 47

• **Exercise 1** •

Desert Temperatures

⬇

- Hot and freezing
- Little water in the air

fluctuation n a change; ups and downs
insulate v to prevent the release of heat

Q1 What is true of deserts?
- Ⓐ They are always hot during the evening.
- Ⓑ They experience big temperature swings.
- Ⓒ They cannot have lakes or rivers.
- Ⓓ They have not always existed on the Earth.

Q2 Why do deserts lack insulation?
- Ⓐ They are too warm.
- Ⓑ They have low humidity.
- Ⓒ They have too much sand.
- Ⓓ They gain too little sunlight.

| **Listening Skills** | Focusing on Structure Words |

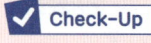 Listen carefully and underline the structure words.

1 We have a lot to go over today.
2 Today, we'll start with the temperatures of most deserts.
3 A desert can get very hot during the day.
4 Water helps block sunshine from reaching the Earth's surface.

48

• Exercise 2 •

The South Pole
⬇
- Coldest environment
- Little sunlight
- High elevation

---

frigid *adj* extremely cold in temperature
altitude *n* a distance up or down from sea level

Q1 Why is the South Pole so cold in winter?
- Ⓐ There is a lot of ice.
- Ⓑ It is always dark there.
- Ⓒ There are high winds.
- Ⓓ It is near the equator.

Q2 What is one reason the South Pole is colder than the North Pole?
- Ⓐ Snow
- Ⓑ Ice
- Ⓒ Tides
- Ⓓ Altitude

Listening Skills Focusing on Structure Words

✓ **Check-Up** Listen carefully and underline the structure words.
1. It is an extremely cold environment.
2. There are a number of reasons for these cold temperatures.
3. During summer, the sun stays low near the horizon.
4. Most of the sunlight is reflected away from the ground.

• **Exercise 3** •

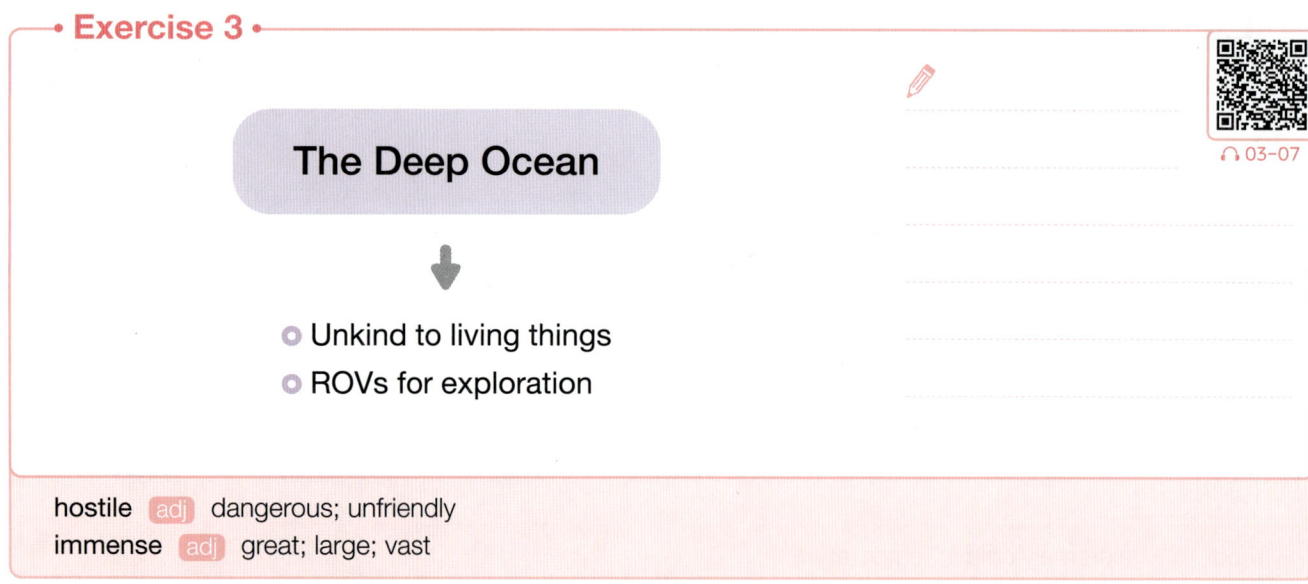

The Deep Ocean
- Unkind to living things
- ROVs for exploration

hostile adj dangerous; unfriendly
immense adj great; large; vast

Q1 Which is NOT a characteristic of the deep ocean?
- Ⓐ High pressure
- Ⓑ Cold temperatures
- Ⓒ Bright light
- Ⓓ Darkness

Q2 What is a reason that few people explore places deep beneath the surface?
- Ⓐ ROVs cannot go too deep underwater.
- Ⓑ It has already been explored very much.
- Ⓒ It is costly to do research there.
- Ⓓ It is too close to the Earth's core.

Listening Skills Focusing on Structure Words

 Listen carefully and underline the structure words.

1 It is one of the most hostile environments to life on the planet.
2 Even with special technology, it's impossible.
3 We are able to explore areas deep beneath the surface.
4 Deep-sea exploration is very expensive.

• **Exercise 4** •

The Atacama Desert

- So dry
- Cold current: so little rain & fog
- Similar to Mars

current n a stream of moving water in an ocean or sea
fog n clouds that are near the ground

Q1 What is the main reason little rain falls in the Atacama Desert?
- Ⓐ The ocean
- Ⓑ The mountains
- Ⓒ The forests
- Ⓓ The sand

Q2 Why has NASA conducted tests in the Atacama Desert?
- Ⓐ Astronauts are preparing to visit the moon.
- Ⓑ The dark sky makes viewing stars easy.
- Ⓒ Conditions there are similar to those on Mars.
- Ⓓ There is no rain to damage scientific instruments.

Listening Skills Focusing on Structure Words

✓ **Check-Up** Listen carefully and underline the structure words.

1 The ocean is the reason so little rain falls there.
2 However, fog is one feature of parts of the desert.
3 Here's something interesting about the desert.
4 NASA, the American space organization, has conducted numerous tests there.

Exercise 5

Yellowstone National Park

⬇

- Volcanic activity
- Magma pool
- Geysers

| hotbed [n] an area of fast growth | crater [n] a large hole; a cavity |
| erupt [v] to explode, as in a volcano | |

Q1 What is Yellowstone National Park on top of?
- Ⓐ A natural spring
- Ⓑ An ancient civilization
- Ⓒ A supervolcano
- Ⓓ A dry lake

Q2 What is true of geysers?
- Ⓐ They contain lava.
- Ⓑ They hold hot water.
- Ⓒ They are not dangerous.
- Ⓓ They were once volcanoes.

Listening Skills | Focusing on Structure Words

✓ **Check-Up** Listen carefully and underline the structure words.

1 First of all, much of the region is full of volcanic activity.
2 It hasn't erupted in more than 600,000 years.
3 Below the surface are hot gases and an enormous magma pool.
4 Some of the gases are highly toxic.

• **Exercise 6** •

The Dangers of Deserts

- Human body sweats
- Lack of fluids
- Dehydration / heatstroke / hypothermia

sweat v to lose body fluids
dehydration n the abnormal loss of fluids by the body
exposure n an uncovering

Q1 What is a big threat in hot deserts?
- Ⓐ Too much humidity
- Ⓑ Dehydration
- Ⓒ Hypothermia
- Ⓓ Sweating

Q2 According to the professor, what is a danger to humans in cold deserts?
- Ⓐ Frostbite
- Ⓑ Snow blindness
- Ⓒ Avalanches
- Ⓓ Hypothermia

Listening Skills | Focusing on Structure Words

✓ **Check-Up** Listen carefully and underline the structure words.
1. Let's begin with hot deserts.
2. Our bodies will sweat a lot in an attempt to keep our body temperature down.
3. In cold deserts, dehydration can be a factor.
4. This happens when the body cannot retain heat.

• **Exercise 7** •

The Tibetan Plateau

⬇

○ Extreme land
○ Cold and dry
○ Tiny population

plateau n a raised, flat surface of land	**remote** adj faraway; distant
inhospitable adj difficult; harsh	

Q1 Where is Tibet?

    Ⓐ In India
    Ⓑ In Nepal
    Ⓒ In Russia
    Ⓓ In China

Q2 What is true of Tibet?

    Ⓐ Few people live in its northwest region.
    Ⓑ Many groups of people live in the area.
    Ⓒ There are no grasslands in it.
    Ⓓ It has more land than Greenland.

Listening Skills Focusing on Structure Words

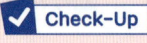 **Check-Up** Listen carefully and underline the structure words.

1 Actually, the southern region isn't too bad.
2 In the northwest part of the plateau is Changtang Province.
3 Another reason, as you can guess, is the temperature.
4 In winter, it is absolutely frigid as the temperature averages about forty degrees below zero Celsius.

• **Exercise 8** •

🎧 03-17

The Sahara Desert

⬇

○ The largest desert
○ Had water during an ice age
○ Rare but heavy rain

shape	n	a form; a condition
monsoon	n	a seasonal wind that often brings heavy rain
torrential	adj	heavy; strong

Q1 What is true about the Sahara Desert?
- Ⓐ It is in southern Africa.
- Ⓑ It is the world's largest hot desert.
- Ⓒ It never rains there.
- Ⓓ It has several rivers flowing in it.

Q2 What area of the Sahara receives the most rainfall?
- Ⓐ The south
- Ⓑ The east
- Ⓒ The west
- Ⓓ The north

Listening Skills Focusing on Structure Words

🎧 03-18

✓ **Check-Up** Listen carefully and underline the structure words.

1 It occupies most of the entire region of northern Africa.
2 However, the Sahara hasn't always been in bad shape.
3 Experts believe that the monsoons eventually shifted to the southern Sahara.
4 The southern region receives a bit more rainfall.

Chapter ❸ 55

Vocabulary Review

A Circle the words that best complete the sentences.

1. The city was built in the (crater / tube) of an extinct volcano.
2. Athletes usually (rest / sweat) a lot, which keeps the body cool.
3. The weather in the Himalayas is often (inhospitable / numerous).
4. Susan is in great (shape / feeling) because she exercises.
5. Too much (experience / exposure) to the sun can be harmful.

B Choose the words to complete the sentences.

1. The southern part of the United States is a football _____.
   - Ⓐ maniac
   - Ⓑ hotbed
   - Ⓒ tournament
   - Ⓓ team

2. The ocean _____ pushed the boat far away from shore.
   - Ⓐ organization
   - Ⓑ condition
   - Ⓒ current
   - Ⓓ rain

3. The size of the new eight-level cruise ship is _____.
   - Ⓐ immense
   - Ⓑ taken
   - Ⓒ risk
   - Ⓓ strength

4. The _____ family stayed at the old hotel in the valley.
   - Ⓐ checked
   - Ⓑ up front
   - Ⓒ entire
   - Ⓓ power

5. The _____ rains caused a lot of trouble for the farmers.
   - Ⓐ left
   - Ⓑ size
   - Ⓒ torrential
   - Ⓓ fake

C Choose the words with the closest meanings to the highlighted words.

1. The volcano could erupt at any moment.
   - Ⓐ explode
   - Ⓑ shake
   - Ⓒ roar
   - Ⓓ threaten

2. Dylan tried to define the idea in his own words.
   - Ⓐ share
   - Ⓑ write
   - Ⓒ explain
   - Ⓓ correct

3. The air in Arizona is extremely arid.
   - Ⓐ dry
   - Ⓑ hot
   - Ⓒ windy
   - Ⓓ heavy

4. The scientist hopes to conduct some tests in his laboratory.
   - Ⓐ confirm
   - Ⓑ consider
   - Ⓒ run
   - Ⓓ examine

5. The stock market experienced great fluctuations that day.
   - Ⓐ gains
   - Ⓑ profits
   - Ⓒ protections
   - Ⓓ changes

D Complete the sentences by filling in the blanks with the best words from the list. Change the forms of the words if necessary. Use each word only once.

> insulate   rover   frigid   hostile   fog

1. The thick _____ made it hard for drivers to see anything.
2. Sleeping bags help keep campers _____ from the cold.
3. An operator uses a remote control to drive the Mars _____.
4. The soldiers are _____, so people should avoid them.
5. The _____ temperatures in August were not normal at all.

Chapter ❸   57

Practice Test

1-4 Listen to part of a lecture in a geology class.

1   What is the lecture mainly about?
    - Ⓐ Fossils in the Petrified Forest
    - Ⓑ The Painted Desert
    - Ⓒ Different desert mountains
    - Ⓓ Animal life in the Petrified Forest

2   What can be inferred about the Painted Desert?
    - Ⓐ It is larger than the Petrified Forest.
    - Ⓑ It was once a large inland ocean.
    - Ⓒ It is one of the coolest places on the Earth.
    - Ⓓ It receives more rain than typical deserts.

3   Why does the professor mention skeletons?
    - Ⓐ To prove that dinosaurs once roamed the Petrified Forest
    - Ⓑ To note the deadly heat in the Petrified Forest
    - Ⓒ To compare the reptiles living in the Painted Desert
    - Ⓓ To explain the hunting techniques of animals in the Painted Desert

4   Are the following characteristics of the Painted Desert or the Petrified Forest?
    Click in the correct box for each sentence.

	Painted Desert	Petrified Forest
1 It is full of colorful mountains.		
2 It contains dinosaur fossils.		
3 It has the remains of ancient trees.		
4 There are distinct strata in this area.		

CHAPTER 04

Service Encounters
(Chunking)

CHAPTER 4 **Service Encounters** (Chunking)

Understanding TOEFL Question Types & Listening Skills

1 Question Types — **Understanding Function of What Is Said Questions**

Understanding Function of What Is Said questions test your understanding of what the speaker is really saying or is asking about. It tests your knowledge of the speaker's intention, not simply a statement the person makes.

- **Example Understanding Function of What Is Said Questions**
  - What does the professor imply when he says this: (replay)
  - Why does the student say this: (replay)
  - What is the purpose of the student's response: (replay)

- **Useful Tips for Your Success**
  - What the speaker says and what the speaker really means may be different.
  - Pay close attention to the overall gist of the dialogue.

Sample Question

Student — ○ Wants to register for a class

⬇

Employee — ○ Puts the student on the waiting list

🎧 04-01

currently *adv* now; at the present time
drop out *phr* to quit; to stop doing something

Q What does the employee imply when she says this: "In most classes, at least a couple of students drop out each semester."

Ⓐ The professor is a very hard grader.
Ⓑ The class material is difficult.
Ⓒ The class is too early for most students.
Ⓓ The class is a popular one with students.

2 Listening Skills — Chunking

Chunking is a way of sorting and organizing information. One way to signal the end of a thought group is to make a pause. A pause gives listeners time to understand what a person just said.

Check-Up

▶ Listen to the sentences and put / marks to divide the sentences into chunks.

1 I need to register for a class.
2 It's being taught by Professor Cole.
3 Let me check on its availability.
4 Then go ahead and sign me up, please.

🎧 04-02

• Exercise 1 •

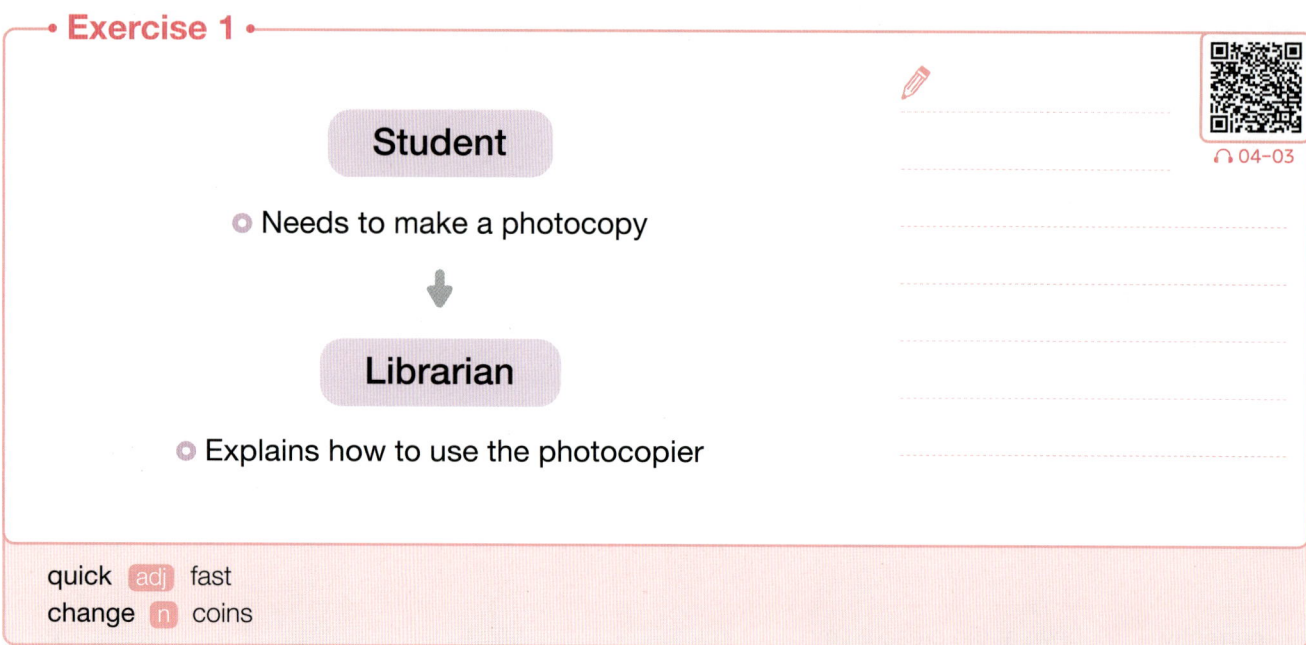

quick [adj] fast
change [n] coins

Q1 What does the student imply when she says this: "It'll take you two seconds."

    Ⓐ The librarian is very honest.
    Ⓑ An activity is easy for the librarian.
    Ⓒ The photocopier is slow.
    Ⓓ The photocopier is on the second floor.

Q2 Why does the librarian say this: "You have to purchase a copy card."

    Ⓐ The student has no money.
    Ⓑ The copier only takes cards.
    Ⓒ The student can use money.
    Ⓓ Copy cards are hard to find.

Listening Skills Chunking

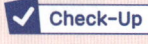 **Check-Up** Listen to the sentences and put / marks to divide the sentences into chunks.

1 It'll take you two seconds.
2 Do you have a copy card?
3 Here's your card, and here's five in change.
4 You forgot your purse.

• **Exercise 2** •

Student
○ Wants to get university housing

⬇

Employee
○ Informs the student of housing options

preference (n) the act of liking one thing more than another
complicate (v) to make difficult or complex

Q1 What does the student imply when he says this: "Roommates really complicate things."
- Ⓐ He has many roommates.
- Ⓑ He thinks roommates are great.
- Ⓒ He enjoys complicated situations.
- Ⓓ He would rather live alone.

Q2 What is the purpose of the employee's response: "I hear you."
- Ⓐ To say the student is speaking clearly
- Ⓑ To indicate she does not understand
- Ⓒ To agree with the student
- Ⓓ To state that the student made a good joke

Listening Skills | Chunking

✓ **Check-Up** Listen to the sentences and put / marks to divide the sentences into chunks.

1 I'm interested in university housing.
2 Are there any studio apartments available?
3 Actually, there are a couple of units open now.
4 You just need to make a deposit, and then it's all yours.

• **Exercise 3** •

Student
○ Wants to change a class to pass-fail

⬇

Employee
○ Helps the student with the change

handle v to manage; to be responsible for
drop v to cancel

Q1 What does the employee imply when he says this: "You're all set."

  Ⓐ The job is done.
  Ⓑ The student can go.
  Ⓒ The class is finished.
  Ⓓ The student paid for tuition.

Q2 Why does the employee say this: "Yes, but you can get a one-month extension if you need it."

  Ⓐ To say that the student can delay her tuition payment
  Ⓑ To tell the student to choose her classes later
  Ⓒ To point out that there is a strict deadline
  Ⓓ To comment that students rarely pay on time

Listening Skills Chunking

✓ **Check-Up** Listen to the sentences and put / marks to divide the sentences into chunks.

1 This window handles class changes.
2 You're only allowed one per semester.
3 When is the deadline to pay tuition?
4 You can get a one-month extension if you need it.

• **Exercise 4** •

Student
- Needs to change shifts with another worker

↓

Manager
- Tells the student to talk to another coworker

shift n a scheduled period of work
replacement n a person who does something in place of another; a substitute

Q1 Why does the manager say this: "Well, school is the reason that you're here."
   Ⓐ To let the student finish work early
   Ⓑ To allow the student to go to class now
   Ⓒ To permit the student to study at work
   Ⓓ To agree to the student's proposal

Q2 What does the manager imply when he says this: "David is always looking for extra hours."
   Ⓐ The student should ask David for assistance.
   Ⓑ David works more than any other student.
   Ⓒ He thinks David is his best employee.
   Ⓓ David does not make enough money at his job.

Listening Skills Chunking

 **Check-Up** Listen to the sentences and put / marks to divide the sentences into chunks.

1 Mr. Jefferson, could I have a quick word with you?
2 I don't think that's ideal.
3 Thank you so much for understanding.
4 He's standing over by the sink.

Exercise 5

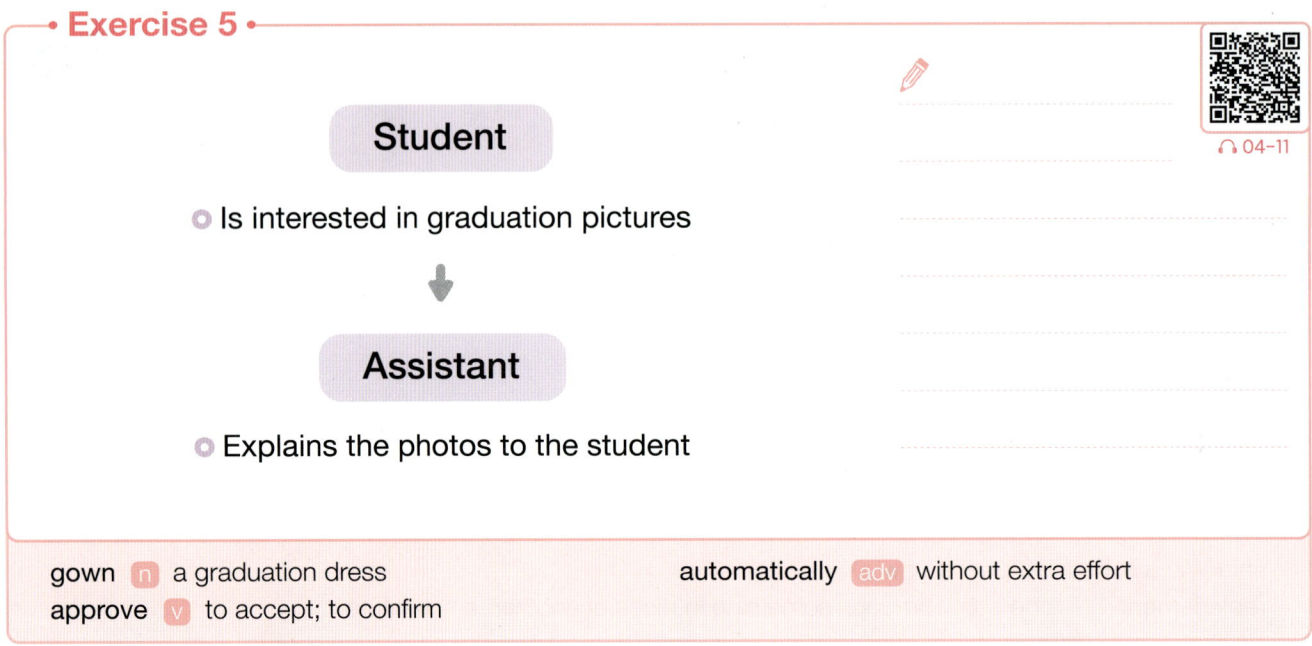

gown n a graduation dress	automatically adv without extra effort
approve v to accept; to confirm	

Q1 What does the assistant imply when he says this: "We have some different ones for you to wear just for the pictures."

- Ⓐ The student can wear anything she wants.
- Ⓑ The student has to prepare a cap and gown herself.
- Ⓒ The assistant has different caps and gowns.
- Ⓓ The cap and gown should be bought first.

Q2 What is the purpose of the assistant's response: "There's no fee."

- Ⓐ To say that the photo shoot costs nothing
- Ⓑ To tell the student she must pay a fee
- Ⓒ To request a fee from the student
- Ⓓ To give the student a discount

Listening Skills **Chunking**

✓ **Check-Up** Listen to the sentences and put / marks to divide the sentences into chunks.

1 Have you applied to graduate?
2 Then you should be on my list.
3 There's no fee.
4 I have class in fifteen minutes.

68

Exercise 6

Student
- Wants to be on the student council

↓

Assistant
- Talks about the requirements

🎧 04-13

---

run for *phr* to compete; to be a candidate
criterion *n* a standard or rule
formality *n* an official procedure

Q1 What does the assistant imply when she says this: "You must take at least twelve hours this semester."

Ⓐ Students rarely take twelve hours of classes.
Ⓑ Students taking more than twelve hours are part time.
Ⓒ Most students attend the school part time.
Ⓓ Students taking fewer than twelve hours are part time.

Q2 Why does the assistant say this: "We'll notify you via email in two or three days. It's just a formality."

Ⓐ To indicate the school must verify the student's information
Ⓑ To state that the student is now on the council
Ⓒ To ask for the student's email address
Ⓓ To advise the student to wear formal clothes

Listening Skills Chunking

 **Check-Up** Listen to the sentences and put / marks to divide the sentences into chunks.

1 What exactly does full time mean?
2 May I see it, please?
3 You can keep that copy.
4 It's just a formality.

🎧 04-14

Chapter ④ 69

• Exercise 7 •

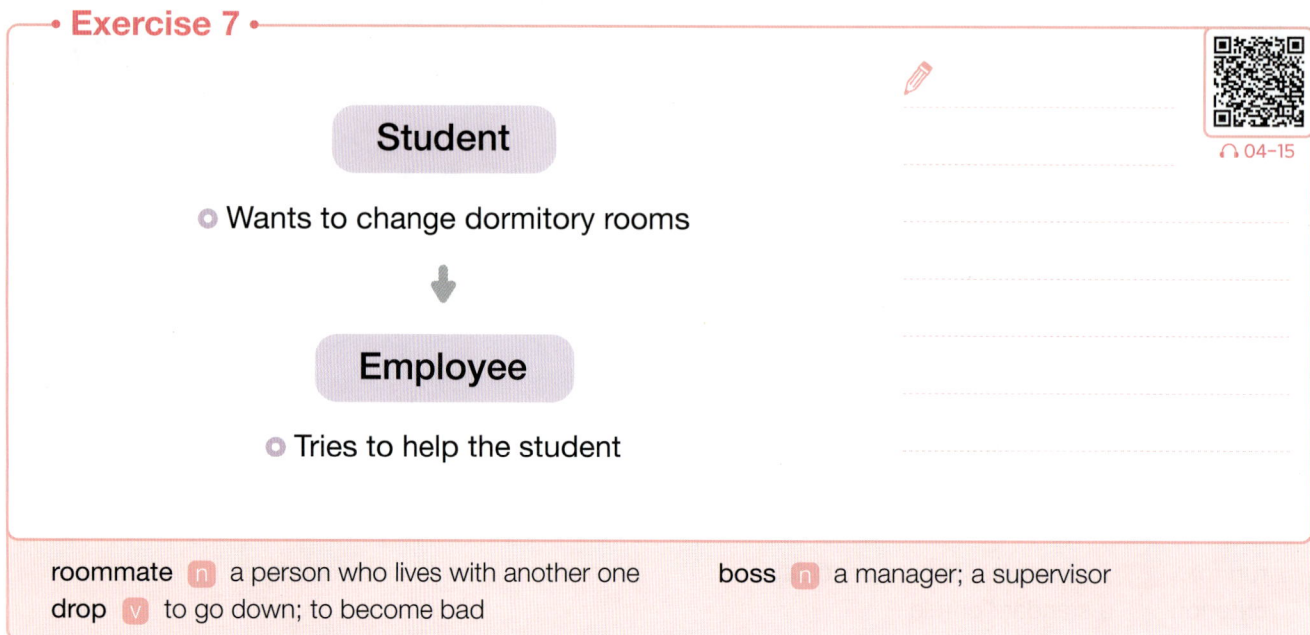

roommate n a person who lives with another one
drop v to go down; to become bad
boss n a manager; a supervisor

Q1 What does the employee imply when he says this: "The date for moving passed a couple of days ago."

Ⓐ He probably cannot help the student.
Ⓑ The student should come back later.
Ⓒ He is too busy right now.
Ⓓ The student has to fill out some forms.

Q2 Why does the employee say this: "I'll be back in a couple of minutes."

Ⓐ To tell the student to take a seat
Ⓑ To give the student some advice
Ⓒ To indicate he will talk to his boss now
Ⓓ To say that he will probably not succeed

Listening Skills Chunking

✓ **Check-Up** Listen to the sentences and put / marks to divide the sentences into chunks.

1 What exactly is the problem?
2 Maybe I can help.
3 Have you asked her to stop doing that?
4 I have to speak with my boss.

• **Exercise 8** •

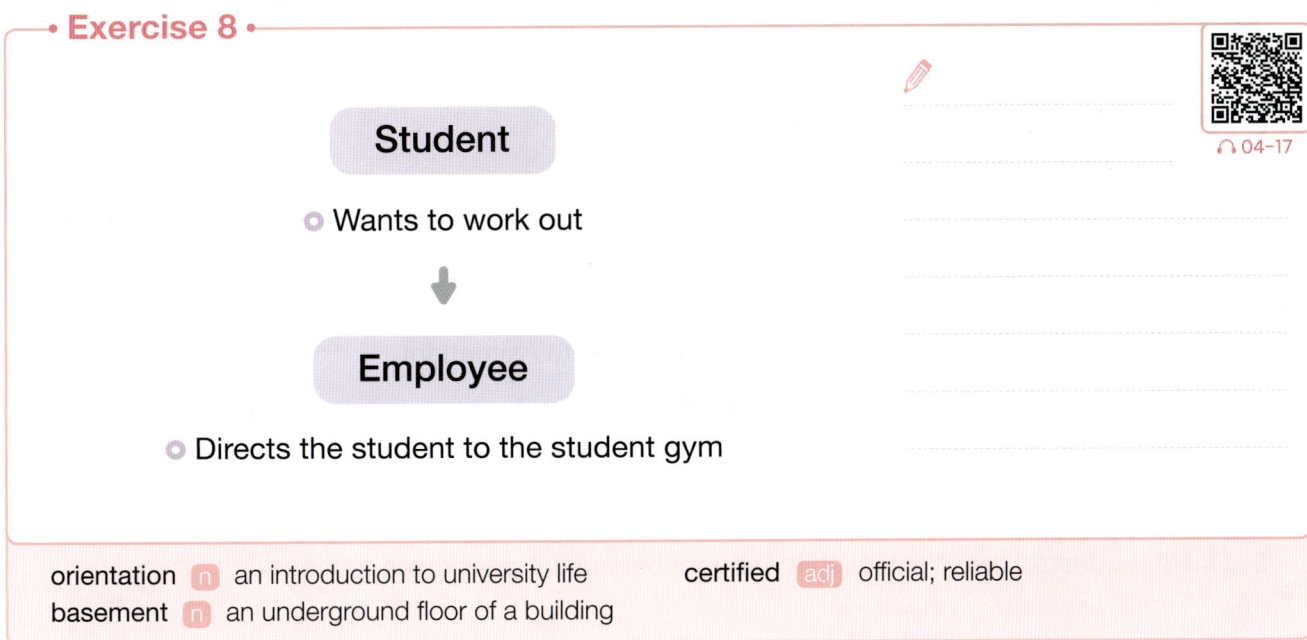

orientation n an introduction to university life
basement n an underground floor of a building
certified adj official; reliable

Q1 Why does the student say this: "Isn't the gym for everybody?"

Ⓐ He thinks anyone can work out at the gym.
Ⓑ He cannot find his student ID.
Ⓒ He wants to find the student gym.
Ⓓ He hopes to work out with other students.

Q2 What does the employee imply when she says this: "Well, if your friend is certified, there's a good chance."

Ⓐ The student has a good chance of becoming a trainer.
Ⓑ The student's friend is not certified.
Ⓒ The university favors certified trainers.
Ⓓ The employee is not a certified trainer.

Listening Skills Chunking

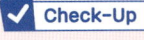 **Check-Up** Listen to the sentences and put / marks to divide the sentences into chunks.

1 I'll have to remind them again.
2 This is the faculty-only fitness center.
3 I think there's an opening in the student center.
4 Yeah, here's an application.

Vocabulary Review

A Circle the words that best complete the sentences.

1 His poor grades have created an unpleasant (situate / **situation**).
2 Petra wants to become a (listed / **certified**) scuba diver.
3 No one in the class wants to (jump / **run**) for president.
4 Because of her SAT score, Nancy was (**automatically** / severally) accepted.
5 David requested the evening (**shift** / shape) because it pays more money.

B Choose the words to complete the sentences.

1 Her father was upset that she _____ the difficult class.
   A scored
   B dropped
   C bought
   D flew

2 He likes to _____ things by making them more difficult.
   A complicate
   B pay
   C advertise
   D research

3 I cannot believe he paid completely with _____ for that book.
   A check
   B certificate
   C full
   D change

4 You need to _____ for the class before you can attend it.
   A drop out
   B take off
   C move up
   D register

5 Diana looks really pretty in her graduation _____.
   A diploma
   B reception
   C gown
   D hairstyle

C Choose the words with the closest meanings to the highlighted words.

1. The department approved the new professor.
   - Ⓐ accepted
   - Ⓑ admired
   - Ⓒ advised
   - Ⓓ addressed

2. Jessica is trying to find a replacement for her job this weekend.
   - Ⓐ a substitute
   - Ⓑ a semester
   - Ⓒ an hour
   - Ⓓ a manager

3. Many students could not handle the stress of final exams.
   - Ⓐ manage
   - Ⓑ realize
   - Ⓒ oversee
   - Ⓓ plead

4. The professor's preference was to avoid punishing the student.
   - Ⓐ fear
   - Ⓑ recess
   - Ⓒ choice
   - Ⓓ comment

5. Because he was so quick, the athlete was able to score.
   - Ⓐ talented
   - Ⓑ strong
   - Ⓒ fast
   - Ⓓ fearless

D Complete the sentences by filling in the blanks with the best words from the list. Change the forms of the words if necessary. Use each word only once.

> criterion   willing   promise   formality   orientation

1. Several people are _____ to help Mr. Davidson.
2. Many freshmen did not attend _____ this year.
3. Eric made a(n) _____ to his family to improve his grades.
4. It was a(n) _____ for the president to sign the document.
5. The _____ for the speech grade was changed by the professor.

Practice Test

1-3 Listen to part of a conversation between a student and a student activities office employee.

1. What are the speakers mainly discussing?
    - Ⓐ Taking part in student government
    - Ⓑ Some different clubs on campus
    - Ⓒ An upcoming school event
    - Ⓓ Sports teams the student can join

2. What can be inferred about the student?
    - Ⓐ He is a first-year student.
    - Ⓑ He is not taking many classes this semester.
    - Ⓒ He does not enjoy doing outdoor activities.
    - Ⓓ He is highly involved in on-campus activities.

3. What does the student imply when he says this: "It's just the kind of thing I'm interested in."
    - Ⓐ He does not have much interest in dinosaurs.
    - Ⓑ He thinks rocks are more interesting than dinosaurs.
    - Ⓒ He is looking forward to learning to play chess.
    - Ⓓ He is thinking about joining the paleontology club.

CHAPTER 05

Office Hours
(Pitch and Intonation)

CHAPTER 5 **Office Hours** (Pitch and Intonation)

Understanding TOEFL Question Types & Listening Skills

1 Question Types — Understanding Speaker's Attitude Questions

Understanding Speaker's Attitude questions test how well you understand the attitude or opinion of the speaker. Usually, they are concerned with how the speaker feels or why the speaker is expressing him or herself in a certain way.

- **Example Understanding Speaker's Attitude Questions**
    - What can be inferred about the student?
    - What does the woman mean when she says this: (replay)
    - What is the professor's opinion of the student?

- **Useful Tips for Your Success**
    - Pay attention to the speaker's tone of voice.
    - Pay attention to the speaker's general attitude during the talk.

Sample Question

Professor — Needs to discuss the student's thesis with her

⬇

Student — Takes the advice of the professor

🎧 05-01

thesis [n] a long academic paper
general [adj] common

Q What does the professor mean when he says this: "Once you revise it, bring it back in."

Ⓐ He wants the student to make changes now.
Ⓑ He wants the student to check the paper again.
Ⓒ He thinks the student's thesis is perfect.
Ⓓ He will revise the thesis for the student.

2 Listening Skills Pitch and Intonation

Pitch and intonation are the way that your voice rises and falls as you speak. A fall in pitch helps listeners recognize the end of a thought group. However, a question may end with a rising or falling pitch.

Check-Up

▶ Listen to the following dialogue and underline the high-pitched words.

Student: Good morning, Dr. Givens.
Professor: Samantha, the reason I called you in is to discuss your thesis.
Student: Did you like it?
Professor: Kind of. I like your idea, but the thesis is too broad and general.

🎧 05-02

Exercise 1

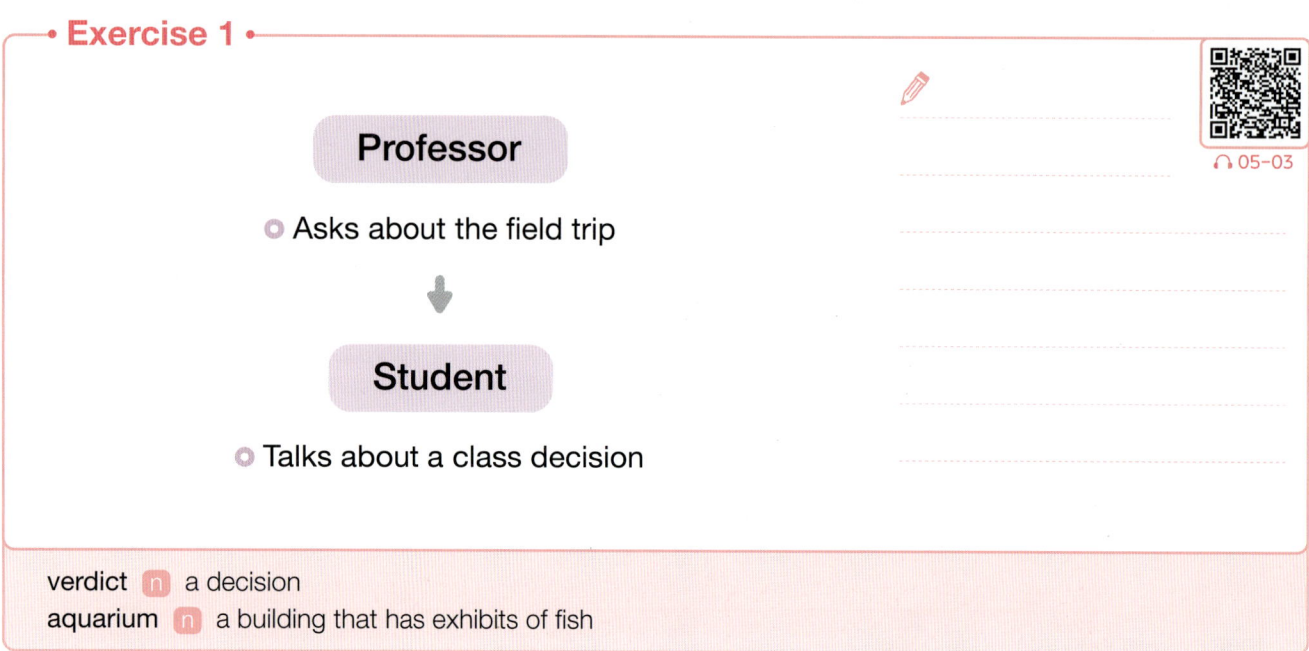

Professor
- Asks about the field trip

Student
- Talks about a class decision

verdict n a decision
aquarium n a building that has exhibits of fish

🎧 05-03

Q1 What can be inferred about the professor when she says this: "Really? That's interesting."

Ⓐ She is tired.
Ⓑ She is surprised.
Ⓒ She is relieved.
Ⓓ She is worried.

Q2 What can be inferred about the professor?

Ⓐ She likes to do things by herself.
Ⓑ She thinks money matters to most students.
Ⓒ She does not like hot weather.
Ⓓ She thinks the aquarium is expensive.

Listening Skills | Pitch and Intonation

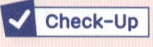 **Check-Up** Listen to the following dialogue and underline the high-pitched words.

Professor: So what's the verdict?

Student: The majority of the students want to go to White Beach for the field trip.

Professor: Really? That's interesting. I thought they would prefer to visit the aquarium.

Student: Me, too. I actually voted for the aquarium.

🎧 05-04

• **Exercise 2** •

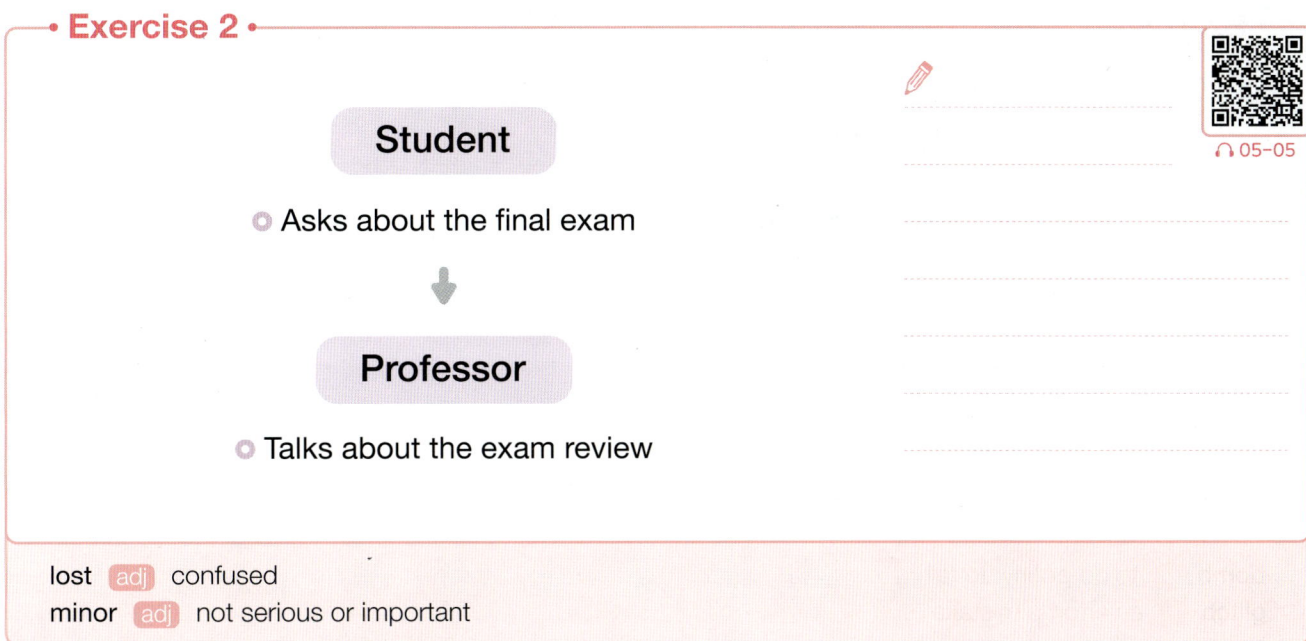

lost **adj** confused
minor **adj** not serious or important

Q1 What does the professor mean when he says this: "You didn't take the time to attend the review?"

Ⓐ He thinks the student is ready for the review.
Ⓑ The student should have attended the review.
Ⓒ He hopes the student will come to every class.
Ⓓ The student ought to apologize to him.

Q2 What can be inferred about the professor when he says this: "I didn't mean to sound like I was blaming you."

Ⓐ He blames the student for missing the review.
Ⓑ He is sorry for not letting the student explain a situation.
Ⓒ He thinks the student should not blame herself.
Ⓓ He believes the student's poor grade is her problem.

Listening Skills — Pitch and Intonation

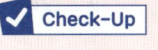 **Check-Up** Listen to the following dialogue and underline the high-pitched words.

Student: Thanks. Do you mind if I sit down?
Professor: Not at all. Go ahead.
Student: I'm a bit lost when it comes to the final examination.
Professor: I see. How so?

• **Exercise 3** •

Student
- Has a question about her grade

⬇

Professor
- Plans to fix the problem

bomb v to do poorly; to fail
glitch n an error; a mistake

Q1 What can be inferred about the student?
- Ⓐ She is upset.
- Ⓑ She is tired.
- Ⓒ She is very busy.
- Ⓓ She does not enjoy school.

Q2 What is the professor's opinion of the student?
- Ⓐ She cares about animals too much.
- Ⓑ She is an excellent student.
- Ⓒ She should try harder in class.
- Ⓓ She cannot keep up with the class.

Listening Skills Pitch and Intonation

✓ **Check-Up** Listen to the following dialogue and underline the high-pitched words.

Professor: Good morning, Karen. What brings you here?
Student: Good morning, Professor Cartwright.
Professor: You look like you lost your favorite pet or something. What's going on?
Student: I just don't get it, sir.

• **Exercise 4** •

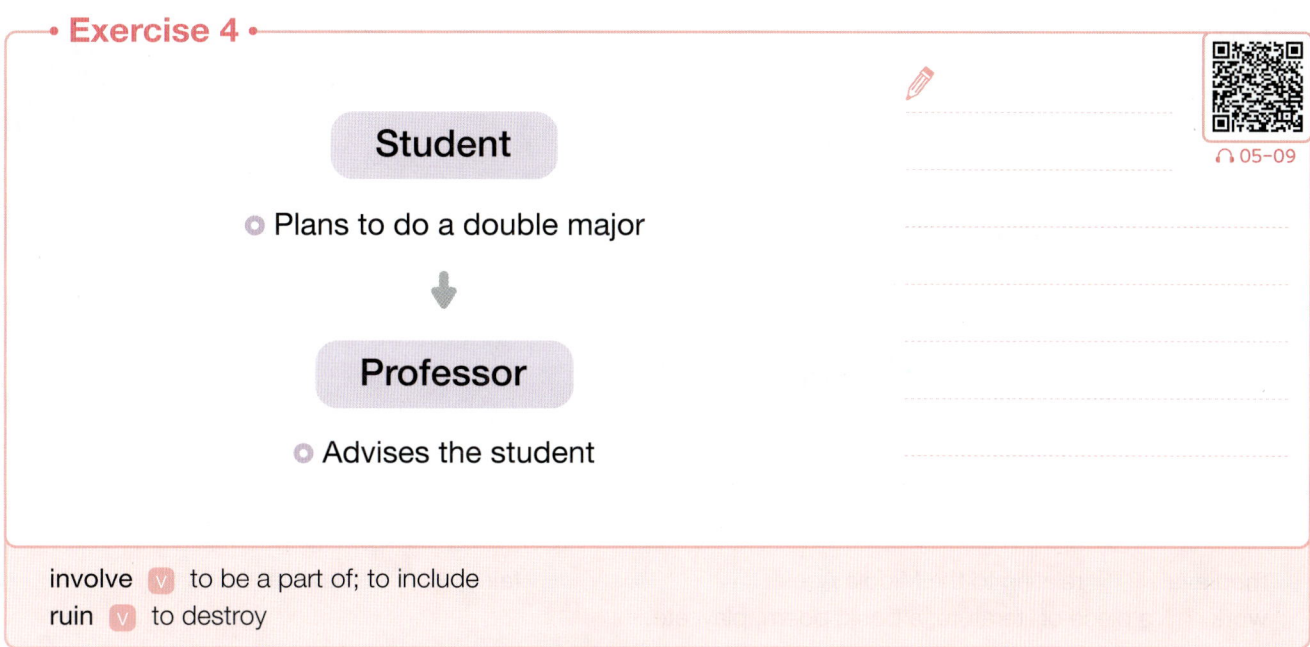

involve v to be a part of; to include
ruin v to destroy

Q1 What does the professor think of the student?

- Ⓐ She thinks he should leave school.
- Ⓑ She considers him a top student.
- Ⓒ She says he cannot do a double major.
- Ⓓ She believes he should change his major.

Q2 What does the student mean when he says this: "Biting off more than I can chew, huh?"

- Ⓐ Very much work is good for him.
- Ⓑ His goals might be too high.
- Ⓒ He is very hungry during class.
- Ⓓ He does not have enough homework.

Listening Skills Pitch and Intonation

 Check-Up Listen to the following dialogue and underline the high-pitched words.

Student: The dean, huh? Sounds important.
Professor: Believe me. It is. So what's up?
Student: I'm thinking about doing a double major.
Professor: You're going to do what?

• **Exercise 5** •

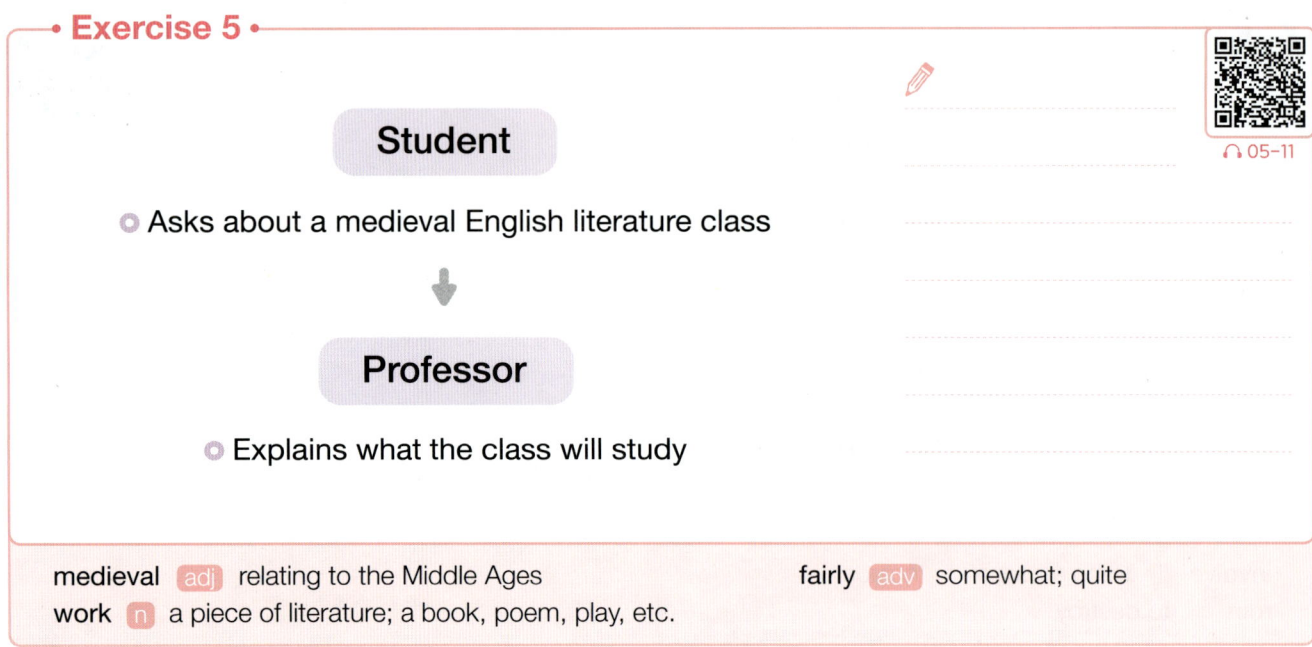

medieval adj relating to the Middle Ages	**fairly** adv somewhat; quite
work n a piece of literature; a book, poem, play, etc.	

Q1 What can be inferred about the professor?

  Ⓐ He thinks the student can get a good grade.
  Ⓑ He has not met the student before.
  Ⓒ He enjoys teaching medieval literature.
  Ⓓ He is going to retire from teaching soon.

Q2 What is the student's opinion of Middle English?

  Ⓐ She finds it an interesting language.
  Ⓑ She believes nobody needs to know it.
  Ⓒ She thinks it might be hard to learn.
  Ⓓ She considers it very important.

Listening Skills Pitch and Intonation

✓ **Check-Up** Listen to the following dialogue and underline the high-pitched words.

Student: Professor Chambers, could I speak with you, please?

Professor: Of course. Um. . . I'm afraid I don't know your name. Are you in my class?

Student: No, sir, but I'm thinking about taking your class next semester. My name is Amber Marston.

Professor: It's a pleasure to meet you, Amber. Which of my classes are you interested in?

• **Exercise 6** •

Student
○ Talks about transferring schools

↓

Professor
○ Helps the student

🎧 05-13

pep talk [n] a chat meant to make a person happier or more confident
get in [phr] to enter; to be accepted
alma mater [n] the school from which one has graduated

Q1 What is the professor's opinion of the student?
  Ⓐ She is glad the student is leaving.
  Ⓑ She enjoyed instructing the student.
  Ⓒ She thinks the student is making a bad decision.
  Ⓓ She believes the student cannot be a finance major.

Q2 What does the professor mean when she says this: "I'll do better than that, Brandon."
  Ⓐ She will help the student.
  Ⓑ She will thank the student.
  Ⓒ She wants the student to do well.
  Ⓓ She thinks the student is the best.

Listening Skills | **Pitch and Intonation**

 Check-Up Listen to the following dialogue and underline the high-pitched words.

Student: I came in to say goodbye, ma'am.
Professor: Yes, I heard that you were transferring schools.
Student: Yeah.
Professor: We're all sorry to see you go, Brandon.

🎧 05-14

• Exercise 7 •

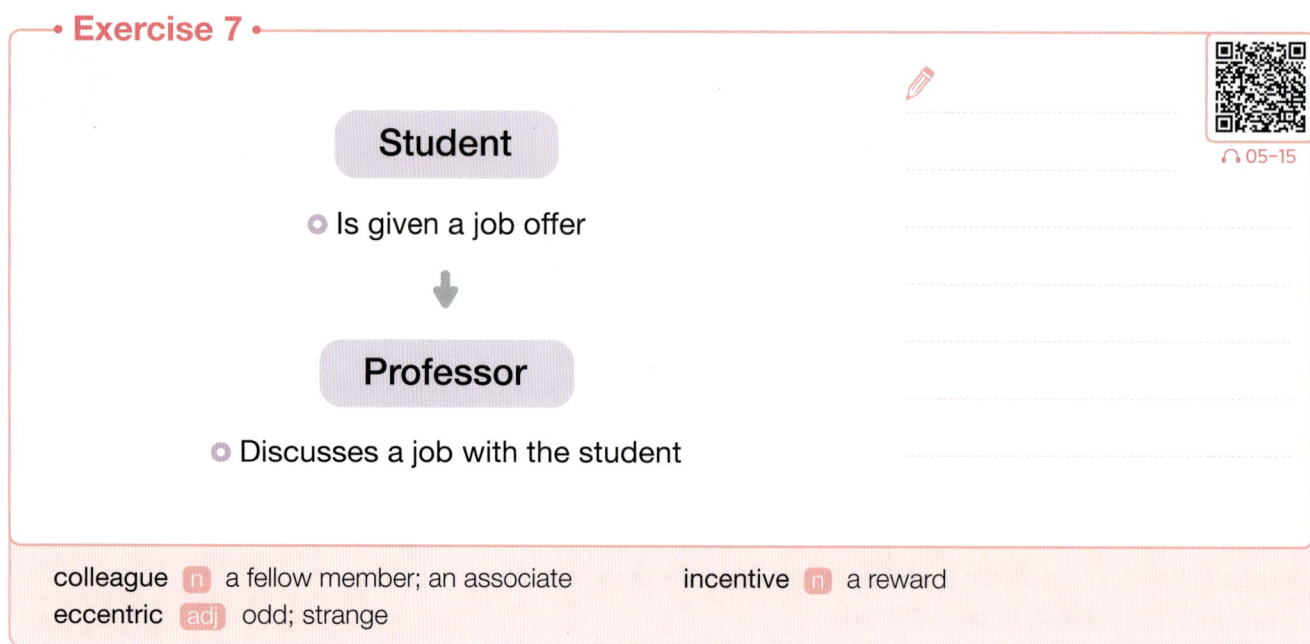

Student
- Is given a job offer

⬇

Professor
- Discusses a job with the student

colleague n a fellow member; an associate	**incentive** n a reward
eccentric adj odd; strange	

Q1 What does the professor mean when he says this: "Dr. Holloway is a bit eccentric."

- Ⓐ Dr. Holloway is an average professor.
- Ⓑ Dr. Holloway is different from most people.
- Ⓒ Dr. Holloway is much older than the professor.
- Ⓓ Dr. Holloway enjoys teaching mathematics.

Q2 What is the student's opinion of the job?

- Ⓐ The pay is too low.
- Ⓑ The working time is too late.
- Ⓒ The work is very easy.
- Ⓓ The wage is fair for that kind of work.

Listening Skills Pitch and Intonation

Check-Up Listen to the following dialogue and underline the high-pitched words.

Professor: But, well, how can I put this . . . ? Dr. Holloway is a bit eccentric.
Student: How so?
Professor: He does most of his work very early in the morning.
Student: How early?

• **Exercise 8** •

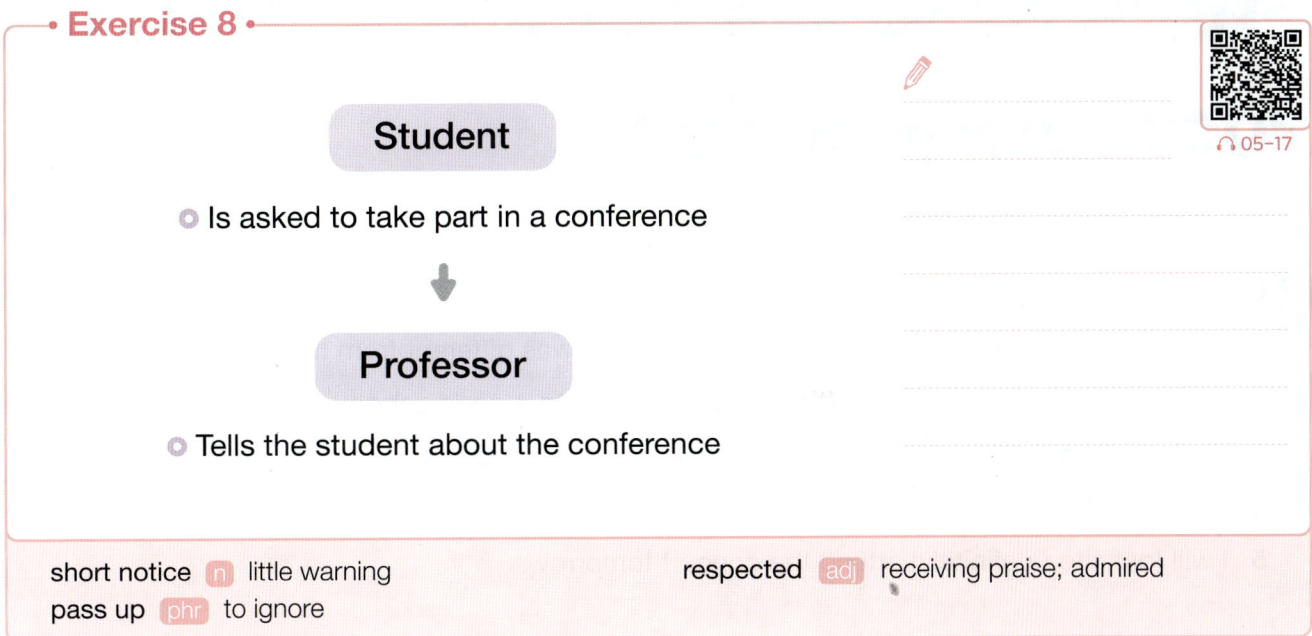

| short notice | n | little warning | | respected | adj | receiving praise; admired |
| pass up | phr | to ignore |

Q1 What can be inferred about the student?

- Ⓐ He has good topic ideas.
- Ⓑ He has a fear of audiences.
- Ⓒ He thinks the professor is joking.
- Ⓓ He wants to be a professor one day.

Q2 What can be inferred about the professor?

- Ⓐ Her lectures are probably boring.
- Ⓑ She makes a good impression on the student.
- Ⓒ She has no confidence in the student.
- Ⓓ She must teach a class soon.

Listening Skills Pitch and Intonation

 Listen to the following dialogue and underline the high-pitched words.

Student: Sure, Professor Walker. Is anything wrong?

Professor: Just the opposite. I have a great opportunity for you.

Student: Really? What is it?

Professor: The university is hosting an academic conference in our department next week.

Vocabulary Review

A Circle the words that best complete the sentences.

1 In (middle / **medieval**) times, the English language was different from today.
2 Ashley was nervous about (**getting in** / passing by) to a good school.
3 Professor Appleby has a reputation for being (familiar / **eccentric**).
4 Landon is highly (**respected** / unlimited) by his peers.
5 I will (definite / **definitely**) attend the concert tomorrow.

B Choose the words to complete the sentences.

1 A cash reward is a good _____ for entering the contest.
   A amount
   B promotion
   C incentive
   D result

2 The task _____ a lot of outside research.
   A involved
   B supported
   C asked
   D found

3 His poor test results _____ his chances of winning a scholarship.
   A increased
   B tried
   C committed
   D ruined

4 The _____ in the computer program caused it to shut down.
   A wire
   B viral
   C glitch
   D hesitation

5 Randy looked _____ while he was taking the test.
   A lost
   B fun
   C standard
   D believed

C Choose the words with the closest meanings to the highlighted words.

1. It was a minor mistake.
   - Ⓐ heavy
   - Ⓑ underage
   - Ⓒ complex
   - Ⓓ small

2. The jury's verdict was not made easily.
   - Ⓐ question
   - Ⓑ decision
   - Ⓒ relation
   - Ⓓ plan

3. The general idea is to exercise as much as possible.
   - Ⓐ captain
   - Ⓑ specifically
   - Ⓒ common
   - Ⓓ tiring

4. Amy has been depressed since she bombed the exam.
   - Ⓐ failed
   - Ⓑ missed
   - Ⓒ studied
   - Ⓓ wrote

5. Kyle thanked the professor for the pep talk.
   - Ⓐ word
   - Ⓑ advice
   - Ⓒ joke
   - Ⓓ friendship

D Complete the sentences by filling in the blanks with the best words from the list. Change the forms of the words if necessary. Use each word only once.

| alma mater | colleague | pass up | short notice | aquarium |

1. The children found the field trip to the _____ exciting.
2. Dr. Cox hopes his daughter will attend his _____.
3. Trent _____ an excellent chance to earn extra money last summer.
4. Chris was not able to attend the party on such _____.
5. Stuart has many famous _____ in the field of chemistry.

Practice Test

1-3 Listen to part of a conversation between a student and a professor.

1. Why does the professor mention the summer session at the end?
   - Ⓐ To show the benefits of taking classes then
   - Ⓑ To advise the student against staying for it
   - Ⓒ To explain why the winter session is better
   - Ⓓ To talk about why he enjoys summer classes

2. What can be inferred about the professor?
   - Ⓐ He does not have time to talk to the student.
   - Ⓑ He teaches more classes than other professors.
   - Ⓒ He feels that summer classes are worthless.
   - Ⓓ He does not like cold weather.

3. What does the professor imply when he says this: "You'll also have the same class just about every day."
   - Ⓐ Students will attend school on weekends.
   - Ⓑ Students do not have the same class every day in spring and fall.
   - Ⓒ Students must pay more for summer classes.
   - Ⓓ Students do better work when they attend class more often.

CHAPTER 06

Infectious Diseases
(Signal Words and Phrases)

CHAPTER 6 | **Infectious Diseases** (Signal Words and Phrases)

Understanding TOEFL Question Types & Listening Skills

1 Question Types — Understanding Organization Questions

Understanding Organization questions check how well you understand the overall organization of the passage and the relationship between ideas in the passage. Some questions test general understanding, and others test more detailed understanding.

- **Example Understanding Organization Questions**
    - How does the professor organize the information about X?
    - How is the discussion organized?
    - Why does the professor mention X?

- **Useful Tips for Your Success**
    - Listen carefully for transitions that indicate a sequence.
    - Pay attention to comparisons made by the professor.

Sample Question

The Common Cold

- Children get more often
- Sore throat, aches, sneezing, fatigue
- No cure

🎧 06-01

sore adj painful
fatigue n feeling tired

Q Why does the professor discuss a cold?

Ⓐ To discuss medications for it
Ⓑ To cover its symptoms
Ⓒ To compare it with other illnesses
Ⓓ To give some prevention tips

2 Listening Skills — Signal Words and Phrases

Signal words and phrases are words that provide you with clues. Their purpose is to help you organize information and recognize key ideas. Signal words and phrases also point to concept shifts in the passage.

Check-Up

▶ Listen carefully and fill in the blanks.

1 _____, the most common symptoms of a cold are a sore throat, sneezing, and fatigue.

2 _____, body aches, a fever, and even the chills might accompany a cold.

🎧 06-02

Chapter 6   95

• **Exercise 1** •

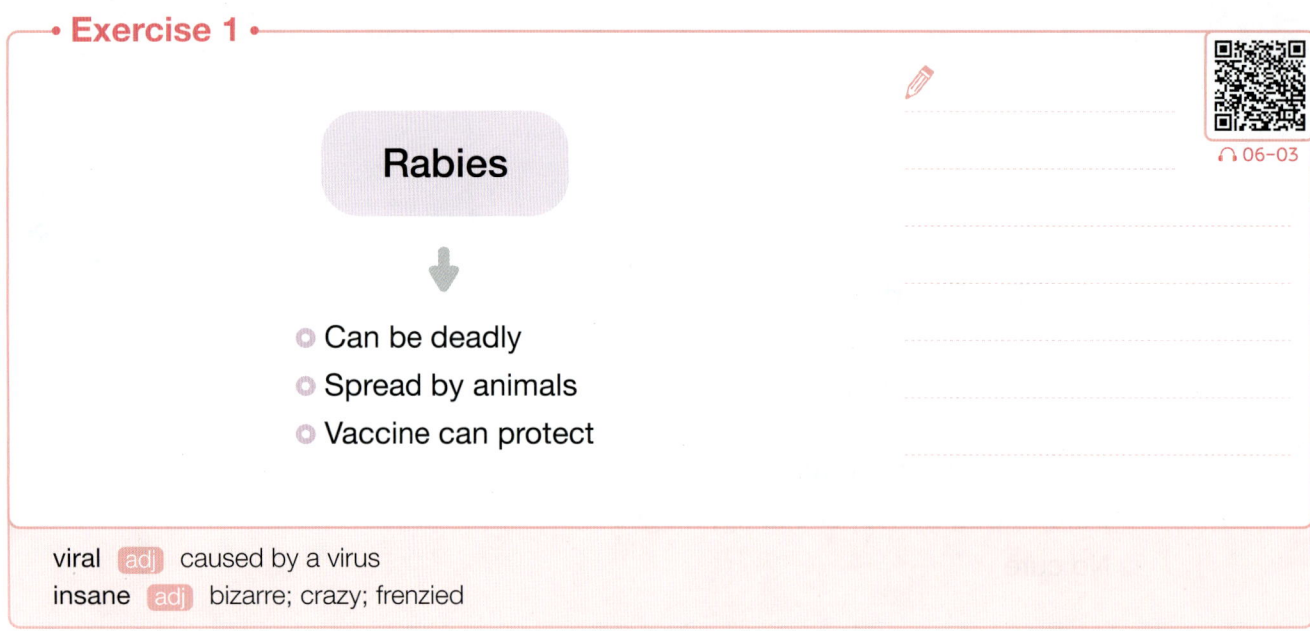

06-03

Rabies

- Can be deadly
- Spread by animals
- Vaccine can protect

viral adj caused by a virus
insane adj bizarre; crazy; frenzied

Q1 How does the professor organize the discussion?

Ⓐ He describes rabies symptoms in humans.
Ⓑ He talks about how rabies is spread.
Ⓒ He explains when rabies first came about.
Ⓓ He follows the textbook definition of rabies.

Q2 Why does the professor mention a rabies vaccine?

Ⓐ To note a defense against rabies
Ⓑ To explain that rabies is not dangerous
Ⓒ To show what makes animals insane
Ⓓ To discuss the low cost of preventing rabies

| **Listening Skills** | **Signal Words and Phrases** |

06-04

✓ **Check-Up** Listen carefully and fill in the blanks.

1 _____ stay clear of animals that are acting funny.

2 _____ _____ _____, I'm talking about animals that act and look insane.

Exercise 2

Chickenpox

- Contagious
- Itchy sores
- Lifetime immunity

contagious *adj* easily spread from person to person
immunity *n* protection; resistance

Q1 How does the professor organize the information about chickenpox?
Ⓐ She discusses its history.
Ⓑ She describes medications for it.
Ⓒ She talks about its contagiousness.
Ⓓ She compares it to smallpox.

Q2 Why does the professor mention immunity?
Ⓐ Some people never get chickenpox.
Ⓑ Most people are immune to chickenpox.
Ⓒ Vaccines make people immune to chickenpox.
Ⓓ Infected people will probably not get chickenpox again.

Listening Skills   Signal Words and Phrases

✓ **Check-Up**   Listen carefully and fill in the blanks.

1 _____, chickenpox cannot be cured by any medications.
2 _____, the good news is that you'll probably never get it again.

• Exercise 3 •

Vaccines

- The best protection against viruses
- Help the body build antibodies
- First one in 1756

🎧 06-07

inoculation n a vaccine shot; an injection
ward off phr to defend against; to turn away

Q1 How does the professor organize the discussion?
- Ⓐ He talks about the earliest vaccine.
- Ⓑ He lists important vaccines in history.
- Ⓒ He explains how vaccines work.
- Ⓓ He contrasts vaccines with medicine.

Q2 Why does the professor discuss smallpox?
- Ⓐ To show how deadly it is
- Ⓑ To note how successful vaccines can be
- Ⓒ To question the strength of vaccines
- Ⓓ To suggest that smallpox still exists

Listening Skills | Signal Words and Phrases

 Listen carefully and fill in the blanks.

🎧 06-08

1 _____ _____, what we call vaccines are the most effective way to protect humans against infectious diseases.

2 _____ _____ _____ in basic terms what a vaccine is.

• **Exercise 4** •

The Spanish Flu
↓
- Twentieth-century killer virus
- Between 50 to 100 million died
- Global disease

conclusive adj convincing; without doubt
outbreak n a sudden increase

Q1 Why does the professor mention AIDS?

 Ⓐ To show how deadly the Spanish flu was
 Ⓑ To note that it is worse than the flu
 Ⓒ To discuss how it is now under control
 Ⓓ To suggest that is can spread very quickly

Q2 Why does the professor discuss the Spanish flu?

 Ⓐ To describe how it was isolated
 Ⓑ To explain why it killed so many people
 Ⓒ To note that it was the world's last pandemic
 Ⓓ To compare pandemics with epidemics

Listening Skills Signal Words and Phrases

✓ **Check-Up** Listen carefully and fill in the blanks.

1 _____ _____, currently, AIDS is one of the most tragic and deadliest.
2 _____ _____, unlike other flu outbreaks, it was extremely contagious.

Chapter ❻ 99

• **Exercise 5** •

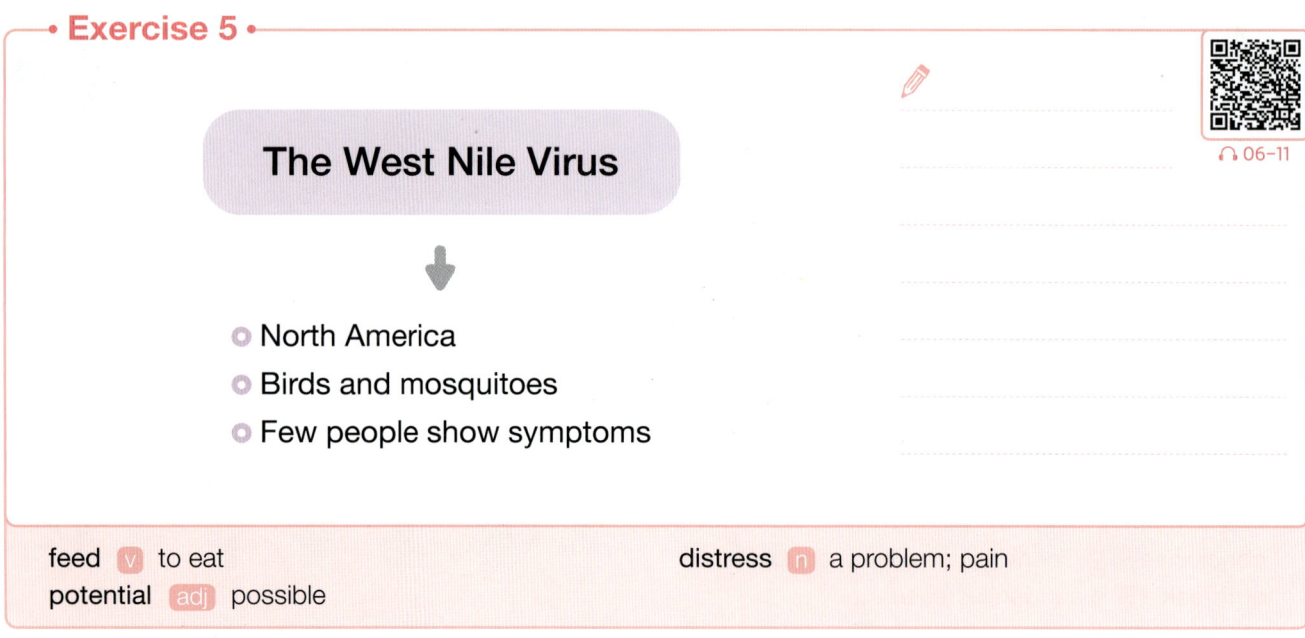

The West Nile Virus

- North America
- Birds and mosquitoes
- Few people show symptoms

feed [v] to eat   distress [n] a problem; pain
potential [adj] possible

Q1 How does the professor organize the discussion about the West Nile Virus?

- Ⓐ He discusses how it is spread and its symptoms.
- Ⓑ He contrasts it with a different virus.
- Ⓒ He talks about how to protect against it.
- Ⓓ He lectures on the symptoms and then its vaccine.

Q2 Why does the professor mention dead birds?

- Ⓐ To warn the students about touching them
- Ⓑ To show that mosquitoes do not feed on them
- Ⓒ To relate a new theory about the West Nile Virus
- Ⓓ To note that birds do not die from the West Nile Virus

| Listening Skills | Signal Words and Phrases |

✓ **Check-Up** Listen carefully and fill in the blanks.

1 _____, I'd like to begin by discussing the West Nile Virus.

2 _____, I'll discuss what it is and how it is spread.

3 _____, I'll get into some of the symptoms if time allows.

Exercise 6

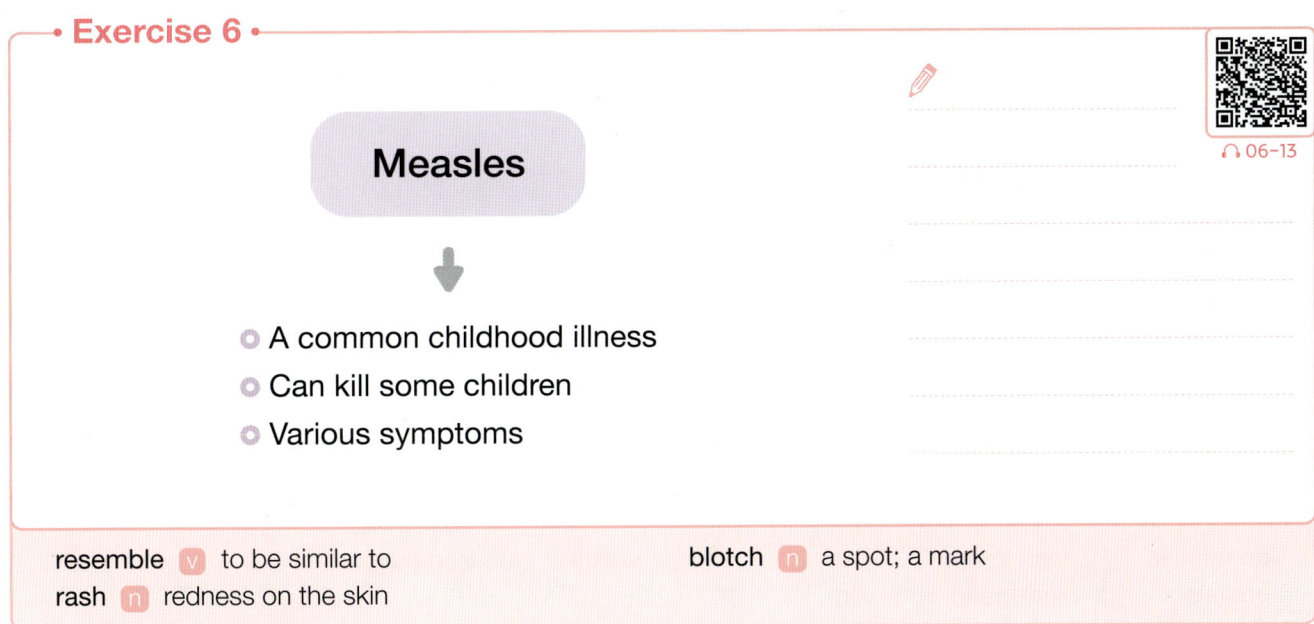

Measles
- A common childhood illness
- Can kill some children
- Various symptoms

🎧 06-13

resemble v to be similar to
rash n redness on the skin
blotch n a spot; a mark

Q1 How does the professor organize the information about measles?
  Ⓐ She asks questions and then answers them.
  Ⓑ She gives information in chronological order.
  Ⓒ She provides a number of facts about it.
  Ⓓ She focuses on ways to cure it.

Q2 Why does the professor mention the number of children who die from measles each year?
  Ⓐ To explain why children need to get vaccinated
  Ⓑ To emphasize how dangerous it can be
  Ⓒ To point out that the number is low
  Ⓓ To compare those deaths with ones from chickenpox

Listening Skills | Signal Words and Phrases

✓ **Check-Up** Listen carefully and fill in the blanks. 🎧 06-14

1 _____, most children get vaccinated for it when they're young.
2 _____, this doesn't happen everywhere in the world.
3 _____, the rash appears on the face first and then spreads elsewhere.

Chapter ❻ 101

• Exercise 7 •

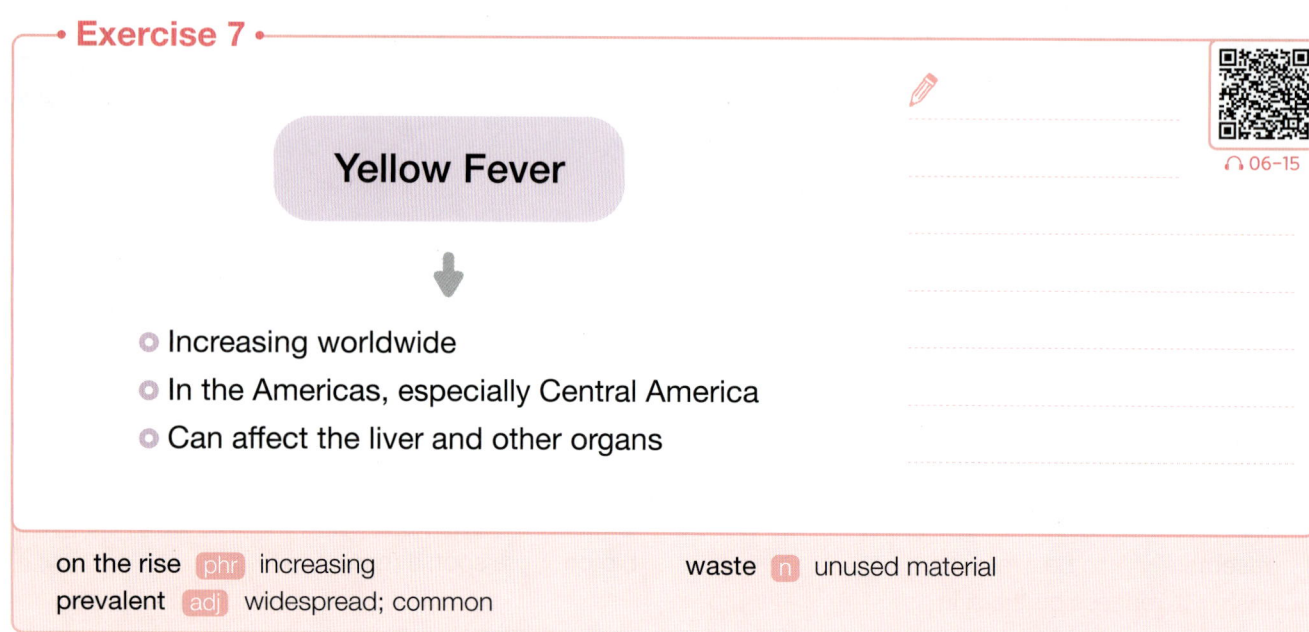

Yellow Fever

- Increasing worldwide
- In the Americas, especially Central America
- Can affect the liver and other organs

🎧 06-15

on the rise `phr` increasing
prevalent `adj` widespread; common
waste `n` unused material

Q1 How does the professor organize the discussion about yellow fever?

Ⓐ He names two vaccines for it.
Ⓑ He discusses North and Central America.
Ⓒ He talks about where and how it affects people.
Ⓓ He explains why it is called yellow fever.

Q2 Why does the professor mention the liver?

Ⓐ To show how yellow fever gets its name
Ⓑ To note the strength of the organ
Ⓒ To explain how it filters oxygen
Ⓓ To suggest the liver and the heart work together

Listening Skills | **Signal Words and Phrases**

✓ **Check-Up** | Listen carefully and fill in the blanks.

🎧 06-16

1 _____, let me give you some background.
2 _____, without protection, people are at risk in many regions around the world.
3 _____, why is it called yellow fever?

• **Exercise 8** •

🎧 06-17

Smallpox
⬇
- Deadly and infected others
- Rashes on the skin
- Vaccine discovered

New World n North and South America   **eradicate** v to wipe out; to eliminate
estimate v to guess; to suppose

Q1 How is the discussion organized?

Ⓐ The professor focuses on the history of smallpox and its vaccine.
Ⓑ The professor discusses the symptoms caused by smallpox.
Ⓒ The professor compares smallpox with some other illnesses.
Ⓓ The professor stresses the medicine that can cure smallpox.

Q2 Why does the professor mention Native Americans?

Ⓐ To claim they helped find a smallpox vaccine
Ⓑ To explain the effects of smallpox on them
Ⓒ To point out that they lived in the New World
Ⓓ To say they are mostly immune to smallpox

| **Listening Skills** | **Signal Words and Phrases** |

🎧 06-18

✓ **Check-Up** | Listen carefully and fill in the blanks.

1 _____, a person with smallpox gets a rash over his or her entire body.

2 _____, a vaccine for it was discovered.

3 _____, it never escapes because it could kill millions of people if it did.

Chapter ❻   103

Vocabulary Review

A Circle the words that best complete the sentences.

1 Many animals in the jungle (feed / relying) on nuts and berries.
2 It was (ironies / ironic) that the math professor made an addition mistake.
3 The elderly are at (risk / risky) of being affected by this disease.
4 The city burns all of its (waste / library) in a remote area.
5 It could take up to three weeks for the patient to (recover / remove).

B Choose the words to complete the sentences.

1 One _____ problem is that the project does not have much money.

   A potential
   B reading
   C speech
   D tear

2 The patient is in _____ and needs some medication.

   A speed
   B turn
   C luxury
   D distress

3 The flu _____ caused hundreds of students to miss class.

   A average
   B outbreak
   C inform
   D ride

4 Because he had chickenpox as a child, he now has _____ to that disease.

   A immunity
   B worker
   C low
   D powerful

5 The patient has some red _____ all over his face.

   A colds
   B illnesses
   C fevers
   D blotches

C Choose the words with the closest meanings to the highlighted words.

1. Bradley has a sore throat and a headache.
   - Ⓐ painful
   - Ⓑ rough
   - Ⓒ perfect
   - Ⓓ large

2. It is difficult for the country to ward off invaders.
   - Ⓐ accept from
   - Ⓑ defend against
   - Ⓒ look for
   - Ⓓ catch up

3. The evidence was not conclusive enough to put him in jail.
   - Ⓐ great
   - Ⓑ specific
   - Ⓒ internal
   - Ⓓ convincing

4. Doctors hope to eradicate this illness from the population.
   - Ⓐ remove
   - Ⓑ cure
   - Ⓒ immunize
   - Ⓓ study

5. This disease can cause death in some cases.
   - Ⓐ sickness
   - Ⓑ symptom
   - Ⓒ medicine
   - Ⓓ vaccine

D Complete the sentences by filling in the blanks with the best words from the list. Change the forms of the words if necessary. Use each word only once.

| on the rise | wipe out | inoculation | contagious | viral |

1. The common cold is caused by a(n) _____ infection.
2. Almost the entire town was _____ by an unknown virus.
3. It is important for children to get _____ before school.
4. Infectious diseases can possibly become _____.
5. Many diseases that were once rare are now _____.

Practice Test

1-4 Listen to part of a lecture in a physiology class.

1 What is the main topic of the lecture?

   Ⓐ The bacteria that causes the bubonic plague
   Ⓑ The bubonic plague and its effects
   Ⓒ The world's worst plague
   Ⓓ The history of the Black Death

2 Why does the professor mention the Black Death?

   Ⓐ To say it was not too deadly
   Ⓑ To describe its effect on European society
   Ⓒ To explain what happened during it
   Ⓓ To name the countries it affected

3 What animals can get infected with the bubonic plague?

   Ⓐ Fleas
   Ⓑ Mice
   Ⓒ Rabbits
   Ⓓ Pigeons

4 What can be inferred about the bubonic plague?

   Ⓐ It only affects people in Europe.
   Ⓑ It kills many people who get it.
   Ⓒ Scientists know little about it.
   Ⓓ It does not kill people anymore today.

CHAPTER 07

Photography
(Distinguishing Consonants)

CHAPTER 7 Photography (Distinguishing Consonants)

Understanding TOEFL Question Types & Listening Skills

1 Question Types — Connecting Content Questions

Connecting Content questions test your ability to relate ideas in the passage. The ideas may be obvious or implied. You may also be asked to fill in a chart which classifies items in categories.

- **Example Connecting Content Questions**
  - What can be inferred about X?
  - What does the professor imply about X?
  - Are the following characteristics of X or Y?
    Click in the correct box for each phrase or sentence.

- **Useful Tips for Your Success**
  - Pay close attention to how you organize your notes.
  - Identify terms and details as well as definitions.

Sample Question

Parts of the Camera
⬇
- The lens
- The aperture

 07-01

component n. a part
adjust v. to change to fit

Q What can be inferred about a camera lens?

Ⓐ It is expensive.
Ⓑ It is made of metal.
Ⓒ It has a hole inside it.
Ⓓ It changes the color of the image.

2 Listening Skills   Distinguishing Consonants

A consonant is a sound such as *p*, *f*, *n*, and *t*. It's important to distinguish some consonants like *r* from *l*, *v* from *b*, and *f* from *p* in lectures and conversations.

Check-Up

▶ Listen carefully and circle the words you hear.

1 focus – pocus   2 rinse – lens
3 picture – fixture   4 right – light

 07-02

Chapter 7   111

Exercise 1

Types of Cameras

⬇

- Film – black and white photos
- Digital – convenience and storage

resolution [n] clearness; quality
get rid of [phr] to throw out; to dispose of

Q1 What can be inferred about photographs?

Ⓐ They are more detailed on film.
Ⓑ Black and white pictures are the most expensive.
Ⓒ Digital photos are larger than film photos.
Ⓓ Film cameras produce more types of photos.

Q2 Are the following characteristics of film or digital cameras?

	Film Cameras	Digital Cameras
① They are capable of storing pictures.		
② People can view the pictures they take quickly.		
③ They are better for black and white photography.		
④ Their pictures have a high resolution.		

Listening Skills Distinguishing Consonants

✓ **Check-Up** Listen carefully and circle the words you hear.

1 fig – big 2 firm – film
3 flack – black 4 while – white

• **Exercise 2** •

Early Photography

↓

- For the privileged
- Kodak made available to all
- Point-and-shoot cameras

founder *n* a creator; the first builder of something
disposable *adj* able to be thrown away after being used

Q1 What can be inferred about early photography?
  Ⓐ Most people had cameras.
  Ⓑ Kodak built the first camera.
  Ⓒ Kodak cameras were fairly cheap.
  Ⓓ Cameras made by Kodak lasted a lifetime.

Q2 Are the following characteristics of pre-Kodak or post-Kodak photography?

	Pre-Kodak	Post-Kodak
① Photography was for the rich only.		
② Cameras could store a hundred images.		
③ Everyone could enjoy photography.		
④ Photography before 1880 was this period.		

Listening Skills **Distinguishing Consonants**

✓ **Check-Up** Listen carefully and circle the words you hear.

1 seat – sheet   2 all – are
3 for – poor   4 it – eat

• **Exercise 3** •

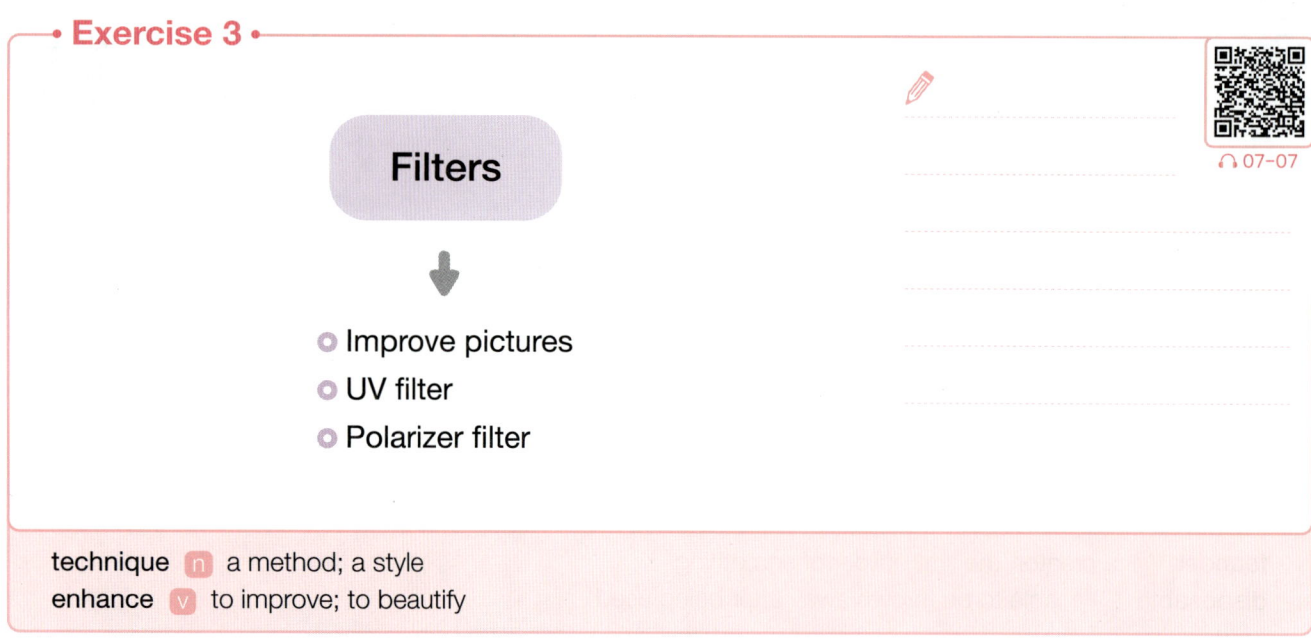

🎧 07-07

technique n a method; a style
enhance v to improve; to beautify

Q1 What is the most likely result if a filter is not used for a picture of a lake?

Ⓐ The lens will not work properly.
Ⓑ The lake will be hard to see.
Ⓒ The sun will not affect the picture.
Ⓓ The camera will filter the picture itself.

Q2 Are the following characteristics of UV filters or polarizer filters?

	UV Filters	Polarizer Filters
① They may reduce unwanted coloring.		
② They reduce reflections.		
③ They are good for pictures of lakes or rivers.		
④ They add depth to pictures.		

Listening Skills Distinguishing Consonants

✓ Check-Up Listen carefully and circle the words you hear.

1 staff – step   2 cheap – cheat
3 crowds – clouds   4 glass – grass

🎧 07-08

• **Exercise 4** •

Underwater Photography

⬇

- Special cameras
- Different techniques
- Color hard to capture

point n a time; a place
shallow adj not deep

Q1 What can be inferred about underwater photography?

  Ⓐ It is easier than land photography.
  Ⓑ It results in very clear photographs.
  Ⓒ Sunlight has a great effect on it.
  Ⓓ It commonly results in out-of-focus pictures.

Q2 Are the following characteristics of underwater photography or land photography?

	Underwater Photography	Land Photography
① A lot of color is lost.		
② Colors are easier to capture.		
③ Distance does not matter much.		
④ Photographers must be near their subjects.		

Listening Skills Distinguishing Consonants

✓ Check-Up   Listen carefully and circle the words you hear.

1 shot – chop   2 we'll – we're
3 fool – pool   4 vision – mission

Exercise 5

Ansel Adams and Annie Leibovitz

- Famous American photographers
- Adams: landscapes
- Leibovitz: portraits of famous people

influential [adj] having a great effect on or power over others
haunting [adj] unforgettable
stun [v] to surprise; to shock

Q1 What does the professor imply about Ansel Adams?

Ⓐ He enjoyed rock music.
Ⓑ He was a cowboy.
Ⓒ He used color film at times.
Ⓓ He influenced Annie Leibovitz.

Q2 Are the following characteristics of Ansel Adams or Annie Leibovitz?

	Ansel Adams	Annie Leibovitz
① Took pictures of the American West		
② Was the last person to photograph John Lennon		
③ Preferred black and white film		
④ Worked for *Rolling Stone*		

Listening Skills Distinguishing Consonants

✓ **Check-Up** Listen carefully and circle the words you hear.

1 west – vest
2 from – plumb
3 subjects – objects
4 couple – cup of

• **Exercise 6** •

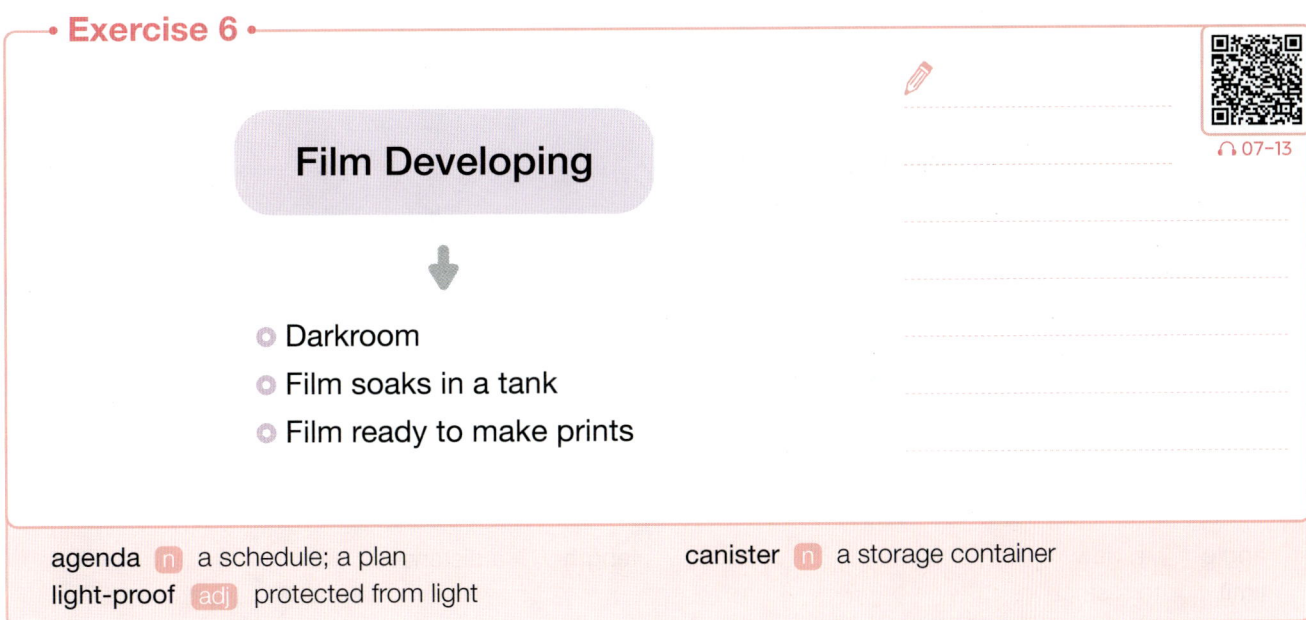

| agenda | n | a schedule; a plan | | canister | n | a storage container |
| light-proof | adj | protected from light |

Q1 What does the professor imply about film?

Ⓐ Some light will not harm it.
Ⓑ Different ones develop in different times.
Ⓒ Safety lights cannot hurt it.
Ⓓ It is highly sensitive to any light.

Q2 The professor mentions several events in film developing. In which order do they occur?

	Order
① Film is placed in a daylight processing tank.	
② All darkroom lights are turned off.	
③ Water is added.	
④ Developer is added.	
⑤ Film is placed on a reel.	

Listening Skills | **Distinguishing Consonants**

✓ **Check-Up** Listen carefully and circle the words you hear.

1 reason – season
2 votes – notes
3 reel – feel
4 view – few

Chapter ❼ 117

Exercise 7

Types of Lenses

- Standard
- Wide-angle
- Telephoto

angle n a view
limit v to restrict

length n a distance

Q1 What does the professor imply about camera lenses?

Ⓐ There are four main kinds of them.
Ⓑ There is only one kind of them.
Ⓒ Most cameras come with a 50mm lens.
Ⓓ Wide-angle ones are the most difficult to use.

Q2 Are the following characteristics of wide-angle lenses or telephoto lenses?

	Wide-Angle Lenses	Telephoto Lenses
① They are excellent for sports.		
② They reduce depth.		
③ They are good for pictures of mountains.		
④ They are good for portraits.		

Listening Skills   Distinguishing Consonants

✓ **Check-Up** Listen carefully and circle the words you hear.

1 angle – anger
2 telephoto – telephone
3 life – like
4 first – thirst

• **Exercise 8** •

Dorothea Lange

⬇

- Native Americans
- Poor people in rural areas
- Visited other countries

apprentice [n] a person learning a skill from another
laborer [n] a worker
caption [n] a title or explanation for a picture

Q1 What can be inferred about Dorothea Lange?

Ⓐ She did not like the picture *Migrant Mother*.
Ⓑ She took pictures in a wide variety of places.
Ⓒ She retired to live in a rural area after World War II.
Ⓓ She became very rich from her photographs.

Q2 Which time period in Dorothea Lange's life do the following refer to?

	Before the Great Depression	During and After the Great Depression
① Photographed Native Americans		
② Visited foreign countries to take pictures		
③ Studied at Columbia University		
④ Took pictures of people in rural areas		

Listening Skills   Distinguishing Consonants

✓ **Check-Up**   Listen carefully and circle the words you hear.

1 greatest – latest
2 wrong - long
3 capture – caption
4 prevention – detention

Chapter ❼ 119

Vocabulary Review

A Circle the words that best complete the sentences.

1. The class (agenda / arrange) will change this summer.
2. The sides of a triangle form three (photos / angles).
3. The Great (Caption / Depression) was a difficult time for most people.
4. At that (even / point), Conner left the room.
5. Dr. Fairchild has an interesting teaching (technique / class).

B Choose the words to complete the sentences.

1. The black dress _____ the woman's beauty.
   - A) saw
   - B) felt
   - C) enhanced
   - D) limit

2. Let's use _____ cups at the party so that we do not have to wash them.
   - A) disposable
   - B) fresh
   - C) steel
   - D) replace

3. Nathan's new digital camera has outstanding _____.
   - A) cost
   - B) resolution
   - C) stylish
   - D) picture

4. It is difficult for kids to _____ to a new school.
   - A) study
   - B) blending
   - C) adjust
   - D) acceptance

5. The class was _____ to hear about the tragedy.
   - A) worry
   - B) warned
   - C) relief
   - D) stunned

C Choose the words with the closest meanings to the highlighted words.

1. The story the man told was haunting.
   - Ⓐ light
   - Ⓑ memorable
   - Ⓒ scaring
   - Ⓓ short

2. The view from the peak of the mountain is amazing.
   - Ⓐ top
   - Ⓑ cliff
   - Ⓒ rock
   - Ⓓ valley

3. He hid the gold in a small canister.
   - Ⓐ room
   - Ⓑ drawer
   - Ⓒ pouch
   - Ⓓ container

4. The length of the field was shorter than expected.
   - Ⓐ size
   - Ⓑ location
   - Ⓒ time
   - Ⓓ material

5. The instructor limited the class time outside.
   - Ⓐ restricted
   - Ⓑ took
   - Ⓒ doubled
   - Ⓓ extended

D Complete the sentences by filling in the blanks with the best words from the list. Change the forms of the words if necessary. Use each word only once.

| detention | shallow | founder | component | light-proof |

1. The student got _____ and had to stay late after school.
2. The _____ of the university spoke at the event.
3. Most of the children swim in the _____ end of the pool.
4. Xavier needs to buy a new _____ for his laptop.
5. The _____ room is an excellent place to process film.

Practice Test

1-4 Listen to part of a lecture in a photography class.

Photography

1. What is the lecture mainly about?
   - Ⓐ Differences between cameras and art
   - Ⓑ The first type of photography
   - Ⓒ Famous pictures taken by daguerreotypes
   - Ⓓ Photography as an art form

2. Why does the professor mention Nicéphore Niépce?
   - Ⓐ To discuss his problems with Louis-Jacques-Mandé Daguerre
   - Ⓑ To name a creator of the daguerreotype
   - Ⓒ To call him an artist who took pictures
   - Ⓓ To state that he developed silver iodide

3. What is the professor's opinion of the daguerreotype?
   - Ⓐ He believes it was inefficient.
   - Ⓑ He likes it more than modern cameras.
   - Ⓒ He thinks it created beautiful pictures.
   - Ⓓ He feels that it had few limitations.

4. What can be inferred about the daguerreotype?
   - Ⓐ It was popular for fewer than two decades.
   - Ⓑ It was too expensive for most people to buy.
   - Ⓒ It is still used by some people today.
   - Ⓓ It required people to be still a long time to take pictures.

CHAPTER

08

Inventions
(Listening for Numbers)

CHAPTER 8 **Inventions** (Listening for Numbers)

Understanding TOEFL Question Types & Listening Skills

1 Question Types — Making Inferences Questions

Making Inferences questions are based on the facts in the listening passage. In many cases, the professor may imply something without directly stating it.

- **Example Making Inferences Questions**
  - What does the professor imply about X?
  - What will the professor probably do next?
  - What can be inferred about X?
  - What does the professor imply when he says this: (replay)

- **Useful Tips for Your Success**
  - Pay attention to what the professor implies.
  - The answer will usually use vocabulary not mentioned in the passage.

Sample Question

The Wheel

- 4000 B.C. Mesopotamia pottery wheel
- Transportation 3500 B.C.

🎧 08-01

invention n a new creation
pinpoint v to locate exactly

Q What does the professor imply about the wheel?

Ⓐ It was probably invented in Mesopotamia.
Ⓑ It was first used for chariots.
Ⓒ No other invention is as important as it.
Ⓓ Early wheels were large, round rocks.

2 Listening Skills — Listening for Numbers

We often hear numbers in lectures. A pause is especially important when you are listening to numbers in measurements, years, and other examples. Notice how spaces and punctuation are used to group the numbers.

Check-Up

▶ **Listen and fill in the blanks with suitable numbers.**

🎧 08-02

1 It dates back to about _____ B.C. in Mesopotamia.
2 There is evidence of the first wheeled vehicle being used around _____ years later in 3500 B.C.
3 Still later, the chariot was definitely present in China sometime between _____ and 1200 B.C.

Chapter 8 127

• Exercise 1 •

Early Watercraft

⬇

- Canoes around 50,000 years ago
- Egyptians built large ships
- Chinese navies

🎧 08-03

craft n a ship or other vessel
barge n a boat with a flat bottom

Q1 What does the professor imply about early humans?

Ⓐ They accidentally invented boats.
Ⓑ They used canoes to reach new lands.
Ⓒ They relied on the ocean for food.
Ⓓ They used sails on early watercraft.

Q2 What can be inferred about the Egyptians?

Ⓐ They used the wind to propel their ships.
Ⓑ They needed slaves to paddle their ships.
Ⓒ They built large barges to transport food.
Ⓓ They learned ship building from the Chinese.

Listening Skills Listening for Numbers

✓ **Check-Up** Listen and fill in the blanks with suitable numbers.

🎧 08-04

1 Around _____ to _____ years ago, humans began venturing out onto the seas.
2 The Egyptians were regularly building ships between _____ and _____ feet in length with great skill.
3 Still later, around _____ B.C., we know the Chinese began assembling navies.

• Exercise 2 •

🎧 08-05

The Compass
⬇
- Invented in China
- Not used by sailors
- Used by sailors after 1000 A.D.

---

determine v to figure out
lose sight of phr to be unable to see something anymore
ancient adj very old

Q1 What can be inferred about compasses in the past?
- Ⓐ They were useful to sailors on cloudy days.
- Ⓑ They used material that was easy to find.
- Ⓒ They were not too expensive for people to buy.
- Ⓓ They were only available to a few people.

Q2 What will the professor probably do next?
- Ⓐ Give the students a homework assignment
- Ⓑ Ask the students questions
- Ⓒ Show the class some pictures
- Ⓓ Take a short break

Listening Skills Listening for Numbers

🎧 08-06

✓ **Check-Up** Listen and fill in the blanks with suitable numbers.
1. We know it was invented in China sometime between _____ B.C. and _____ A.D.
2. They started doing that between the years _____ and _____.
3. In the West, the compass was first used around _____.

• **Exercise 3** •

🎧 08-07

Gunpowder

⬇

- Chinese invention
- Used for small bombs

gunpowder n an active explosive ingredient
saltpeter n potassium nitrate; a material used for fireworks and gunpowder
sulfur n a nonmetallic element that burns

Q1 What can be inferred about gunpowder?

Ⓐ It decreased the number of deaths during wars.
Ⓑ It will not work without saltpeter.
Ⓒ The Chinese used it for guns first.
Ⓓ It was a minor invention for the Chinese.

Q2 What can be inferred about the Chinese?

Ⓐ Gunpowder gave them an advantage in wars.
Ⓑ They preferred guns over exploding arrows.
Ⓒ They designed metal grenades in the tenth century.
Ⓓ They shipped gunpowder to other countries.

Listening Skills Listening for Numbers

🎧 08-08

✔ **Check-Up** Listen and fill in the blanks with suitable numbers.

1 They did this sometime during the _____ century.
2 The oldest gun ever found dates back to _____.
3 The recipe was _____% saltpeter, _____% sulfur, and _____% other nonessential ingredients.

• **Exercise 4** •

Leonardo da Vinci

⬇

- Interested in flight
- Designs for flying machines
- Designs for bridges

🎧 08-09

practical *adj* useful
fanciful *adj* unreal; not serious

Q1 What does the professor imply about Leonardo's designs?

　Ⓐ All of them could be successfully made today.
　Ⓑ He created all of them from his imagination.
　Ⓒ Some of them were modeled on things in nature.
　Ⓓ He invented the first successful airplane.

Q2 What does the professor imply about the Ottomans?

　Ⓐ They believed in Leonardo's bridge design.
　Ⓑ They never made the bridge that Leonardo designed.
　Ⓒ They lacked the money to complete Leonardo's project.
　Ⓓ They hired a new architect to build Leonardo's bridge.

Listening Skills Listening for Numbers

🎧 08-10

✓ **Check-Up** Listen and fill in the blanks with suitable numbers.

1 Leonardo lived in the _____ .

2 In _____ , he came up with a design for a bridge more than _____ feet long.

Chapter ❽   131

• Exercise 5 •

Bell and Edison

⬇

- The first telephone
- Both contributed important patents
- 1876: first voice via telephone

🎧 08-11

patent n the legal right to a design
grant v to give; to allow
crucial adj essential; important

Q1 What can be inferred about the invention of the telephone?

Ⓐ Bell did not need Edison's invention.
Ⓑ Bell designed it all by himself.
Ⓒ It relied on the work of both Bell and Edison.
Ⓓ The microphone Edison used in it was soon replaced.

Q2 What does the professor imply when she says this: "Please make note of that."

Ⓐ She considers the patent number to be important.
Ⓑ It is not important for the students to remember dates.
Ⓒ The students should not rely only on her lectures.
Ⓓ Edison wrote many notes when working on new inventions.

Listening Skills Listening for Numbers

✓ **Check-Up** Listen and fill in the blanks with suitable numbers.

1 Its patent number is _____.
2 In _____, Edison was granted a patent for the invention of the carbon microphone.
3 It was U.S. patent number _____.

🎧 08-12

132

• **Exercise 6** •

08-13

The Wright Brothers

- First successful flight
- Kitty Hawk, North Carolina
- 4 flights total

continuous *adj* nonstop; without pause
wingspan *n* the length of two wings from tip to tip

Q1 What can be inferred about early flight?

Ⓐ People built airplanes before the Wright brothers.
Ⓑ Gliders were successful before powered planes.
Ⓒ Many early inventors could control their airplanes.
Ⓓ Airplane engines caused many problems for inventors.

Q2 What can be inferred about the Wright brothers?

Ⓐ They planned to make one test flight at Kitty Hawk.
Ⓑ They encountered bad weather at Kitty Hawk.
Ⓒ They were not concerned about flying at a high altitude.
Ⓓ Their first plane crashed soon after it took off.

Listening Skills | Listening for Numbers

08-14

✓ **Check-Up** Listen and fill in the blanks with suitable numbers.

1 The engine weighed _____ pounds and had _____ horsepower.
2 The total weight of the plane was _____ pounds.
3 Wilbur flew the plane _____ feet down the sand dunes.

• Exercise 7 •

Coca-Cola

- Georgia, U.S., 1886
- Advertised as health drink
- Global company

fizzy adj having many bubbles; carbonated
pharmacy n a place that sells medicine
staggering adj amazing; overwhelming; outstanding

Q1 What does the professor imply about John Pemberton?

  Ⓐ He was a talented scientist and professor.
  Ⓑ He was not honest about Coke's benefits.
  Ⓒ He became very rich overnight.
  Ⓓ He stole the Coca–Cola recipe from Native Americans.

Q2 What can be inferred about Coca-Cola?

  Ⓐ It is made from natural plants.
  Ⓑ It came in plastic bottles before cans.
  Ⓒ It is the largest company in the United States.
  Ⓓ It does not cure health problems.

Listening Skills | Listening for Numbers

Check-Up Listen and fill in the blanks with suitable numbers.

1 He came up with the recipe for Coke in _____ or _____.
2 The first bottled Coke came out in March of _____, and it was put in cans much later in _____.
3 Its global revenues amounted to more than _____ - _____ billion dollars in _____.

• Exercise 8 •

Nails

⬇

- Invented by the Romans
- Made by blacksmiths
- Mass produced and made from steel

🎧 08-17

incredibly adv highly; very	**blacksmith** n a person who makes objects with iron
interlock v to fit into each other	

Q1 What can be inferred about the Romans?

Ⓐ They made a large number of inventions.
Ⓑ They preferred using wood to concrete.
Ⓒ They made wooden buildings that still exist today.
Ⓓ They made some buildings with wood.

Q2 What does the professor imply about nail-making machines?

Ⓐ They were not difficult to invent.
Ⓑ They made nails faster than blacksmiths.
Ⓒ They were invented by the Romans.
Ⓓ They were made of iron and steel.

Listening Skills Listening for Numbers

✓ **Check-Up** Listen and fill in the blanks with suitable numbers.

🎧 08-18

1 Most experts agree that the Romans did that more than _____ years ago.
2 Fortunately, in the _____, nail-making machines were invented.
3 This started in the mid-_____ and continued throughout the early _____.

Chapter ❽ 135

Vocabulary Review

A Circle the words that best complete the sentences.

1 The (invention / station) helped people save money on energy.
2 The boys used a small (craft / paddle) to get to the island.
3 The (sailors / sellers) kept the ship from sinking in the storm.
4 (Gunpowder / Strategic) allowed the men to defeat the archers.
5 The pieces of wood are cut to (interact / interlock) with one another.

B Choose the words to complete the sentences.

1 Diane had a _____ dream of attending an Ivy League school.
   A fanciful
   B pleasure
   C hope
   D title

2 The scientists made a _____ error in the rocket's design.
   A wanted
   B crucial
   C regular
   D formal

3 The _____ noise bothered the test takers.
   A sweet
   B silent
   C continuous
   D actually

4 The bubbles in _____ drinks really bother Erin.
   A fizzy
   B flat
   C thirsty
   D vitamins

5 The project cost the country a(n) _____ three billion dollars.
   A cheap
   B bonus
   C staggering
   D exacted

C Choose the words with the closest meanings to the highlighted words.

1. The pharmacy did not have the necessary medicine.
   - Ⓐ company
   - Ⓑ supermarket
   - Ⓒ drugstore
   - Ⓓ doctor

2. Fortunately, there will not be heavy rain in the area today.
   - Ⓐ Seriously
   - Ⓑ Happily
   - Ⓒ Probably
   - Ⓓ Apparently

3. Dr. Lowe granted Manny a five-day extension.
   - Ⓐ allowed
   - Ⓑ loaned
   - Ⓒ asked
   - Ⓓ developed

4. He learned to navigate a ship when he was young.
   - Ⓐ fly
   - Ⓑ build
   - Ⓒ drive
   - Ⓓ sail

5. The barge carried the old airplane down the river.
   - Ⓐ boat
   - Ⓑ jet
   - Ⓒ tractor
   - Ⓓ machine

D Complete the sentences by filling in the blanks with the best words from the list. Change the forms of the words if necessary. Use each word only once.

| pinpoint | direction | patent | magnetic | wingspan |

1. The doctor could not _____ the cause of the patient's problem.
2. The new _____ made the inventor a rich man.
3. Only _____ rocks such as iron can be used for magnets.
4. The _____ they should be going now is south.
5. The _____ of the new plane is longer than a football field.

Practice Test

1-4 Listen to part of a lecture in an engineering class.

Engineering

1 What aspect of concrete does the professor mainly discuss?

　Ⓐ How people use it
　Ⓑ Why it is effective
　Ⓒ When it was invented
　Ⓓ How long it can last

2 Why does the professor mention cement?

　Ⓐ To name its ingredients
　Ⓑ To explain how useful it is
　Ⓒ To say who invented it
　Ⓓ To discuss its characteristics

3 According to the professor, what did the Egyptians use concrete for?

　Ⓐ Statues
　Ⓑ Ships
　Ⓒ Pyramids
　Ⓓ Homes

4 How is the lecture organized?

　Ⓐ The professor reads from the textbook and then explains the passage.
　Ⓑ The professor covers information in reverse chronological order.
　Ⓒ The professor shows pictures to the class and then explains them.
　Ⓓ The professor focuses on the inventions of the Romans and the Egyptians.

Actual Test

Actual Test 1

Questions 1-4 Listen to part of a conversation between a student and a professor.

09-01

1. What problem does the student have?
    - Ⓐ She has not turned in her homework yet.
    - Ⓑ She does not know how to study for a test.
    - Ⓒ She cannot find a book she needs at the library.
    - Ⓓ She does not understand a class assignment.

2. What does the professor tell the student her paper needs?
    - Ⓐ A bibliography
    - Ⓑ A conclusion
    - Ⓒ A thesis statement
    - Ⓓ Some quotations

3. What is the professor's opinion of the student's paper?
    - Ⓐ It should be fun for her to write.
    - Ⓑ It does not require much research.
    - Ⓒ It is very well written.
    - Ⓓ It has quite a few mistakes.

4. What will the student probably do next?
    - Ⓐ Attend her next class
    - Ⓑ Go to the library
    - Ⓒ Ask another question
    - Ⓓ Visit one of her friends

Questions 5-9 Listen to part of a lecture in an environmental science class.

Environmental Science

5 What aspect of the Himalaya Mountains does the professor mainly discuss?
   - Ⓐ Their appearance
   - Ⓑ Their conditions
   - Ⓒ Their height
   - Ⓓ Their location

6 Why does the professor mention Base Camp?
   - Ⓐ To discuss the oxygen level there
   - Ⓑ To point out its exact location
   - Ⓒ To say how many people go there each year
   - Ⓓ To state that people have died there

7 What is a likely outcome of a climber on Mount Everest not using bottled oxygen?
   - Ⓐ The climber will not reach the top.
   - Ⓑ The climber will be more likely to fall.
   - Ⓒ The climber will suffer a permanent disability.
   - Ⓓ The climber will take a long time to reach the top.

8 What is the professor's opinion of the Himalaya Mountains?
   - Ⓐ They look beautiful.
   - Ⓑ They should be avoided.
   - Ⓒ They kill too many people.
   - Ⓓ They are very dangerous.

9 What will the professor probably do next?
   - Ⓐ End the class
   - Ⓑ Take a break
   - Ⓒ Show some pictures
   - Ⓓ Continue to lecture

Actual Test 2

Questions 1-4 Listen to part of a conversation between a student and a librarian.

09-03

1. Why does the student visit the librarian?
   - Ⓐ To have his library card renewed
   - Ⓑ To ask about some books he checked out
   - Ⓒ To inquire about the availability of a book
   - Ⓓ To try to find the location of a book

2. Why is the student unable to check out a book?
   - Ⓐ The library cannot find it.
   - Ⓑ Another person has borrowed it.
   - Ⓒ It is from the reference section.
   - Ⓓ He forgot his library card.

3. What can be inferred about the student when he says this: "I thought I only had five."
   - Ⓐ He only brought five books with him.
   - Ⓑ He is not permitted to borrow any more books.
   - Ⓒ He remembers returning a book yesterday.
   - Ⓓ He believes the librarian made a mistake.

4. What is the purpose of the student's response: "You don't need me to bring the books in?"
   - Ⓐ To disagree with the woman
   - Ⓑ To request assistance
   - Ⓒ To make a comparison
   - Ⓓ To express his surprise

Questions 5-9 Listen to part of a lecture in an art history class.

Art History

5 According to the professor, where did the Maya live?

- (A) In Asia
- (B) In Europe
- (C) In Central America
- (D) In South America

6 What aspect of Mayan cave art does the professor mainly discuss?

- (A) The styles that were used
- (B) The figures that were painted
- (C) The colors that were used
- (D) The places they were painted

7 What happened to the Maya?

- (A) They were destroyed in a major war.
- (B) They failed to develop an advanced culture.
- (C) They built few temples and other buildings.
- (D) They died out prior to the arrival of Columbus.

8 What does the professor say about cave art in Europe?

- (A) It can be very colorful.
- (B) It looks somewhat different from Mayan cave art.
- (C) It was created thousands of years ago.
- (D) It is only found in a few countries.

9 What does the professor imply when she says this: "They don't care about preserving cave art."

- (A) Mayan cave art is sometimes destroyed.
- (B) Few people know about Mayan cave art.
- (C) It is difficult to find some Mayan cave art.
- (D) Mayan cave art is becoming more popular.

Actual Test 3

Questions 1-4 Listen to part of a conversation between a student and a professor.

09-05

1. What are the speakers mainly discussing?
   - Ⓐ A midterm exam
   - Ⓑ The most recent class
   - Ⓒ An extra-credit project
   - Ⓓ A biology lab

2. Why does the professor apologize to the student?
   - Ⓐ He does not know her name.
   - Ⓑ He forgot their appointment.
   - Ⓒ He did not return her paper.
   - Ⓓ He cannot sign a form for her.

3. What is the professor's opinion of the student?
   - Ⓐ He believes she will be a good biologist.
   - Ⓑ He thinks she has a good idea for a topic.
   - Ⓒ He is frustrated by her poor grade.
   - Ⓓ He is impressed with her desire to learn.

4. What does the student imply when she says this: "No problem at all."
   - Ⓐ She is willing to visit the professor later.
   - Ⓑ She can submit some work on time.
   - Ⓒ She will be sure to take better notes.
   - Ⓓ She is going to study hard for the exam.

Questions 5-9 Listen to part of a lecture in a history of technology class.

History of Technology

5 What is the main topic of the lecture?
   Ⓐ Carl von Linde and Fred Wolf
   Ⓑ Modern refrigerators
   Ⓒ The Industrial Revolution
   Ⓓ The history of refrigeration

6 What can be inferred about refrigeration methods in the past?
   Ⓐ They were only useful in certain seasons.
   Ⓑ They were not difficult to use.
   Ⓒ They could be used anywhere on the Earth.
   Ⓓ They did not always keep food cold.

7 What happened during the Industrial Revolution?
   Ⓐ People began moving to large cities.
   Ⓑ Many scientific advances took place.
   Ⓒ There was a greater need for refrigerated food.
   Ⓓ People learned how to make money from new machines.

8 Do the following refer to Carl von Linde or Fred Wolf?
   Click in the correct box for each sentence.

	Carl von Linde	Fred Wolf
1 Liquified gases in large amounts		
2 Caused a breakthrough in refrigeration technology		
3 Made the first refrigerator to be used in homes		
4 Is called the father of modern refrigeration		

9 What is the professor's opinion of modern refrigerators?
   Ⓐ They have become too small.
   Ⓑ They are very effective.
   Ⓒ They can cost too much money.
   Ⓓ They need to be improved.

Appendix

Dictation Exercises

Dictation Exercises

Chapter 1

Sample Question

W Professor: When you think of France, along with the Eiffel Tower, perhaps _____ _____ . _____ _____ prehistoric cave art, too. _____ _____ Chauvet Cave in the south of France. The cave _____ _____ , fossils of animals, and even animal and _____ . In a sense, it's _____ . Experts estimate that _____ about 30,000 years old. The stunning artwork is _____ . For example, _____ bears, lions, and even panthers.

Exercise 1

M Professor: This morning, we will begin our discussion of _____ . I'd like to talk about _____ _____ . _____ , pictures of cave art _____ _____ such as bison, horses, cattle, and deer. We can _____ _____ the types of animals that were drawn were _____ _____ . Surprisingly, drawings of _____ _____ are _____ . There are also _____ _____ of tracings of _____ . But remember that each cave drawing _____ its environment and the habitat _____ . _____ _____ , a group of early humans _____ _____ , like a river or lake, _____ _____ . The reason was that _____

156

_____. Other examples are _____ and _____. For these reasons, the subjects of most cave art are _____ of _____ _____ _____.

Exercise 2

M Professor: Good morning, class. It is good to see everyone so bright and early. Today, we are going down under to _____, and we will _____ and _____ _____ there. Australia is just _____ containing _____ Aboriginal cave and rock art. You are _____ the Aborigines, right . . .? To clarify, they are _____ of Australia. Continuing, _____ _____ is Kakadu National Park in northern Australia. _____ _____ in the park is Ubirr. It is _____ _____ with outcrops that were used by Aborigines _____. Lots of types of fish, such as mullet and catfish, _____ _____ along with turtles and wallabies. _____ is the main gallery, where _____ _____ a Tasmanian tiger. _____ _____ for about 20,000 years.

🎧 01-05

Exercise 3

W Professor: That was a very good explanation, Laura. Now, I'd like to _____ _____, which is a very broad category. However, we can _____ rock art _____ _____: petroglyphs and pictographs. _____, I'll explain petroglyphs. These are basically _____ and _____. Images were _____, _____,

🎧 01-07

_____, and _____ into various surfaces _____ _____ _____ _____. On occasion, petroglyphs were even _____ and _____.

_____ pictographs. These involved the use of pigments. Pigments are _____ used for rock art. Early humans would _____ and _____ like crayons or coloring sticks. _____ _____ they used paintbrushes as well to form pictographs. One of the most common pictographs discovered is _____ _____. A pigment _____ _____, and the hand was then _____ _____ a rock. _____ _____ _____.

Exercise 4

W Professor: Perhaps two or three thousand years ago, _____ _____ the Baja Peninsula in Mexico and _____ in rocks and caves. Or so the legend goes.
I'm talking about Sierra de San Francisco, _____ _____ in Mexico. Actually, it was designated as a World Heritage Site in the 1990s. Now, were they giants? We're not sure, but some of the paintings are of _____ and _____ and _____ _____ in actual size. _____ _____ for a work of cave art. _____, the motifs of the art _____ human _____ animal representations. It is _____ and very well _____. The paintings at Sierra de San Francisco _____ _____ as well. _____ such as deer, sheep, and rabbits _____ _____. Octopi and whales are, too. _____, _____ eagles and pelicans can also _____ _____.

Exercise 5

M Professor: _____ _____ that have rock and cave art _____ _____. We have only begun _____ _____, if you will, of what is out there. You can bet that _____ _____. _____ by the elements, by weather, and by other natural occurrences.

Moving on, the Apollo 11 cave in southern Africa is often considered _____ _____ on the Earth. _____ _____ it is around 30,000 years old. Please be aware that Apollo 11 is the name of the cave, but _____ _____ _____ of the cave. Actually, the rock art _____ _____ brought from another location in Africa.

_____ a kind of _____ or _____ for the rock art. But _____ made it, and _____ was it made? Well, there are many theories, but _____ to either question. Recently, new finds in Africa suggest that rock art _____ _____ the age of the Apollo 11 find. That makes some of it _____ _____. Okay. We'll discuss that some more during the next class.

Exercise 6

W Professor: Okay, _____ _____ of cave art in Europe. Now, let's ask a very important question . . . _____ _____ prehistoric people _____ _____? It's hard to say because _____ _____ then. So they _____

_____ _____. However, there are _____

_____.

_____, some people believe prehistoric people were making art _____

_____. _____ _____, they

were just _____ who created art. As a result, _____

_____. That's why

_____. Another

theory is that these paintings were like _____

_____. The pictures were painted _____ _____

_____ _____ _____ they would hunt. In fact,

some cave art _____ _____ _____

_____. The cave at Lascaux has _____ _____

_____. A third theory is that the pictures had _____ _____

_____. Perhaps prehistoric people believed they could

_____ _____

_____. Then, they _____ _____

_____. Of course, we can't know for sure _____ _____

_____. It's just a theory.

Exercise 7

M Professor: _____ _____ _____

_____ is the Altamira cave in Spain. If any of you are backpacking through Europe this

summer, you should try to visit it. It will _____ _____

_____. _____ _____ nearly

1,000 feet in length, and paintings extend _____ the mouth of the cave _____

_____.

_____ the

Paleolithic Age, or the Old Stone Age. The dating of artifacts _____ the

cave art _____ _____

_____. The inhabitants of Altamira _____

_____ for coloring and drawing, but _____ _____

160

_____. There's _____ _____ about the Altamira paintings and the methods _____ _____ _____. Now, listen closely to this. _____, the inhabitants used _____ and _____ _____ to their subjects. They also used the contours of the cave _____. Contours are _____ _____ of the cave walls. They used them _____ _____-_____. Pretty cool, huh? Actually, I have some images of cave art from Altamira. Everyone, _____ _____ at the screen.

Exercise 8

M Professor: I went to the Lascaux cave in France with a few grad students _____ _____ _____ _____ there a couple years ago. The cave is _____ of France. Check the map on page 352 of your books to see where. Lascaux is _____. It was actually _____ in 1940. Most of the paintings are of _____, and they are _____ _____. Now, here's _____. The fame of Lascaux, which came right after its discovery, _____ _____. It was _____ _____, and the cave received nearly 2,000 visitors every single day. Lots of people in the cave meant a lot of, well, _____, _____, CO2, which was _____ to _____. _____, in 1963, the French government _____ to preserve the paintings. A few years ago, that _____ _____ my students and me. We

Dictation Exercises   161

couldn't believe _____ _____ _____. But we also believed it was _____ _____ _____ these ancient paintings. Don't you agree, class?

Practice Test

W Professor: Let's take a look at the Sahara Desert now. There are _____ _____ _____ archaeological sites that _____ _____ there. So far, we _____ _____ more than 2,000 sites.

_____ _____ _____ _____ _____ located in Morocco and Algeria. _____ _____ _____ in Algeria is Tassili. Actually, I was _____ _____ _____ _____ a few years ago. Much of the rock art in the caves shows _____ _____ _____ such as crocodiles. Yes, crocodiles in the Sahara. _____ _____ _____ to you? Well, the Sahara in prehistoric times was _____ _____ _____ _____. We'll talk more about that in a minute though. Oh, at Tassili, some of the rock carvings also _____ _____ and _____. _____ _____ _____ in Morocco _____ _____ in the Figuig Mountains. _____ _____ _____ found there show rhinos, antelopes, and felines. The felines represented _____ _____ _____. However, animal rock art is _____ _____ _____ at Figuig. There are also, um, _____ _____, including dotted lines, parallel lines, semicircles, and rectangles. _____, much of this art was actually _____ _____ and then _____, uh, probably _____ _____. Prehistoric artists _____ _____ _____ when they painted. Now, uh, I want to talk about _____ _____ _____ in Chad and

_____ it _____ _____ _____ I just talked about.

Chapter 2

Sample Question

W Professor: Mr. Archer, _____. Come in.

M Student: Hello, Professor Chapman. Can I talk to you for a minute?

W: Sure. _____. _____ _____ your paper for me yet?

M: No, _____ _____. Actually, I _____ _____ _____ _____ _____ about our group project.

W: I see. And I detect from your voice that _____ _____.

M: No, it isn't. We _____ _____ Stephen _____ _____, but it _____ _____ very well.

W: Really? How?

M: Well, he _____ our _____ _____ _____, and we're really _____ _____.

Exercise 1

W Student: Hi, Professor Madison. _____ _____?

M Professor: Um, yes, for the moment . . . You're, um . . .

W: Sandy. I'm _____ _____.

M: Oh, yes. Sandy. Right . . . _____ _____ today?

W: _____, and I was hoping you could give me some tips on _____.

M: A job, huh? _____ _____?

W: _____. I _____ my mind.

M: Well, you're young. _____ sometimes. _____?

W: What?

M: _____ on the university bulletin board this morning. The university is _____ _____ this weekend, and _____ _____.

W: Really? That's great.

M: You can talk with _____ _____. That might _____.

W: I'm sure it will. I _____ my résumé _____. See you in class. Thanks.

Exercise 2

W Professor: Thanks for coming to see me, Matt. Do you know _____ _____?

M Student: Actually, _____. _____ _____?

W: As you know, _____ _____. And, um, you _____ on the midterm exam.

M: Yeah, I guess _____. I hope to _____ this time.

W: I'm _____.

164

M: Thanks.

W: But I want to tell you _____.

I think _____ _____.

M: Yes? What is it?

W: Your tests are _____ _____ _____, of course. However, I _____ other factors _____ _____.

M: _____ _____ _____ factors?

W: Some are _____ _____ and your _____. Your marks for both of those are good, so you _____ _____ _____ _____.

M: _____ _____ _____ _____. Thanks so much.

Exercise 3

W Student: Excuse me, Professor Hamilton.

M Professor: Just a minute, please . . . Okay. All finished. _____ _____ _____ _____?

W: Hello. Um, do you _____ _____ _____ I can borrow?

M: A course catalog . . .? I, uh, _____ _____ _____. Why?

W: I just want to _____ _____ _____ _____ for a psychology class.

M: That's it?

W: Yes. I need to _____ _____. Then, we can _____ _____ _____.

M: I see. Well, I'm sorry, but I don't have one. I'm sure _____ _____ _____ at the Registrar's office.

W: Yes, _____ _____ that, but it's _____ _____ _____ campus. I thought I'd just _____ if you happened to have one.

M: _____ _____ the

Psychology Department office? It's in this building.

W: Is it? Oh, I feel so silly! I _____. Thanks, sir. _____.

M: You're welcome. Good luck.

Exercise 4

M Professor: Good afternoon, Natalie. _____ _____ ?

W Student: I'm all right. I wonder _____ _____ to talk.

M: _____ ?

W: We have _____ _____ next week, but I'm not sure _____ _____ _____.

M: First, _____ in class and doing the reading?

W: I try to _____ in class. I'm a bit _____, but I _____ by tomorrow.

M: In that case, I suggest _____ every day.

W: What else?

M: You should _____ in the book. Several questions on the test will _____, so you need to _____.

W: Wow. Thanks for the tip. Is there _____ _____ ?

M: It might not _____ _____. If you don't understand something, perhaps your friend _____.

W: My roommate is in the class, so I'll see _____ _____. Thanks a lot, sir.

Exercise 5

W Professor: Yes?

M Student: Oh, hi, Professor Gilbert.

W: Jeremy Ginn. I was hoping _____ .

M: Yes, I'm sorry I _____ _____, but I _____ _____ the chemistry lab.

W: That's fine. _____ _____.

M: I'm glad to hear that.

W: Actually, Jeremy, I _____ _____. If you agree, I will _____ _____.

M: Sure. _____ _____?

W: I'm _____ _____ in my freshman anatomy class next Thursday. It's a small class with _____ _____ _____.

M: Yes . . . ?

W: Well, all of my graduate assistants are _____ _____, so I was wondering if you _____ _____ for me.

M: Me, a proctor? _____ _____?

W: I sure am. _____ _____ is _____ the quizzes from me in the morning and then _____ to the class. Of course, you need to _____ at the end of the class.

M: No problem. _____ _____.

W: I know, Jeremy. _____ _____ the quizzes, just _____ in my mailbox.

M: You've got it, Professor.

Exercise 6

🎧 02-13

W Student: Um, Professor Burgess? _____ _____ _____ _____ _____ for a moment, or do you have a lecture now?

M Professor: If you can _____ _____ _____, I can talk. I _____ _____ _____ in five minutes.

W: Okay. Well, _____ _____ _____ . . .

M: You want to _____ _____ _____. Well, the add-drop period is over, so I guess . . .

W: Oh, no. I really enjoy your class.

M: Really? I don't hear that too often.

W: Um, I was hoping you could _____ _____ _____ _____ _____ in the laboratory. I need to _____ _____ _____ _____ from class today.

M: Extra time in the lab? I think that's another first. Most students run away _____ _____ _____ _____ from my lab class.

W: Really. I'm being serious! _____ _____ _____?

M: Actually, I think _____ _____ now, but you cannot mix any chemicals _____ _____ _____.

W: I _____ _____ _____ like that. I just want to _____ _____ _____.

M: That's fine. But please _____ _____ _____. Okay?

W: No problem. It will only _____ _____ _____ _____ or so.

M: That's fine.

W: Thanks a lot, Professor Burgess.

Exercise 7

02-15

W Professor: Andrew, I think you know _____ _____ _____ _____ _____ _____.

M Student: Yes, ma'am. _____ _____ _____ lately.

W: _____ _____. Is there _____ _____ _____?

M: There is, actually. I _____ _____ of my fraternity, and _____ _____ almost all of my time.

W: I see . . . Well, I think fraternities are fine, Andrew, but academics _____ _____ _____. _____ _____ _____?

M: Yes, ma'am.

W: The syllabus _____ _____ if you miss three or more classes, _____ _____ by five points. You _____ _____ _____, right?

M: Yes, I am. I'm really sorry. This month, I _____ _____ and _____ _____. I _____ _____ from now on.

W: That's _____ _____.

M: Yes . . .

W: Andrew, _____ _____ your grade; however, I'd like you to _____ _____ _____. Please _____ _____ the habits of dolphins. That should _____ _____ _____. Got it?

M: I'll _____ _____ by Wednesday, Professor Starling. Thank you.

W: Good. I'm glad _____ _____.

Dictation Exercises 169

Exercise 8

02-17

W Professor: Hello, Brad. _____ with you?

M Student: Hello, Professor Watson. I'm _____ _____, but everything is _____ _____.

W: That's good news. I want to _____ _____ _____ that has just come up.

M: Yes? What's that?

W: _____ that will be held two months from now.

M: A speech contest?

W: That's right. And I think you _____ _____ _____.

M: Hmm . . . _____ _____ _____ before though. I don't know _____ _____ _____.

W: _____ at all. You'll _____ _____ ahead of time, and you have to _____-_____ on it.

M: That _____.

W: _____. If you get selected _____ _____, you'll _____ _____ about _____ _____ before you go up on stage to speak.

M: That's _____. But it _____ _____.

W: Oh, there are _____ _____, but there usually _____ _____.

M: Okay. _____. I think _____ _____.

W: That's great news. I'll email you a link _____ _____.

_____. I'm sure you'll _____, and you _____.

M: Thanks for _____, Professor Watson.

Practice Test

W Student: Good afternoon, Professor Nelson. _____ for a minute?

M Professor: Well, actually, I have class at 3:00, and it's 2:45 right now . . .

W: _____.

M: Okay. But _____, please.

W: Great. Thanks. _____ an academic conference next month.

M: Right. I'm _____.

W: Yes, well, uh, I was hoping I _____.

M: Submissions _____ undergraduate _____ graduate students. However . . .

W: Yes?

M: The competition _____.

W: I see.

M: This conference is _____ in the country. _____ will be chosen to speak at it.

W: Okay.

M: Last year, we had about _____. I think we _____ only five or six.

W: _____.

M: Yeah. Anyway, _____ by 5:00 PM. So you _____

_____.

W: Actually, _____ _____ _____. I came by here to _____ _____ _____ with you.

M: Finished? Well, _____ _____. You know, I could _____ _____ _____ for you and _____ _____.

W: That _____ _____.

M: That way, you will _____ _____ _____ I suggest.

W: Great. In that case, I'll _____ _____ _____ tomorrow afternoon.

Chapter 3

Sample Question

W Professor: Deserts are _____, uh, _____ _____. They are _____ _____. Dry is _____ _____. But how dry? Just because an area is arid, _____ _____ _____? Not always. Scientists have come up with a formula that _____ _____. According to them, deserts are areas that _____ _____ of precipitation each year. However, please note that _____ _____. Some areas _____ _____, but scientists still _____ _____.

🎧 03-01

Exercise 1

M Professor: Okay, let's settle down everyone. We have _____ _____ today. Oh, remember we have a quiz next week. Please don't forget.

🎧 03-03

Today, we'll _____ of most deserts. You all know that _____, but can you tell me why . . . ? Let me explain. Many deserts have a big fluctuation _____ and _____. For example, a desert can _____ during the day, but that night, it _____ almost to freezing. Why is this? Well, _____ humidity, which is _____ in the air. You see, _____ from reaching the Earth's surface. _____ also _____ insulate, that is, _____ to the Earth's surface at night. With deserts, this lack of humidity _____ and _____ easily. This is the reason _____ _____.

Exercise 2

W Professor: _____ on the Earth? Without a doubt, _____ is one of the most frigid places. It is _____. Think of it this way. _____, the average temperature at the South Pole is about _____ _____ Fahrenheit. Cold, huh? But that's beach weather _____. Winter temperatures average—are you ready for this— _____ - _____ Fahrenheit. There are _____ these cold temperatures. _____, during winter, the South Pole _____. It's _____ _____. During summer, the sun _____ _____, and with _____ _____, most of the sunlight _____

🎧 03-05

Dictation Exercises   173

_____ _____ _____. _____, the South Pole is at a relatively _____ _____ around _____ _____. This altitude is one of the reasons why the South Pole is _____ _____.

Exercise 3

W Professor: First, I want to _____ _____ _____. Well done, and I hope you keep it up. Now, this morning, we'll continue our discussion on _____ _____. One place I'd like to talk about is one _____ probably _____ _____: _____ _____. It is one of _____ _____ to life on the planet. _____ _____, _____, and _____ atmospheric _____ characterize the deep ocean. Of course, it is one of _____ _____ and _____ _____ as well because _____ _____ simply _____ _____ in that type of environment. _____, it's impossible. Still, we are able to _____ _____ the surface. We can use ROVs. ROV _____ _____ remotely operated vehicle. Usually, an ROV is _____ _____ installed with cameras and built to _____ _____. But deep-sea exploration is _____ _____. That's another reason why _____ _____ _____ has been explored.

Exercise 4

M Professor: Imagine a place _____ _____ parts of it _____ _____ in more than 400 years. Yes, that place _____ _____. It's the Atacama Desert, and _____ _____ Chile in South America.

174

Interestingly, the desert is located _____ _____ _____. The ocean is the reason _____ _____ _____ _____. There is a _____ - _____ alongside Chile. _____ _____ _____, there's cold air at the surface while _____ _____ _____ _____. This means that _____ _____ _____. However, _____ _____ _____ of parts of the desert. The desert, by the way, is _____ _____. Depending on the season, the temperature can be _____ _____ and _____ _____ _____ Celsius.

Here's something interesting about the desert. Because it is _____ _____ there, the conditions in the Atacama Desert are _____ _____ _____. NASA, the American space organization, _____ _____ _____ _____ there. _____ _____ _____, _____ _____ currently on Mars _____ _____ in the Atacama Desert to see _____ _____ _____ _____ there.

Exercise 5

M Professor: Yellowstone National Park in the northwest part of the United States is _____ _____ _____ _____ _____. First of all, much of the region is _____ _____ _____ _____ _____. In fact, _____ _____ _____ _____ a supervolcano, one of the largest and most volatile types of volcanoes. It _____ _____ in more than _____ _____, but _____ _____ _____ are hot gases and an enormous magma pool.

Now, the Yellowstone Caldera, which is _____ _____ _____ at the top of the volcano, _____ _____ _____ _____. In fact, it's _____ _____ _____. Well, I suppose it's actually more

Dictation Exercises 175

dormant. After all, it _____ _____ _____ _____. Nevertheless, hot rocks are _____ _____ _____ and _____ through vents or geysers throughout the park. Some of the gases are _____, so they're dangerous to animals and humans _____ _____. Many of the geysers _____. It's often _____ _____ Fahrenheit. So _____ _____ to any geysers if you ever visit the park.

Exercise 6

W Professor: As you should know, there are _____ _____ _____. Antarctica is _____ _____ _____ _____, and the Sahara in North Africa is a hot desert. I'd like to discuss _____ _____ these hostile environments _____ _____ _____. Let's begin with _____. _____ and _____ as well as _____ _____ _____ are not a healthy combination for humans. Our bodies will _____ _____ in an attempt to _____ _____. However, after even a few hours of _____ _____ _____, a number of conditions _____ _____. Of course, dehydration is _____ _____ _____ heatstroke, and after a few punishing days, _____. In cold deserts, _____ _____. Sure, you could _____ or _____, but without a source of heat, you'll _____ _____. _____ that humans face in cold deserts _____ _____ is hypothermia. This happens _____ _____ _____ _____ and _____ _____.

Exercise 7

W Professor: In Asia, the Tibetan Plateau in western China is one of _____ _____ for people _____ _____. Actually, _____ _____ isn't too bad. _____ _____, and the temperatures and the altitude are _____ _____.

However, in the north and the northeast, it is _____ _____ _____. Moving to the north, the plateau increases in elevation, and _____ _____ and _____. In the northwest part of the plateau is Changtang Province. It's _____ _____ of Tibet. _____ _____? Well, the average altitude is _____ _____. That's one reason. Another reason, as you can guess, _____ _____. Annually, the temperature averages _____ _____ Celsius. _____, it is absolutely frigid as the temperature averages _____ _____ Celsius. Chilly, huh? It is _____, especially humans, _____ _____. It should _____ _____ that it is _____ _____ in all of Asia. Only Antarctica, and perhaps Greenland _____.

Exercise 8

M Professor: North Africa is the winner _____ _____ _____ _____ _____ in the world. _____ _____ _____ _____ the Sahara, and it _____ _____ _____. Yes, I said million, class. It occupies most of _____ _____ _____. However, the Sahara _____ _____ _____ _____. An ice age long ago _____ _____ _____, but once it ended, the Sahara _____ _____ _____. In addition, monsoon rains _____ _____ the southern _____ northern regions of the Sahara, but that _____ _____ _____. Not times of the year. I'm talking about _____ _____ _____ _____. Experts believe that the monsoons _____ _____ _____ Sahara, and they _____ _____ today. Let me _____ _____ _____. Most of the Sahara is very dry, but _____ _____ _____ a bit _____ _____, which still _____ _____, than the north. Another funny thing about the Sahara is that _____ _____ _____, _____ _____ _____. We call these torrential rains, and they can _____ _____ or even _____.

Practice Test

M Professor: _____ _____ _____ is the Painted Desert in northern Arizona. It's absolutely beautiful. The landscape of mountains and hills _____ _____ brightly colored _____. _____, which we call strata, in the mountains are _____ _____ and _____. Reds, oranges, yellows, and other earth tones _____ _____ _____ _____ over thousands and thousands of years. Wind and rain are _____ _____ which _____ _____ _____ _____. Of course, sunrise and sunset are _____ _____ the brilliant colors of the Painted Desert.

_____ _____ _____ _____ parts of the Painted Desert is the Petrified Forest. It is _____ petrified, you know, _____, _____, _____, and even dinosaur bones and _____. Most of the petrified items _____ _____ _____ _____ and were petrified _____ _____. Ash and sand _____ _____ trees and wood _____ _____ leaves and other items _____ _____ _____.

The Petrified Forest also contains some of _____ _____ in North America. _____ _____ _____ is the phytosaur. This was _____ _____ that was somewhat _____ _____ _____ or _____. It _____ _____ _____. But that's not all. There are also _____ _____ invertebrates _____ _____ _____ and _____ in the forest.

Chapter 4

Sample Question

M Student: Excuse me. I _____ _____ for a class.
W Registrar's Office Employee: Sure. _____ _____ _____ ?
M: The class is History 26. It's _____ _____ _____ Professor Cole.

W: _____. Let me check on _____.

M: Sure.

W: I'm sorry, but that class _____.

M: Full? Oh, no. That's bad news.

W: Yes, it's full, but I can _____. _____ if you do that.

M: What are the chances of _____?

W: In most classes, at least _____ each semester.

M: That's _____. Then go ahead and _____, please.

W: All right. May I see your student ID?

Exercise 1

W Student: Hello. Could you _____ for me?

M Librarian: You need to use the photocopiers _____.

W: Oh, come on, please. It'll _____.

M: _____, _____ my manager is standing right there.

W: Oh, I see. Well, thanks . . .

M: Wait a minute.

W: What?

M: Do you _____?

W: _____ change or bills or a credit card?

M: _____. You have to _____. You can _____

the card and then _____ _____ _____ _____

_____.

W: _____ a copy card?

M: From me.

W: Okay. I'll take one _____ _____ of credit on it.

M: Okay. Here's your card, and _____ _____ _____

_____.

W: Great. Thanks a lot. Second floor, right?

M: _____ _____.

W: See you later.

M: What a minute. You _____ _____. Here you are . . .

W: Oh, thanks.

Exercise 2

W Housing Office Employee: Hi. Can I help you?

M Student: Yes, I'm _____ _____ _____.

W: You have _____ _____. Do you prefer on- or off-campus housing?

M: On campus. The off–campus housing is _____ _____

_____ _____, and I don't like buses.

W: You don't like buses? Okay. Then _____ _____

_____ an on–campus apartment _____ a dormitory?

M: Are there _____ _____?

I _____ _____. Roommates really

_____.

W: _____ _____. There sure are.

M: _____ can I _____ the studio?

W: Actually, there are _____ _____

_____ now. You just need to _____ _____, and

then _____.

M: Great. _____?

W: Let me _____, and we'll _____. Okay?

M: Sounds good. Let's do it.

Exercise 3

M Employee: Uh, number twenty-two is next, please . . .

W Student: Hello. Um . . . I'm not sure _____ _____.

M: Okay. This window _____.

W: Oh, good. I'd like to _____ _____ to the pass-fail option.

M: Okay. Student number, please.

W: 2-1-5-7-8-8.

M: Hmm . . . It looks like _____-_____ this semester. You're _____.

W: I know. So I'd like to do this. I want to _____ _____ from my schedule. Then, I'd like to _____ _____ to _____-_____. Can I do that?

M: You sure can. Biology 414 . . . dropped . . . _____ Japanese II _____ pass-fail. Okay. _____. Anything else?

W: Oh, one more thing. When is _____ _____? Next Friday, right?

M: Yes, but you can _____-_____ if you need it.

W: Oh, good. Thanks.

182

Exercise 4

04-09

W Student: Mr. Jefferson, could I _____ _____ _____ _____ _____ ?

M Cafeteria Manager: Sure, Stephanie. What do you want to talk about?

W: It's about _____ this Thursday evening.

M: What about it?

W: Is it _____ _____ with someone else?

M: For _____ ? _____ that's ideal.

W: Oh, _____ for the rest of the semester. I'm talking about _____ .

M: _____ ?

W: I've got _____ _____ _____ to give _____ _____ , and the group wants to _____ _____ on Thursday.

M: Hmm . . . Well, _____ that you're here.

W: Thank you so much _____ _____ .

M: However, you need to _____ _____ _____ as your replacement. If you don't do that, you'll _____ _____ _____ .

W: I don't really know _____ _____ _____ here. _____ do you think _____ _____ ?

M: David is always _____ .

W: _____ is David?

M: He's _____ by the sink. _____ _____ with him now?

Exercise 5

W Student: Good morning. _____

_____? A celebrity photo shoot?

M Assistant: Um, actually, we're _____

_____ _____ this morning. You know, for graduating students . . . Cap and gown. That kind of thing.

W: Oh, really? Nobody told me. This is _____ _____ _____ .

M: _____ _____ _____ graduate?

W: Yes.

M: _____ _____ _____ ?

W: Of course.

M: Then you _____ _____ _____

_____ . What's your name?

W: Heather Hampton.

M: Hampton, Hampton . . . Yes, _____ _____ . Would you like

to _____ ?

W: _____ _____ , but I don't have a cap or a gown.

M: _____ . We have some different ones for you _____

_____ just _____ _____ .

W: Great. _____ ?

M: _____ _____ . Your picture will automatically

_____ _____ , and the

university will _____ _____ via regular or

email . . .

W: Okay.

M: Once you preview your picture, you can _____

_____ on the request form.

W: I see. _____ , will it? I have class

in fifteen minutes.

M: No, _____ . Here, have a seat . .

Exercise 6

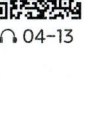
04-13

M Student: Hello. I'm _____ _____ _____ student council.

W Assistant: _____ - _____ can do that. You're full time, right?

M: _____ _____ _____ full time _____?

W: You must _____ _____ _____ this semester.

M: Oh, I'm taking five classes _____ _____ _____.

W: Wonderful. The other criterion is that you must _____ _____ _____ and _____ _____.

M: I have that, too.

W: _____ _____ _____, please? Okay, um, this looks fine. Actually, I had Dr. Jensen last year. He's great.

M: Yeah, _____ _____ for my undergraduate thesis.

W: _____ on the student council _____ _____ _____?

M: Secretary.

W: Do you _____ _____?

M: Here you go. You can _____ _____ _____.

W: Thanks. _____ _____ _____—your address, email, and phone number— _____ _____?

M: Yes, it is.

W: Perfect. Then could I please _____ _____ and _____ _____ on this line?

M: There you go.

W: Okay. We'll _____ _____ in two or three days. It's just a formality.

M: Sounds good. Thanks a lot.

Exercise 7

W Student: Excuse me. I wonder _____

_____ my housing situation.

M Housing Office Employee: _____

_____?

W: I would like to _____

_____. Is that possible?

M: The date for moving _____

_____.

W: Oh, that's too bad.

M: _____

_____ you want to move? Maybe I can help.

W: It's my roommate. She and I simply _____

_____.

M: In _____?

W: I go to bed early, but she _____.

She's _____ and always _____

_____.

M: Have you _____

_____ that?

W: Yes, I have, but she _____

_____ because of my horrible living situation.

M: Hmm . . . We could probably _____

_____.

W: You could? That _____.

M: I have to _____.

I _____ though.

W: _____, I'll

186

appreciate it.

M: Let me talk to my boss. I'll _____ _____ _____ _____ _____ .

Exercise 8

W University Fitness Center Employee: Hello. Can I see _____ or _____ , please?

M Student: Um . . . what do you mean? _____ _____? Faculty and students?

W: Oh, you must be a freshman. They never remember to tell you guys during orientation, do they? I'll _____ .

M: _____ , please?

W: This is _____ - _____ . Actually, university employees can work out here, too.

M: Then _____ _____?

W: You're _____ . It's _____ of this building. You can just _____ _____ .

M: Thanks. By the way, _____ in the fitness centers?

W: Sure. Are you _____ _____?

M: Oh, no. I'm _____ .

W: Well, _____ , there's a good chance. I think _____ in the student center.

M: Wonderful. _____ .

W: Yeah, _____ . Just tell her _____ _____ and _____ _____ in sometime soon.

M: I will. Thanks for your help.

W: Have a good workout.

Practice Test

M Student: Hello. _____
_____ clubs at the school?

W Student Activities Office Employee: We had _____
_____. Is that _____?

M: It was yesterday? _____
_____.

W: There were _____ all around campus.
_____?

M: I guess I _____ the dates _____.

W: Anyway, clubs are _____. So
you have time to _____ or _____
_____ if you are interested.

M: That's great news. _____ are
there?

W: _____ clubs.

M: Hmm . . . Do you know _____?

W: The movie club is _____
_____. _____ the cycling club and the jogging club.

M: Those last two clubs _____. Are
there any clubs that _____
_____?

W: _____ the chess club? It _____
_____. There's also a computer programming club.

M: Those _____. I might check out _____
_____.

W: Is there anything else _____?

M: I _____ rocks. Is there a geology
club?

188

W: _____, but there is a paleontology club. _____ dinosaurs and fossils. Sometimes they even _____

_____.

M: Woah, that _____. It's just _____

_____.

W: You're in luck. The club _____

_____ of the year this evening at six thirty.

M: _____?

W: It's going to be in room 203 in Carmichael Hall. _____

_____, the club _____

_____. Good luck.

Chapter 5

Sample Question

M Professor: Samantha, please _____.

W Student: Good morning, Dr. Givens.

M: Samantha, the reason I called you in is _____

_____.

W: _____?

M: Kind of. I like your idea, but the thesis is _____ and _____.

W: I see. I _____.

M: It _____. Here's your paper. I've _____ there at the bottom in blue. That'll _____.

W: Thanks so much, Dr. Givens.

M: My pleasure, Sam. _____, bring it back in. Okay?

W: Sure. _____ with you?

M: _____.

W: Thanks a lot.

Exercise 1

W Professor: Come in, Lance. _____ _____ ?

M Student: Yes, I did.

W: So what's the verdict?

M: _____ want to go to White Beach _____ .

W: Really? That's interesting. _____ _____ visit the aquarium.

M: Me, too. I actually _____ . _____ twenty-two for White Beach and five for the aquarium.

W: Hmm . . . You told them that _____ _____ 75 dollars _____, right? I mean to White Beach.

M: I did, and I told them _____ the aquarium _____ . Still, as I said, _____ _____ White Beach.

W: _____ ? Well, then _____ _____ . We'll journey to White Beach next Saturday _____ _____ .

M: I guess so.

W: Okay. Lance, can you _____ and _____ from everyone? Tell them they ____ _____ . If they _____ , _____ . Okay?

M: You're the boss, Professor Shamrock.

190

Exercise 2

W Student: Hi, Professor Gibson. May I _____, or are you _____?

M Professor: Sure, I've got a few minutes.

W: Thanks. _____ sit down?

M: _____. Go ahead.

W: I'm _____ the final examination.

M: I see. _____?

W: Um, _____?

M: Were you _____ yesterday?

W: No, sir.

M: You _____ the review? So tell me _____ to explain everything again.

W: _____, I was in a minor car accident yesterday.

M: Oh, my. Are you okay? I didn't mean to _____.

W: That's okay. And yes, I'm fine. Thanks.

M: Right. Then, um, let me explain _____ for you. Do you have _____ and _____?

Exercise 3

M Professor: Good morning, Karen. _____?

W Student: Good morning, Professor Cartwright.

M: _____ your favorite pet or something. _____?

W: I just _____, sir.

M: Get what?

W: It's _____.

M: Um, what are you talking about, Karen?

W: I just _____, and I received a D in your class! Did I _____ or what because I thought _____?

M: Hold on now. Calm down. We'll _____ _____. First, you had one of _____ in the class on the final. Second, your final grade _____.

W: It was?

M: Yes, I distinctly remember _____ _____.

W: So _____?

M: _____ a computer glitch. It _____. I'll tell you _____. I'll call the Registrar's office _____ _____.

W: Gee, thanks, sir. _____.

Exercise 4

W Professor: Come in.

M Student: Do you have a moment, Professor Stevens? I _____ about something.

🎧 05-09

W: All right, Mr. Chambers, but _____. I've _____ the dean at noon.

M: The dean, huh? _____.

W: _____. It is. So what's up?

192

M: I'm thinking about _____.

W: You're _____?

M: _____ a double major.

W: Hold on a second. Are you _____? Do you know _____ and _____ _____?

M: Well, _____. So _____ it's a good idea?

W: For students _____, I think it's great, but _____ you're _____ _____.

M: _____ _____, huh?

W: Look. You're a good student, but a double major _____ _____. I just don't think you're _____ _____.

M: Thanks for _____ me.

Exercise 5

W Student: Professor Chambers, could I speak with you, please?

M Professor: Of course. Um . . . _____ _____ your name. Are you in my class?

W: No, sir, but I'm thinking about _____ _____. My name is Amber Marston.

M: It's _____, Amber. Which of my classes _____?

W: It's the class on medieval English literature. I was wondering _____ _____.

M: Sure. Basically, we're going to read some of _____ _____ from the Middle Ages.

W: _____ Chaucer?

Dictation Exercises   193

M: _____. We'll also _____ such as *Pearl* and *Sir Gawain and the Green Knight*. We'll _____ about King Arthur, too.

W: Are we going to read them _____ or _____?

M: Middle English.

W: Oh, I don't know _____.

M: Don't be worried. It's actually _____. _____ for fifteen years. In my experience, students _____ Middle English _____.

W: That's _____. I'll definitely _____ in that case.

M: I'm _____ in class in the fall.

Exercise 6

M Student: Professor Watson, may I come in?

W Professor: Yes. Hi, Brandon.

M: I _____, ma'am.

W: Yes, I heard that _____.

M: Yeah.

W: We're all sorry _____, Brandon. I hope _____.

M: Me, too. I want you to know I _____, and I _____ during the past few months.

W: You're very welcome. Is there _____?

🎧 05-13

M: I want to _____ as a finance major _____ _____ _____, but it is really _____ _____ _____ _____ to the program.

W: _____ _____ _____. It's one of the top programs in the country. I actually _____ _____ _____ in the department. _____ _____ _____ it is my alma mater?

M: I didn't know that. In that case, _____ _____ _____ _____ to the department head _____ _____? It might _____ _____ _____.

W: I'll _____ _____ _____ _____, Brandon. I'll _____ _____ _____ this evening and give her _____ _____ for you. How does that sound?

M: That's _____ _____ _____.

Exercise 7

M Professor: Hey, Jamie. Are you _____ _____ – _____ _____?

🎧 05-15

W Student: Yes, I am. Why?

M: I think I _____ _____ _____ _____, but the hours are _____ _____ _____.

W: _____ _____ _____ _____ the job?

M: You _____ _____ _____, Dr. Holloway in the Religion Department.

W: So far, _____ _____ _____.

M: You'd _____ _____, _____ _____, and maybe _____ _____ for him. Those kinds of things . . .

W: Yes . . .

M: But, well, _____ _____ _____

_____ . . . ? Dr. Holloway is a bit eccentric.

W: _____ _____ ?

M: He _____ _____ _____ _____ very early in the morning.

W: How early?

M: Four AM, Jamie. He believes that's when _____ _____ _____. You would assist him _____ _____ in the morning _____ _____.

W: Four? Are you kidding? Is _____ _____ _____ _____ ?

M: _____ _____ _____ _____. Yes, I think _____ _____ at 40 dollars per hour.

W: Forty an hour, huh? Well, that's _____ _____ _____ _____.

M: _____ _____ _____ _____, Jamie, and please _____ _____. Okay?

W: I will. Thanks!

Exercise 8

W Professor: Derrick, come in and have a seat . . . Coffee?

M Student: No thanks, ma'am.

W: Not a coffee drinker, huh? Anyway, thanks for _____ _____ _____.

M: Sure, Professor Walker. _____ _____ _____ ?

W: Just _____ _____. I have _____ _____ _____.

M: Really? What is it?

W: The university _____ _____ in our department next week, and I'd like you _____ _____ _____.

🎧 05-17

M: Wow. That is _____. Thank you.

W: So do you _____? It will be _____

_____ and _____ to

your résumé. _____?

M: Of course. I _____ this kind of an opportunity.

W: You're right. You can't. You'll meet _____ _____

_____ in the field. _____ _____? Perhaps

someone will _____ _____ _____

_____ and _____.

M: _____ _____, Professor.

W: You _____ _____. _____ _____

_____ beginning tomorrow morning? Does that sound good?

M: All right, Professor. _____ _____ at nine in the morning.

Practice Test

M Professor: Jamie, come in, please.

W Student: Hello, Dr. Mears. That test today _____.

M: I know. But don't worry. The next one _____.

W: I sure _____. Anyway, I _____ _____

_____ _____.

M: Sure. Go ahead.

W: I'm trying to decide _____

_____ during the summer session.

M: I see. _____ during a summer or

winter session _____?

W: No, I haven't.

M: Well, _____

sometime, right?

W: _____.

M: Then why are you _____

_____? You should _____ _____

_____.

W: Well, _____ summer classes _____ _____ those during the regular term.

M: _____ they're more difficult. More information _____ _____. You'll also have the same class _____ _____.

W: Right.

M: But you'll only take one or two classes _____ _____ four or five _____ _____ in fall and spring.

W: _____ _____ the summer _____ winter sessions?

M: The courses are the same, but _____. The weather is _____. It's _____.

W: Yeah, I _____.

M: Oh, wait. I _____ the courses. I believe there's _____ _____ offered _____.

W: I didn't know that. Then I think _____ _____. Thanks, sir.

Chapter 6

Sample Question

M Professor: Achoo. Sorry, everyone, but it looks like _____ _____. It's kind of ironic because _____ _____ I plan to discuss today. Generally, adults _____ between _____ and _____, but _____ get them _____. They might _____

_____ each year. Moreover, _____ of a cold are a sore throat, sneezing, and fatigue. Coughing _____. _____, body aches, a fever, and even the chills _____. _____ with the symptoms of a cold, but it _____ actually _____. You basically just have to _____.

Exercise 1

M Professor: Rabies is a deadly viral infection. If it's _____, it will _____. So _____, especially dogs, bats, raccoons, and skunks that _____.
Now, I don't mean _____ in _____ or _____. _____, I'm talking about animals that _____ and _____ in their eyes. _____ the animals have _____ _____ around their mouths.
Actually, rabies is _____. It usually _____ _____ by an infected animal, but a person can sometimes _____ just _____ on the body. Scary, huh?
Fortunately, _____. In most countries, a vaccine _____ _____ against rabies since the late nineteenth century. There's a vaccine _____. Consequently, rabies is _____ in _____.
However, it still _____ every once in a while, so always _____ extremely _____.

Dictation Exercises   199

Exercise 2

W Professor: Good afternoon, class. I'm sure _____ _____ when you were children. Yes, I _____ _____ out there. It wasn't fun, was it? Well, let's discuss it some, shall we?

First, it is _____ and is _____. _____ you had to stay home from school and _____ _____ when you had it. It can _____ _____ the sores on the skin or by _____ and _____. Next, _____ in the form of small, circular spots _____ _____ on the body. They're _____, but it isn't good to scratch them because _____.

Ultimately, chickenpox _____ _____. It _____ _____, which takes about a week or so. However, the good news is that you'll probably _____ because the body develops _____.

Exercise 3

M Professor: So far, what we call vaccines are _____ _____ against infectious diseases and viruses. Let me explain in _____ _____.

A vaccine is most often an inoculation. That is, _____. It's an injection or a series of injections into a person's body. The inoculation contains some form of the virus _____. Usually, it is _____ or even _____ _____. Afterward, the body _____ _____ the given virus.

Antibodies are _____ _____ against diseases. They are usually _____ _____ and _____ _____. Because of antibodies, _____ viruses and infectious diseases _____ _____. The first vaccine _____ Edward Jenner in 1756. It was _____. Since 1979, _____ _____ of smallpox in a human being. Now, that's good medicine. Don't you agree?

Exercise 4

W Professor: Maybe you are all aware of _____ _____. Of course, currently, AIDS is one of _____ and _____. However, _____. The statistics are not concrete or conclusive, but _____ _____, there was the Spanish flu. It _____ than most other diseases in history. Some experts estimate that _____ _____ while others think it was more likely _____. _____ the Spanish flu was _____ that it was a pandemic. This means that _____ and that _____ from it. _____, unlike other flu outbreaks, it was _____. _____, it _____ the young, strong, and healthy _____ the old and weak. _____, _____ for a flu virus, causing even more deaths. _____, around June 1920, the Spanish flu _____.

_____ _____ _____ it arrived.

Exercise 5

M Professor: Today, I'd like to begin by discussing the West Nile Virus, or WNV. First, I'll discuss _____ and _____ _____. Then, I'll _____ _____ if time allows. How does that sound for a plan? The West Nile Virus is often a serious, seasonal virus in North America that _____ _____ _____. Although some people think _____ _____ _____, they are incorrect. On the contrary, it _____ _____ mosquitoes. Mosquitoes become infected _____ infected birds and _____ _____, touching dead birds is _____ _____. Just remember, class, to _____ _____ and mosquitoes. Now, uh, a West Nile Virus infection can _____ _____ _____, the majority of infected people _____ _____. That's right. You heard me correctly. Experts estimate that _____ _____ infected with WNV _____ _____. They have _____ _____ _____. However, _____ _____ _____ such as nausea, fever, vomiting, and body aches.

Exercise 6

W Professor: Let's talk about _____ _____. There are some diseases that _____ _____ _____.

chickenpox. But we've already covered it. _____ _____ measles. Let me tell you about it.

Measles is _____ _____ _____ _____ that's _____ _____ _____ _____.

Nowadays, most children _____ _____ when they're young. However, this _____ _____ _____ in the world. As a result, _____ _____ _____ from measles each year. That's _____ _____ _____ I hope comes down soon.

_____ _____ _____ _____? Well, the symptoms _____ _____ _____ _____ _____ after a child gets infected. Lots of them _____ _____ _____ _____. So children may have a _____, a _____ _____, and a _____. But they might also _____ _____ _____ _____ in their mouths. _____ _____ _____ with large blotches _____ _____ _____. Usually, the _____ _____ _____ first and then _____ _____ _____.

The rash normally _____ _____ _____ _____. The other symptoms might _____ _____ _____ _____. Children with measles _____ _____ _____ _____, but, uh, _____ _____ _____ _____.

Exercise 7

M Professor: _____ _____ is another viral infection, and, unfortunately, it's _____ _____ _____. I say unfortunately, but I should say sadly because there's _____ _____ _____ _____ that's ninety-five-percent effective. If only more people would get the vaccine, they _____ _____ _____ _____ this disease.

First, let me _____. Yellow fever is _____ the Americas and Africa. I would say that _____ in Central America. Still, _____, people are _____ around the world. That's especially _____. So you definitely want to get the vaccine for yellow fever if you have _____.

Now, _____ yellow fever? The answer can _____. Some unfortunate people _____ with the _____ and _____ in the body. The liver, by the way, _____. Sometimes _____ if that individual has yellow fever. This means that person's body cannot _____ or _____.

Exercise 8

W Professor: I'm sure that everyone here _____. You probably know that _____ in the 1500s. This happened when Europeans visited the New World. They _____. Native Americans had _____. So they _____. In some cases, entire villages _____ by smallpox. But _____? Let me tell you. Smallpox _____. It has been around _____. Basically, a person with smallpox _____ his or her _____. It especially affects the face, the arms, and the legs. Smallpox is _____. In the past, it killed at least _____

🎧 06-17

204

_____ it infected. Scientists estimate it has killed _____ _____ throughout history. Fortunately, _____ for it _____. Edward Jenner _____ this vaccine. Since then, incidents of smallpox _____. Today, smallpox _____ _____ from the world. It can only _____ _____. Hopefully, it never escapes because it _____ _____ _____.

Practice Test

W Professor: In the mid-1300s, a horrible plague hit Europe. It _____ _____ 1347 _____ 1351. During that time, _____. Some people believe 🎧 06-19 _____ _____ from this plague. The entire continent _____ _____. The plague _____ the Black Death. It _____ the bubonic plague.
The bubonic plague is an infectious disease _____. It can _____. That's _____. Fleas _____ _____ and _____ _____. Rats would then _____ and _____, where the fleas would _____ _____. _____ of the bubonic plague _____. _____ under their arms, behind their ears, and in other places. The swollen areas were _____ or _____. _____ it the Black Death. There were other symptoms, but the swelling was _____.

The bubonic plague was _____ _____. Between _____ _____ _____ _____ of people who get it nowadays _____ _____ _____ _____. In the Middle Ages, _____ many people died _____ it basically _____ _____ _____. The bubonic plague _____ _____ today. Fortunately, there are vaccines for it. It can also _____ _____. So if there are _____ _____, most people should _____ _____.

Chapter 7

Sample Question

W Professor: Today, I'd like to focus on _____ _____ _____ _____: the lens and the aperture. I think most of you already _____ _____. Its main function is _____ _____ as an image _____ _____. The lens _____ _____ and _____ to create a sharp, clear image of _____ _____ _____ _____. Next is the aperture. It is typically a circular, adjustable _____ _____, and it regulates _____ _____. Together, the lens and the aperture _____ _____.

🎧 07-01

Exercise 1

M Professor: Well, I guess the big question many of you are asking is _____ _____, _____ _____ or _____ _____. That's _____ _____.

🎧 07-03

Let me _____ _____ _____ _____ _____

_____. There is no question that _____ _____ _____

_____ _____ _____ a digital for black and white photography. It

creates _____ _____ _____ _____ while a digital

camera loses a lot. Another advantage of film is that it _____ _____

_____ _____ than the megapixels of a digital camera. Sure, as technology

advances, this could change, but currently, film _____ _____

_____ digital.

Let's move on to _____ _____ _____

_____. First, is an obvious one: _____. Digital cameras can _____

_____ _____ _____ _____ _____ film ever

can. You also have the option of immediate viewing, and then you _____ _____

_____ _____ _____ _____ _____

_____ _____ _____. _____ _____

_____, you are _____ _____ _____ _____

as if it were set in stone.

Exercise 2

W Professor: Everyone, please take a seat. Now, uh, I'd like to _____ _____

_____ _____ _____ the last time with the

history of modern photography.

You all remember that photography pre–1880s _____ _____

_____. Only the rich _____ _____ _____

_____ and _____ and then _____

_____ _____ _____. Thankfully, during the late nineteenth century,

_____ called Eastman Kodak _____.

George Eastman was, of course, _____ _____ of the company, and he is

_____ the world of photography _____

_____ just about _____. He _____

_____ _____ _____ on the inside that could

_____ _____. It was _____

🎧 07-05

_____ _____ and required _____ _____

_____ or _____. A person would simply _____ _____

_____ and _____. Simple, huh? Yes, it was just _____

_____ _____ of today. _____ _____

_____ _____ _____ a person would

_____ _____ _____ to the Kodak Company. Then, the pictures

would _____ _____ and _____ _____

_____ _____ who took them.

Exercise 3

W Professor: There are _____ _____ _____

upon the pictures you take. Of course, technique, camera quality, film quality, and lighting

_____ _____ _____ _____. But

_____ _____ _____. Let's step back for a minute.

What else? I'll give you a hint. It starts with an F . . . That's right . . . Filters. Please _____

_____ _____ when you take pictures.

They'll _____ _____ _____.

Filters are plastic or glass discs which are usually screwed onto a lens _____

_____ _____ _____. They're

pretty cheap, _____ _____

_____. Anyway, there are _____ _____

_____ I want to discuss. They are UV filters and polarizer filters. UV filters basically

_____ _____ and _____.

Some photographers claim they can also _____ _____

_____ _____ that sometimes appears in digital images. Polarizer filters are

_____ _____, for example, between

_____ and _____ _____. They are also useful because they can

_____ _____ or _____

_____, creating _____ _____.

Exercise 4

W Professor: All of you are pretty _____ _____ _____ now, right? Well, at least more than at the beginning of the semester. I sure hope so. Now, at this point, I would like to _____ _____ by _____. How does that sound? On your desks is _____ for _____. Aren't you all excited? We're going to _____ _____ and _____ them _____ the pictures that we've taken on land. Don't worry. You _____ _____ a great swimmer or really a swimmer at all. We'll _____ _____ of the university pool. Okay. _____ between _____ and _____ is _____. _____, and we _____ _____ in our vision when we're _____ _____. Another is _____. On land, we can be _____ _____, but underwater, you've got to _____ _____.

Exercise 5

M Professor: This morning, we will be discussing _____ _____: Ansel Adams and Annie Leibovitz. Ansel Adams was _____ _____, and he, more often than not, _____ _____. The American West was his canvas, and from it, he _____ haunting _____ _____ of deserts, mountain peaks, and woodlands. He _____ absolutely _____. If you _____ _____, go online and check it out. You will _____ _____ the pictures that Adams took.

Leibovitz, _____ _____, is mostly _____ _____ _____ _____ of famous people. She _____ _____ _____ _____ such as actors and singers. Her photography is _____ _____ and _____ _____. It was _____ _____ _____ _____ with the music magazine, *Rolling Stone*. Her most famous photo is arguably _____ _____ _____ John Lennon and Yoko Ono on the morning of December 8, 1980. Sadly, Leibovitz became _____ _____ _____ Lennon professionally. Okay. I didn't mean to ruin the mood in class, but _____ _____ _____, I'll now discuss _____ _____.

Exercise 6

W Professor: Last on the agenda today is a brief review of _____ _____ _____. And, yes, there's an important reason for this: We're having a quiz on it next Thursday. If you don't already _____ _____ _____ of this, please listen carefully and take notes. First, the film _____ _____ from the camera and _____ _____ _____. Now, this occurs where . . . ? That's right. It is done _____ _____ and _____ _____, preferably _____ _____ _____. The key here is _____ _____ _____. There should be none at all because _____ _____ _____.

Next, the reel of film _____ _____ _____. This is a special light-proof canister. Again, _____ _____ the canister to allow for proper developing. Then, _____ _____ _____ to soak the film for a couple of minutes, and after that, _____ _____ _____. When the developer is in the tank, the tank _____ _____. After the

🎧 07-13

developer _____, the film can be _____ and _____. At this point, the film should _____ _____ and _____.

Exercise 7

M Professor: There are _____ of camera lenses. _____ . . . Did I just say four? I _____. Sorry. There are _____. They are standard, wide-angle, and telephoto lenses.

Right now, I'd like to _____ wide-angle and telephoto lenses, but _____ _____ standard lenses _____. You see, _____ of each kind of lens _____ in millimeters. Pros like myself call this the focal length. _____ of the lens. So a standard lens for a 35mm camera is typically 50mm. Um, is everyone _____ _____ okay? Very good.

Okay, let's _____ - _____. They are _____ and especially for _____. Finally, um, telephoto lenses are _____ because they _____ and are _____ _____.

Exercise 8

M Professor: _____ _____ in the 1900s was Dorothea Lange. Some of you have probably _____. She _____ the Great Depression in the 1930s. However, she was _____ _____.

After finishing high school, Lange _____ _____. She studied it at Columbia University and _____ _____ _____ as an apprentice. In the 1920s, she _____ _____ _____ of the country. She _____ _____ Native Americans.

Then, in the 1930s, _____ _____. She started _____ _____. She _____ _____ _____ and _____ _____ around the country. Her photographs showed _____ _____ _____. There were also usually _____ _____. Most of the time, they were _____ _____ she had photographed. Lange _____ _____ during the depression. It was called *Migrant Mother*. Later, during World War II, she _____ _____ _____ in detention camps. She also _____ _____ to take pictures. Let's look at some of her most famous pictures now.

Practice Test

M Professor: Today, if you have a mobile phone, you have a digital camera. People everywhere _____ _____. But camera technology _____ _____. In fact, people have _____ _____ from cameras since the 1800s.

🎧 07-19

_____ that was invented _____ _____ the daguerreotype. That's spelled D-A-G-U-E-R-R-E-O-T-Y-P-E, uh, just so you know. _____ _____? _____ Louis-Jacques-Mandé Daguerre _____ with some help from Nicéphore Niépce. They _____ _____ in the 1830s and _____ _____

_____ in the year 1839.

The two men _____ _____ _____ _____. Here's _____ _____ _____. They _____ _____ _____ with silver iodide. Then, they _____ _____ _____ by using a camera. Then, they used some other chemicals _____ on the plate. Unfortunately, there were _____ _____ _____. So _____ _____ made with a daguerreotype _____ _____. Still, _____ _____ _____ were beautiful.

The daguerreotype _____ _____ very quickly. Just a few years later, there were _____ _____ _____ _____ in big cities. _____ _____ _____ with people. _____ _____, the only way to capture a person's image was _____ or _____ _____. The daguerreotype _____ _____ though. _____ _____ happened, and _____ and _____ to take pictures _____ _____ starting at the end of the 1850s.

Chapter 8

Sample Question

W Professor: I think many of you will _____ _____ this one. _____ _____ perhaps _____ _____ in human history. _____ _____?

Well, that's _____ _____ _____ although many experts believe it _____ about 4000 B.C. in Mesopotamia. But _____ _____ most likely a pottery wheel, _____. There is

Dictation Exercises 213

evidence of _____ _____ _____ _____

_____ _____ around 500 years later in 3500 B.C. This was _____

_____ _____ _____ Western Europe.

_____ _____, the chariot was definitely _____ _____

_____ sometime between 2000 and 1200 B.C.

Exercise 1

M Professor: Around 50,000 to 60,000 years ago, _____

_____ _____ onto the seas. _____ _____ similar to

canoes were probably _____ _____ _____

_____. However, these watercrafts _____

_____ _____ _____. Still, they _____

_____ _____ and other lands.

Much later, there is evidence that _____ _____ _____

_____ around 2500 B.C. You see, uh, an entire ship was entombed _____

_____ _____ at Giza. Then, about 1,000

years later, the Egyptians _____

between eighty and ninety feet in length _____ _____.

But _____ _____ _____. The Egyptians also _____

_____ _____ onto their ships. Still later, around 700 B.C., we

know the _____ _____ _____ _____. They

_____ _____ - _____ with

numerous levels or decks. Around 1100 A.D., _____

_____ _____ during the Song Dynasty.

Exercise 2

W Professor: _____ _____

_____ in history is right here _____

_____. Take a look. Do you know what it is . . . ? Anyone . . . ? It's _____

_____. We use it _____ _____.

214

Why was it _____ _____ _____ _____? In the past, _____ _____ was _____ _____.

Most ships _____ _____ of land. Why? If they lost sight of land, they _____ _____ _____. Sure, some sailors were able _____ _____ _____ _____. But they couldn't do that _____ _____ _____. They also couldn't do that _____ _____.

So... _____ _____. _____ _____ for sure _____ _____. We know it was _____ _____ _____ between 200 B.C. and 200 A.D. It used a lodestone. That's a type of iron ore, _____ _____ _____. _____ _____, the compass always _____ _____. However, the Chinese _____ _____ _____ for many years. They _____ _____ the years 1000 _____ 1200. In the West, the compass _____ _____ _____. Let me show you _____ _____ now.

Exercise 3

M Professor: It's mostly likely true that gunpowder was _____ _____ _____. They did this sometime _____ _____ _____. Guns were invented _____ _____ _____ in the 1100s. _____ _____ ever found _____ _____ 1288 by the way. But let me get back to gunpowder.

Ancient Chinese texts prove that the Chinese _____ _____ with mixtures of substances _____ _____ _____. The actual recipe _____ _____ from one of these texts is in your book on page 454. The recipe was 48.4% saltpeter, 25.6% sulfur, and 21% other

🎧 08-07

nonessential ingredients. _____ _____, the Chinese _____ that they used during battles. Ah, what is saltpeter? It is _____ of nitrogen, which we all know can _____. Now, uh, by _____ _____ saltpeter, the Chinese eventually _____, and _____ that could _____. Around the twelfth century, the Chinese _____ metal-encased grenades as well.

Exercise 4

W Professor: He could just about do it all. I'm _____ _____ Leonardo da Vinci. He was _____ _____, sculptor, musician, _____, scientist, _____ _____. What I'd like _____ today, though, is Leonardo _____. He was _____ _____. He was _____. Yes, flight. He studied the flight of birds, and he _____ that _____ _____ _____. He even designed a helicopter as well as a hang glider. Now, some of his designs _____ while _____ _____. By the way, Leonardo lived in the 1500s. So _____, please. Leonardo was also _____. In 1502, he _____ for a bridge _____ for the Ottomans. However, the Ottomans _____ _____. They thought his bridge was _____. They considered _____. However, he did _____ that were able to _____ _____.

216

Exercise 5

W Professor: Okay. Let's get started. I'd like you to _____ _____ your textbooks today. Please turn to page ninety-six and look at the top of the page. You'll notice that two men _____ primarily _____ _____ .

Yes, I know that _____ _____ Alexander Graham Bell _____ . _____ in 1876. Its patent number is 174,465. However, you all are certainly _____ Thomas Edison. We know him for _____ , but he did _____ . He also _____ concerning telephone technology. In 1877, Edison was _____ _____ of the carbon microphone, _____ until the 1980s. It was U.S. patent number 474,230. Please make note of that. Now, _____ for you _____ is March 10, 1876. And yes, I do expect you to remember _____ . Anyway, this was the day that _____ of speech by telephone _____ . It was _____ , a man named Watson.

Exercise 6

M Professor: Let me make something clear. The Wright brothers, Orville and Wilbur Wright, were _____ and _____ . What they did do, however, was _____ , _____ - _____ .

_____. Sure, other inventors _____ _____ _____, but they _____ _____ _____ _____. Basically, these inventors _____ _____ _____ _____

_____.

_____ _____ _____ at Kitty Hawk, North Carolina, on December 17, 1903. The name of the plane was the *Wright Flyer I*, and it had _____ _____ _____ _____. The engine weighed 170 pounds and _____ _____.

_____ _____ of the plane was 625 pounds.

_____ _____ _____ _____

_____ _____ Orville, who covered about 120 feet in twelve seconds. The Wrights _____ _____ _____ after that. _____

_____ about 200 feet, and _____ _____

_____ about ten feet. But _____ _____

_____ _____ just test runs. _____

_____ _____ of the day was _____ _____

_____ _____. Wilbur _____ _____

852 feet down the sand dunes. With that, _____ _____

_____ _____.

Exercise 7

M Professor: I want to talk about Coca-Cola, the fizzy cola drink _____ _____ _____

_____ _____ _____ _____ _____

_____. It all started in Georgia in the southern United States _____

_____ _____ _____ _____

_____ John Pemberton. He _____ _____

_____ _____ for Coke in 1885 or 1886.

_____ _____ _____ _____, believe it or not, _____ _____ in 1886. A glass of Coke _____

_____ _____ _____. At that time, _____

_____ _____ _____ in the U.S., and there were often soda fountains

🎧 08-15

_____ _____ _____. Back then, people believed carbonated beverages _____ _____, and Pemberton _____ _____ _____ _____.

He claimed that Coca-Cola was _____ _____ _____ _____. He _____ _____ _____ _____ such as addictions and headaches. Anyway, _____ _____ in March of 1894, and it was _____ _____ _____ in 1955. Today, of course, _____ _____ _____. It _____ 79,000 employees, and _____ _____ _____ _____ _____ more than thirty-eight billion dollars in 2021. Staggering, isn't it?

Exercise 8

W Professor: Let's talk about _____ _____ _____ incredibly _____. It's _____ _____. Yes, that's right. The nail. I'm talking about that thing you _____ _____ _____ _____ _____ to each other. _____ _____ _____? Most experts agree that _____ _____ more than 2,000 years ago. The Romans were _____ _____, so it should _____ _____ that they _____ _____ _____. You're probably wondering how _____ _____ _____ in the past, aren't you? It's simple. They _____ _____ so that they _____ _____ _____. Using nails was _____ _____ _____ and _____ _____. For centuries, people _____ _____. Basically, a blacksmith had to _____ _____ _____. Then, he _____ _____ he created a single nail. Again, that was _____

_____ and _____. Fortunately, in the 1790s, _____-_____. These were able to _____-_____ _____. Another improvement was _____ _____ rather than iron. This _____ _____ the mid-1800s and _____ the early 1900s.

Practice Test

M Professor: All around the world, people _____ _____. What is concrete? It's _____ cement, small stones, sand, and water. When it dries, it creates _____ _____ and _____. Ah, cement, by the way, is basically _____ _____ and _____. So _____ _____? More than 2,000 years ago, _____. They _____ the Colosseum _____. Most of their famous structures _____ _____. Many are _____ _____. Roman concrete was _____. But the Romans _____ _____. _____ used a type of concrete _____ _____ 3000 B.C. In fact, it's believed that they used concrete _____ _____ _____. Yet the Egyptians _____ _____. Right now, many experts say that Göbekli Tepe might be _____ _____.

Göbekli Tepe is believed to be _____ _____ ever made. _____ modern-day Turkey. _____ _____ 9500 B.C. The people there used terrazzo, which is _____ _____. Of course, the Egyptians, the Romans, and other people _____ _____

_____. But _____
_____ people have been working with concrete _____
_____ now. Isn't that amazing?

Actual Test

Actual Test 1 | Conversation

W Student: Professor Morris, could I _____
_____? You don't have class now, do you?

M Professor: Hello, Amy. Sure, I can talk to you _____.
What's going on?

W: I'm curious about _____
yesterday.

M: What about it?

W: Well . . . I don't know _____.
I mean, uh, you said _____
_____. But, um, _____ _____
_____?

M: The easiest thing to do is _____
we _____ in class. Then, write about it.

W: So you mean I should just write about, er . . . _____
_____ we have covered? I just need to _____
_____?

M: No, _____.

W: Then what should I do?

M: Your paper _____. You know,
decide what exactly you're going to write about and _____
_____.

W: Oh, I see.

M: _____ your introduction _____
_____. That means you explain _____

Dictation Exercises 221

_____.

W: Ah, sure. I _____ _____ in high school.

M: Great. Is there anything else?

W: One more thing. _____ _____ do I _____ _____ _____?

M: It's a five-page paper, so you _____ _____ _____ _____. But you should still _____ _____ _____ or _____ from the library _____ _____ _____.

W: Okay. I guess I'll _____ _____ _____ since I have some free time. Thanks.

M: Good luck. Come back here _____ _____ _____.

Actual Test 1 — Lecture

M Professor: The Himalaya Mountains _____ _____ _____ India, Pakistan, China, Bhutan, Tibet, and Nepal. _____ _____, Mount Everest, is there. There are _____ _____. In fact, more than 100 mountains in the Himalayas are _____ _____ _____.

The environment in the Himalayas is _____ _____. The mountains rise _____. There are _____ that can drop a thousand meters or more _____ _____. with powerful winds _____ _____. Avalanches _____ _____ as well and _____ _____ within their paths.

In addition, _____ _____ in the Himalayas can be

_____. For instance, _____

_____, a large number of people _____

Mount Everest. Base Camp on the mountain is about _____

_____. There, the oxygen level is approximately

_____

_____. That can _____ people

_____. _____

_____, the amount of oxygen in the air _____

_____. Climbers need to _____ just

_____. Most _____

_____ because they become _____.

Sudden gusts of wind can _____

_____. Each year, _____. Their bodies _____

_____, forever frozen _____

_____ and _____. Okay, uh, let's take a short break now. When we come back,

we'll _____ climbing Mount Everest.

Actual Test 2

Actual Test 2 Conversation

M Student: Good morning. Could you tell me _____

_____?

W Librarian: Sure. _____

_____, please? I need to see it.

M: Of course. Uh . . . Here you are.

W: Thank you. Okay . . . Brian Robinson . . . It looks like you _____

_____.

M: Six? Hmm . . . I thought I _____.

W: Here. Take a look at the screen. You can _____

_____.

M: Thanks. Ah, the book by Matthias Dunston. I _____

Dictation Exercises 223

_____. I need to _____ _____ _____ _____.

W: According to this, _____ are _____ _____. If you _____ _____ by then, you'll have to _____ _____. It's twenty-five cents a day _____ _____ _____.

M: I definitely _____ _____ _____ _____.

W: _____ _____ _____ _____ for you now?

M: You don't need me _____ _____ _____?

W: _____ _____ _____. I can do it from here.

M: Great. Please _____ and _____ _____.

W: All right . . . Your books _____ _____ _____ December 14. Please remember that date _____ _____ _____ in the back of the books.

M: I will. Thanks. Oh, since I'm here, can I _____ _____ _____, please?

W: Sorry, but that's a reference book.

M: Right. I _____ _____ the reference section right over there. This book _____ _____ _____ I'm doing for my economics class.

W: Sure, but books in the reference section are _____ _____ _____ from the library. You can only _____ them _____ _____.

M: So I _____ just _____ the _____ I need?

W: Sure. Or you could _____ _____ _____ with your phone. That _____ _____ _____.

224

Actual Test 2 Lecture

W Professor: We all know about _____ _____ _____ _____. We studied them in our last class. They're really _____ _____. But you should know that there are _____ _____ _____ _____ _____, too. In fact, you can find cave paintings _____ _____ _____. Right now, I'd like to talk about _____ _____ _____.

The Maya _____ in _____ in _____. They had _____ _____, but they _____ before _____ in the Americas. They _____ _____ _____ and _____ _____ in the jungle. They also _____ _____ _____.

Recently, _____ _____ _____ in the Yucatan. Here's a picture of some of the art . . . Notice _____ _____ . . . You can see _____ _____ here . . . There are also _____ _____ . . . as well as _____ _____ . . . Here is _____ . . . And check out these geometric figures . . .

As you can see, the Mayas _____ _____ _____. Many of the paintings are _____ _____ _____ that we studied. Of course, _____ _____ _____ _____ are different, _____. And like cave art in Europe, Mayan cave art _____ _____. People often _____ _____. They _____ _____ cave art. So archaeologists are _____ _____ Mayan cave art before _____. Let's check out some art from another cave now.

∩ 09-04

Actual Test 3

Actual Test 3 Conversation

M Professor: Good afternoon. _____
_____?

W Student: Yes, Professor Stabler. My name is Erika Jackson, and I'm _____
_____.

M: Which one?

W: _____ a few minutes ago.

M: Ah, yes. I _____ in class. Sorry, but I'm teaching three classes this semester. It's _____
_____.

W: Sure. I understand.

M: So _____
_____ today, Erika?

W: In today's class, you mentioned the possibility of _____
_____.

M: That's right.

W: Could you tell me _____? I'm a bit _____, so I'd like _____
_____
_____.

M: _____ on the midterm?

W: I got a ninety-five.

M: That's pretty good. You probably _____
_____-_____.

W: Well, I want to _____
_____ in the class. I also _____, so this will be _____ a bit more _____
_____.

226

M: Good attitude. I like that. Okay. Here's _____ _____ _____ _____.

W: Yes?

M: Go to _____ in the library. Ask to see the folder for Biology 62. Inside the folder, you will find _____ _____ _____ topics that you can research.

W: All right. Do I need _____?

M: No, you don't. But you need to _____ _____ on a topic and then write an eight-page paper.

W: That _____. By when do you need it?

M: _____ before the last class of the semester. I _____ _____ the last class finishes.

W: _____. Thank you for your time, sir.

Actual Test 3　Lecture

M Professor: Today, _____ _____ has a refrigerator. _____ most of you _____ in your dorm room. We _____ _____. But people in the past _____ _____. Centuries ago, people had to use _____ _____. In cold places, people _____. They could _____. In other places, they _____. Some people used _____ to keep food cold. Of course, these _____, so it was _____ _____.

Then, in the 1700s, the Industrial Revolution began. People began _____ _____
_____ _____ _____ _____. Some of them were
_____ _____ _____ _____. Still, there were
_____ _____ _____ for quite a while. Then, in 1876, Carl von Linde
_____ _____ _____ _____. He learned
_____ _____ _____ _____ in large amounts. This
_____ _____ _____ _____ in refrigeration technology.
Linde is _____ _____ _____ modern refrigeration.
_____ _____ _____ _____, Fred Wolf invented the first
refrigerator _____ _____ _____. In the year 1927, refrigerators
_____ _____ _____ _____. _____
_____ _____ _____. _____ _____
_____, which made refrigerators _____ and
_____. Today, as you know, refrigerators are _____ and are extremely
_____ _____ _____ _____.

228

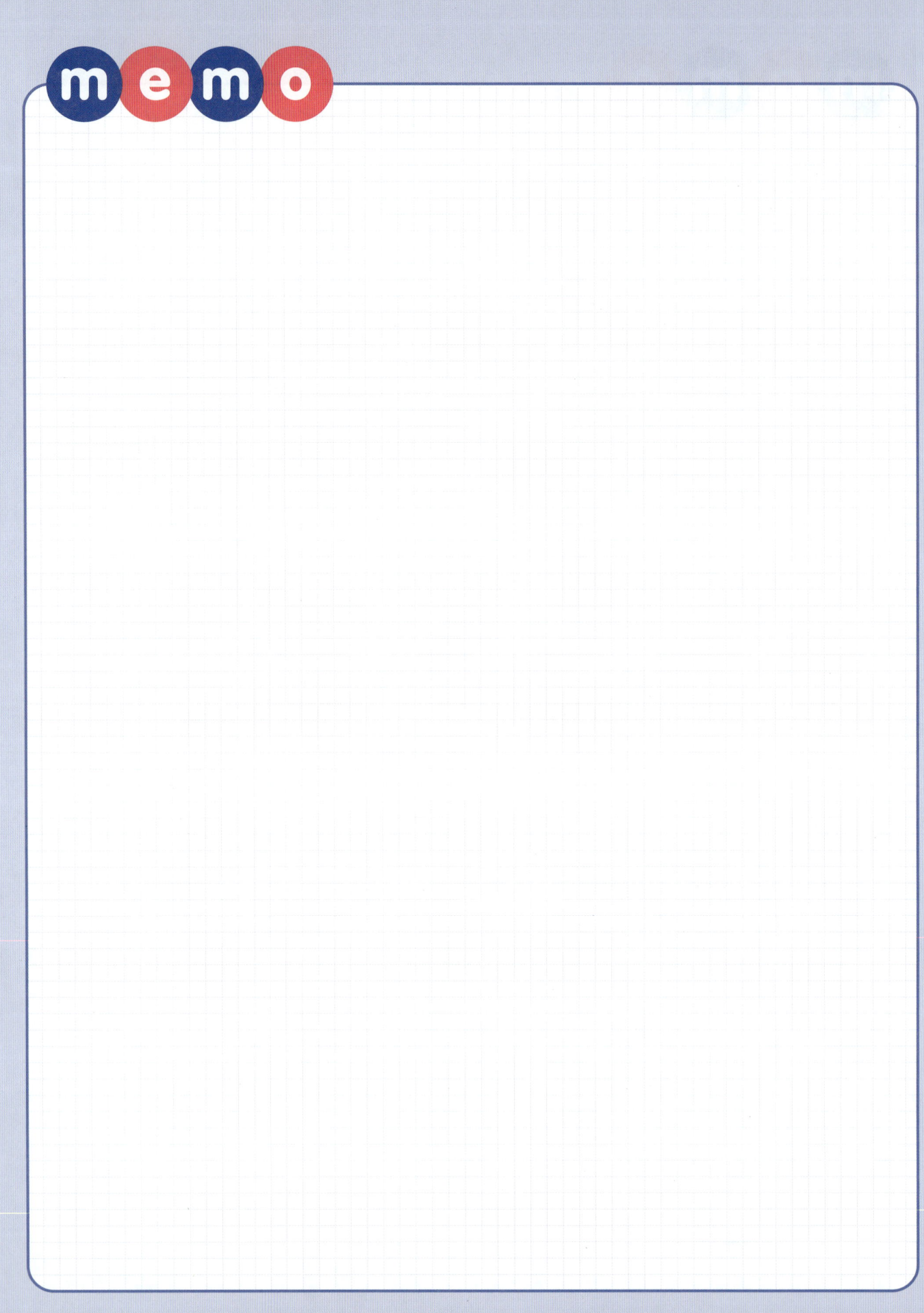

Publisher Kyudo Chung
Editors Woonhee Park, Sangik Cho
Author William Link
Designers Minji Kim, Kyuok Jeong

First published in April 2008 by Happy House
Second edition first published in August 2023 by Darakwon, Inc.
Darakwon Bldg., 211, Munbal-ro, Paju-si, Gyeonggi-do 10881
Republic of Korea
Tel: 82-2-736-2031 (Ext. 250)
Fax: 82-2-732-2037

Copyright © 2008 Happy House, 2023 Darakwon

All rights reserved. No part of this publication may be reproduced, stored in a retrieval system, or transmitted in any form or by any means, electronic, mechanical, photocopying or otherwise, without the prior consent of the copyright owner. Refund after purchase is possible only according to the company regulations. Contact the above telephone number for any inquiries. Consumer damages caused by loss, damage, etc. can be compensated according to the consumer dispute resolution standards announced by the Korea Fair Trade Commission. An incorrectly collated book will be exchanged.

ISBN 978-89-277-8062-5 14740
      978-89-277-8056-4 14740 (set)

www.darakwon.co.kr

Photo Credits
Shutterstock.com

Components Main Book / Answer Key
8 7 6 5 4 3 2   25 26 27 28 29

High Score iBT TOEFL LISTENING For Junior

2nd Edition

High Intermediate

Answer Key

DARAKWON

High Intermediate

Answer Key

CHAPTER 1 Cave and Rock Art

Understanding TOEFL Question Types & Listening Skills
p.14

1 Question Types ▶ Sample Question

스크립트 🎧 01-01

W Professor: When you think of France, along with the Eiffel Tower, perhaps art comes to mind. That goes for prehistoric cave art, too. One special place is Chauvet Cave in the south of France. The cave contains spectacular artwork, fossils of animals, and even animal and human footprints. In a sense, it's a living museum. Experts estimate that most of the art is about 30,000 years old. The stunning artwork is mostly of animals. For example, there are pictures of bears, lions, and even panthers.

해석

W Professor: 프랑스에 대해 생각해볼 때, 에펠탑과 함께 아마도 예술이 떠오를 거예요. 또한 선사 시대의 동굴 벽화도 그럴 것이고요. 한 특별한 장소는 바로 프랑스 남부의 쇼베 동굴입니다. 그 동굴에는 다채로운 벽화와 동물의 화석, 심지어는 동물과 인간의 발자국도 있습니다. 어떤 의미에서 그곳은 살아 있는 박물관이라 할 수 있습니다. 전문가들은 벽화의 대부분이 3만년 정도 되었다고 추정하고 있습니다. 그 놀라운 예술 작품 대부분은 동물에 대한 것입니다. 예를 들어 곰, 사자, 심지어는 흑표범의 그림도 있습니다.

2 Listening Skills ▶ Check-Up

1. That goes for prehistoric cave art, too.
2. One special place is Chauvet Cave in the south of France.
3. In a sense, it's a living museum.
4. The stunning artwork is mostly of animals.

• Exercise 1 •
p.16

정답 Q1 ⓒ Q2 ⓑ
스크립트 🎧 01-03

M Professor: This morning, we will begin our discussion of cave art. I'd like to talk about the subject matter of prehistoric artists. In general, pictures of cave art focus on large animals such as bison, horses, cattle, and deer. We can conclude that the types of animals that were drawn were important to early humans. Surprisingly, drawings of actual human beings are quite rare. There are also occasional examples of tracings of human hands.
But remember that each cave drawing was influenced by its environment and the habitat surrounding it. For example, a group of early humans that lived near water, like a river or lake, would have drawn that. The reason was that it was central to their lives. Other examples are mountains and forests. For these reasons, the subjects of most cave art are very revealing of early human cultures.

해석

M Professor: 오늘 아침, 우리는 동굴 벽화에 대해 토론을 시작할 것입니다. 저는 선사 시대 예술가들이 다뤘던 주제에 대해 이야기하고 싶습니다.
일반적으로 동굴 벽화의 그림들은 들소, 말, 소떼, 사슴과 같이 몸집이 큰 동물들에 초점을 맞춥니다. 우리는 동물 벽화에 그려진 동물 종들이 초기 인류에게 중요했다고 결론지을 수 있습니다. 놀랍게도 실제 인간을 그린 그림은 매우 드뭅니다. 간혹 인간의 손을 모사한 예가 있기도 합니다.
그러나 각 동굴 그림이 그 환경과 그것을 둘러싼 거주 환경의 영향을 받았다는 것을 기억하세요. 예를 들어, 강이나 호수와 같은 물가에서 살았던 초기 인류 집단은 그 모습을 그렸을 것입니다. 그 이유는 그곳이 그들의 삶의 중심이었기 때문입니다. 다른 예로는 산과 숲이 있습니다. 이러한 이유로 대다수 동굴 벽화의 주제들은 초기 인류 문화를 아주 잘 드러낸다고 할 수 있습니다.

Listening Skills

1. Surprisingly, drawings of actual human beings are quite rare.
2. For example, a group of early humans that lived near water, like a river or lake, would have drawn that.
3. The reason was that it was central to their lives.
4. Other examples are mountains and forests.

• Exercise 2 •
p.17

정답 Q1 ⓒ Q2 ⓑ
스크립트 🎧 01-05

M Professor: Good morning, class. It is good to see everyone so bright and early. Today, we are going down under to the continent of Australia, and we will explore some early cave and rock art there. Australia is just full of sites containing early and later Aboriginal cave and rock art. You are all familiar with the Aborigines, right . . .? To clarify, they are the original indigenous people of Australia.
Continuing, one of the most significant sites is Kakadu National Park in northern Australia. A very prominent site in the park is Ubirr. It is a rock formation with outcrops that were used by Aborigines for shelter. Lots of types of fish, such as mullet and catfish, are represented in the paintings along with turtles and wallabies. A highlight of the site is the main gallery, where there is a painting of a Tasmanian tiger. It has been extinct for about 20,000 years.

해석

M Professor: 좋은 아침이에요, 여러분. 여러분 모두를 아침 일찍 밝은 모습으로 보게 되니 좋군요. 오늘은 오스트레일리아 대륙 깊숙이 내려가 그곳의 초기 동굴과 암각화 몇 곳을 탐험해 볼 것입니다. 오스트레일리아는 초기와 후기의 토착 동굴과 암각화를 간직하고 있는 유적지로 그야말로 가득합니다. 여러분 모두 어보리진 원주민에 대해서는 익히 알고 있지요, 그렇죠…? 명확하게 설명하자면, 그들은 오스트레일리아에 원래 살던 토착민입니다.
계속해서, 가장 중요한 유적지 중 한 곳은 오스트레일리아 북부의 카카두 국립공원입니다. 그 공원에서 가장 유명한 유적지는 유버입니다. 그곳은 어보리진 원주민들이 주거지로 이용했던 노두 암석층입니다. 숭어와 메기와 같은 많은 종류의 물고기들이 거북이와 왈라비와 함께 그림 속에 표현되어 있습니다. 가장 흥미로운 곳은 태즈메이니아 주머니늑대 그림이 있는 주전망대입니다. 그것은 약 2만년 전에 멸종했습니다.

Listening Skills

1 It is good to see everyone so bright and early.
2 You are all familiar with the Aborigines, right . . .?
3 To clarify, they are the original indigenous people of Australia.
4 A very prominent site in the park is Ubirr.

• Exercise 3 • p.18

정답 Q1 Ⓑ   Q2 Ⓐ
스크립트 🎧 01-07

W Professor: That was a very good explanation, Laura. Now, I'd like to move on to rock art, which is a very broad category. However, we can break rock art down into two main areas: petroglyphs and pictographs.
First, I'll explain petroglyphs. These are basically carvings in rock and stone. Images were scratched, drilled, carved, and sculpted into various surfaces to create the desired designs. On occasion, petroglyphs were even polished and painted.
Second are pictographs. These involved the use of pigments. Pigments are natural colored minerals used for rock art. Early humans would grind up minerals and make them into devices like crayons or coloring sticks. There is evidence that they used paintbrushes as well to form pictographs. One of the most common pictographs discovered is the human hand. A pigment was applied to a hand, and the hand was then pressed against a rock. Ancient human handprints.

해석

W Professor: 아주 좋은 설명이었어요, 로라. 이제, 암면미술로 넘어가고 싶은데요, 암면미술은 아주 광범위한 범주입니다. 하지만 우리는 암면미술을 암각화와 상형문자라는 두 가지 주요 영역으로 나눌 수 있습니다.
첫째, 암각화에 대해 설명해보겠습니다. 이것은 기본적으로 바위와 돌에 새긴 그림을 말합니다. 다양한 표면 위에 이미지들을 긁어 내고, 구멍 뚫고, 파고, 조각하여 원하는 디자인을 만들었습니다. 어떤 경우에는, 암각화에 윤을 내거나 색칠을 하기도 했습니다.
두 번째는 상형문자입니다. 이것은 안료의 사용과 관계가 있습니다. 안료는 암면미술에 사용되는 색깔이 있는 천연 광물질입니다. 초기 인류는 광물질을 가루로 빻아 크레용이나 색연필과 같은 도구를 만들곤 했습니다. 색칠 붓 또한 사용해 상형문자를 만든 흔적도 있습니다. 가장 흔하게 발견되는 상형문자 중 하나는 바로 인간의 손입니다. 안료를 손에 묻힌 다음, 바위에 손을 눌러 찍었습니다. 고대 인류의 손자국이지요.

Listening Skills

1 I'd like to move on to rock art, which is a very broad category.
2 On occasion, petroglyphs were even polished and painted.
3 Pigments are natural colored minerals used for rock art.
4 One of the most common pictographs discovered is the human hand.

• Exercise 4 • p.19

정답 Q1 Ⓒ   Q2 Ⓐ
스크립트 🎧 01-09

W Professor: Perhaps two or three thousand years ago, a race of giants roamed the Baja Peninsula in Mexico and painted images of themselves in rocks and caves. Or so the legend goes.
I'm talking about Sierra de San Francisco, an important site of rock art in Mexico. Actually, it was designated as a World Heritage Site in the 1990s. Now, were they giants? We're not sure, but some of the paintings are of humans and are about six and a half feet in actual size. That is a huge size for a work of cave art.
In addition, the motifs of the art include both human and animal representations. It is an isolated area and very well preserved. The paintings at Sierra de San Francisco represent a great variety as well. Land animals such as deer, sheep, and rabbits are present. Octopi and whales are, too. Interestingly, images of eagles and pelicans can also be seen there.

해석

W Professor: 아마도 2천년 내지 3천년 전에, 한 거인종이 멕시코의 바하 반도를 돌아다니다가 그들 자신의 모습을 바위와 동굴에 그렸던 것 같습니다. 전설에 따르면 말이죠.
저는 멕시코의 중요한 암각화 유적지인 시에라 데 산 프란시스코에 대해 이야기하고자 합니다. 실제로 그곳은 1990년대에 세계문화유산으로 등재되었습니다. 자, 그들은 거인종이었을까요? 확실하지는 않지만, 어떤 그림들은 인간을 묘사하는데 이들의 그 실제 크기가 6피트 반 정도 됩니다. 동굴 벽화로서는 매우 큰 크기죠.
게다가 그 벽화는 주제로서 인간과 동물을 모두 표현하고 있습니다. 그곳은 고립된 장소이며 매우 잘 보존되어 있습니다. 시에라 데 산 프란시스코의 벽화들은 또한 매우 다양한 모습들을 묘사하고 있습니다. 사슴, 양, 토끼와 같은 육지 동물들이 등장하고요. 문어와 고래도 있지요. 흥미롭게도, 독수리와 펠리칸의 모습 또한 그곳에서 볼 수 있습니다.

Listening Skills

1 Or so the legend goes.
2 Actually, it was designated as a World Heritage Site in the 1990s.
3 That is a huge size for a work of cave art.
4 The paintings at Sierra de San Francisco represent a great variety as well.

• Exercise 5 • p.20

정답 Q1 Ⓑ   Q2 Ⓑ
스크립트 🎧 01-11

M Professor: New sites that have rock and cave art are still being discovered. We have only begun to scratch the surface, if you will, of what is out there. You can bet that some will never be found. Others will be destroyed by the elements, by weather, and by other natural occurrences.

Moving on, the Apollo 11 cave in southern Africa is often considered one of the oldest examples of rock art on the Earth. Dating has determined that it is around 30,000 years old. Please be aware that Apollo 11 is the name of the cave, but the work is not on the walls of the cave. Actually, the rock art exists on large slabs of rock brought from another location in Africa.

The cave itself was chosen as a kind of tomb or protective chamber for the rock art. But who made it, and when was it made? Well, there are many theories, but there is no precise answer to either question. Recently, new finds in Africa suggest that rock art dates back to more than three times the age of the Apollo 11 find. That makes some of it nearly 100,000 years old. Okay. We'll discuss that some more during the next class.

해석
M Professor: 암각화와 동굴 벽화가 있는 새로운 유적지들이 여전히 발견되고 있습니다. 우리는 말하자면, 그러한 곳의 극히 일부에 대해서만 조사해 왔습니다. 어떤 곳들은 전혀 발견되지 않을 거라고 단언할 수 있습니다. 또 어떤 곳들은 비바람, 날씨, 기타 자연 현상에 의해 파괴될 것입니다.
계속해서 이야기하자면, 남아프리카의 아폴로 11호 동굴은 종종 지구상에서 가장 오래된 암각화 중 하나가 있는 곳으로 여겨지고 있습니다. 약 3만 년 정도로 그 연대를 추정하고 있습니다. 그 동굴의 이름이 아폴로 11호이지만, 그림이 동굴의 벽에 있지 않다는 것을 알아두세요. 사실 그 암각화는 아프리카의 다른 지역에서 가져온 커다란 바위 판 위에 새겨져 있습니다.
그 동굴 자체는 암각화를 위한 일종의 무덤 혹은 보호실로서 선택된 것입니다. 그렇다면 누가 그것을 만들었고, 언제 그것이 만들어졌을까요? 글쎄요, 많은 이론이 있지만 두 질문에 대한 명확한 답은 없습니다. 최근 아프리카에서 새롭게 발견된 암각화의 연대는 아폴로 11호의 암각화보다 세 배 더 오래되었을 것으로 추측되고 있습니다. 암각화 중 어떤 것들은 거의 10만년이 되었다는 말이지요. 좋아요. 다음 시간에 그 부분에 대해 좀 더 이야기해 보도록 하죠.

Listening Skills
1 You can bet that some will never be found.
2 Dating has determined that it is around 30,000 years old.
3 Actually, the rock art exists on large slabs of rock brought from another location in Africa.
4 We'll discuss that some more during the next class.

• Exercise 6 • p.21

정답 Q1 Ⓓ   Q2 Ⓑ
스크립트 🎧 01-13

W Professor: Okay, those are a few pictures of cave art in Europe. Now, let's ask a very important question . . . Why did prehistoric people make cave art? It's hard to say because they didn't have written language then. So they couldn't write their thoughts down. However, there are a few theories.

First, some people believe prehistoric people were making art for art's sake. In other words, they were just talented individuals who created art. As a result, they painted what they saw. That's why they painted so many animals. Another theory is that these paintings were like instruction manuals for hunting. The pictures were painted to make hunters familiar with the animals they would hunt. In fact, some cave art does show people hunting animals. The cave at Lascaux has several images of hunting. A third theory is that the pictures had some sort of religious significance. Perhaps prehistoric people believed they could please their gods by painting pictures. Then, they might have successful hunts. Of course, we can't know for sure if that's true. It's just a theory.

해석
W Professor: 좋아요, 저기에 있는 몇 장의 사진들은 유럽의 동굴 벽화에 관한 것입니다. 자, 매우 중요한 질문을 하나 하자면… 왜 선사 시대 사람들이 동굴 벽화를 그렸을까요? 답을 하기가 어려운데, 그 이유는 당시에 글자가 없었기 때문입니다. 따라서 생각을 기록해 둘 수가 없었죠. 하지만 몇 가지 이론들이 있습니다.
첫째로, 어떤 사람들은 선사 시대 사람들이 예술 그 자체를 목적으로 그림을 그렸다고 생각해요. 다시 말하면, 그들은 그저 그림을 그리는 재능이 뛰어났던 사람들이었던 거죠. 그 결과, 그들은 자신이 본 것을 그렸습니다. 바로 그러한 이유 때문에 그처럼 많은 동물들을 그렸던 것이죠. 또 다른 이론에서는 이러한 그림들이 사냥을 위한 지침서와 같은 것이었다고 해요. 사냥을 하는 사람들이 사냥하려는 동물들을 잘 익히도록 그림이 그려졌던 것이죠. 실제로 어떤 동굴 벽화는 정말로 동물을 사냥하고 있는 사람들의 모습을 보여줍니다. 라스코 동굴 벽화에 여러 사냥 장면들이 있습니다. 세 번째 이론에서는 그림들이 일종의 종교적인 의미를 가지고 있었다고 합니다. 아마도 선사 시대 사람들은 그림을 그림으로써 신을 기쁘게 할 수 있다고 믿었던 것 같습니다. 그러면 사냥에 성공할 수도 있다고 믿었을 것입니다. 물론 그것이 사실인지는 확실히 알 수가 없습니다. 이론일 뿐이죠.

Listening Skills
1 Why did prehistoric people make cave art?
2 First, some people believe prehistoric people were making art for art's sake.
3 The pictures were painted to make hunters familiar with the animals they would hunt.
4 Perhaps prehistoric people believed they could please their gods by painting pictures.

• Exercise 7 • p.22

정답 Q1 Ⓒ   Q2 Ⓐ
스크립트 🎧 01-15

M Professor: Another famous spot in Europe is the Altamira cave in Spain. If any of you are backpacking through Europe this summer, you should try to visit it. It will be worth your while. The cave itself is nearly 1,000 feet in length, and paintings extend from the mouth of the cave all the way to the back.

The cave art is from the Paleolithic Age, or the Old Stone Age. The dating of artifacts has established the cave art as being about 16,000 years old. The inhabitants of Altamira used natural mineral pigments for coloring and drawing, but that's not all. There's something unique about the Altamira paintings and the methods used to create them. Now, listen closely to this. First, the inhabitants used light and dark colors to add depth to their subjects. They also used the contours of the cave to their advantage. Contours are the uneven surfaces of the cave walls. They used them to give their pictures a 3-D look. Pretty cool, huh? Actually, I have some images of cave art from Altamira. Everyone, take a look up here at the screen.

해석
M Professor: 유럽의 또 다른 유명한 장소는 스페인의 알타미라 동굴입니다. 여러분 중 누구든 올 여름 유럽으로 배낭여행을 갈 예정이라면 그곳에 방문해 보도록 하세요. 정말 가볼 만한 곳이에요. 동굴 자체는 길이가 거의 1,000피트에 이르며, 벽화가 동굴 입구에서부터 끝까지 가는 내내 그려져 있습니다. 그 동굴 벽화는 구석기 시대, 즉 원시돌 시대의 유적입니다. 유물의 연대로 보아 동굴 벽화는 약 16,000년 정도 된 것으로 밝혀졌습니다. 알타미라 원주민들은 천연 광물 안료를 사용하여 채색하고 그림을 그렸지만, 그것이 전부는 아닙니다. 알타미라 벽화와 그것을 만들어내는 데 사용한 방법들에는 독특한 특징이 있습니다. 자, 잘 들어보세요.
먼저, 원주민들은 밝은 색과 어두운 색을 사용하여 대상에 깊이감을 주었습니다. 또한 그들은 동굴의 등고선을 장점으로 이용하였습니다. 등고선이란 동굴 벽면의 울퉁불퉁한 표면을 말합니다. 그들은 이 등고선을 이용해 그림이 3차원으로 보이게 했습니다. 정말 멋지지 않나요? 사실 저는 알타미라 동굴 벽화에 대한 이미지를 몇 장 가지고 왔어요. 모두들 여기 화면을 봐 주세요.

Listening Skills
1 The dating of artifacts has established the cave art as being about 16,000 years old.
2 Now, listen closely to this.
3 First, the inhabitants used light and dark colors to add depth to their subjects.
4 They used them to give their pictures a 3-D look.

• Exercise 8 • ———————————— p.23

정답 Q1 Ⓐ Q2 Ⓐ
스크립트  01-17
M Professor: I went to the Lascaux cave in France with a few grad students to view the cave paintings there a couple years ago. The cave is in the southwestern region of France. Check the map on page 352 of your books to see where.
Lascaux is a very famous site. It was actually discovered by some teenagers in 1940. Most of the paintings are of animals, and they are about 16,000 years old. Now, here's the interesting thing. The fame of Lascaux, which came right after its discovery, proved to be very damaging. It was opened to the public, and the cave received nearly 2,000 visitors every single day. Lots of people in the cave meant a lot of, well, breathing, which meant a lot of carbon dioxide, CO2, which was very harmful to the delicate paintings.
As a result, in 1963, the French government closed the cave to the public to preserve the paintings. A few years ago, that came as quite a surprise to my students and me. We couldn't believe it was closed. But we also believed it was more important to preserve these ancient paintings. Don't you agree, class?

해석
M Professor: 저는 몇 년 전에 대학원생 몇 명과 프랑스의 라스코 동굴에 갔는데, 그곳의 동굴 벽화들을 보기 위해서였습니다. 그 동굴은 프랑스 남서부 지역에 있습니다. 책의 352쪽의 지도를 보고 그곳이 어디에 있는지 확인해 보세요.
라스코는 아주 유명한 유적지입니다. 그곳은 사실 1940년에 몇몇 10대 아이들에 의해 발견되었습니다. 대부분의 그림들이 동물에 대한 것이며 약 16,000년 정도 되었습니다. 자, 흥미로운 점이 있습니다. 그것이 발견된 직후 얻은 라스코의 명성은 매우 치명적인 것으로 증명되었습니다. 그것이 일반인들에게 공개되면서 그 동굴은 매일 같이 거의 2,000여명의 방문객들을 수용했습니다. 동굴 속에 많은 사람들이 있다는 의미는 그러니까, 많은 호흡 즉, 이산화탄소인 CO2가 많다는 것을 의미했고, 이것은 섬세한 그림에 아주 해로웠습니다.
결과적으로, 1963년에 프랑스 정부는 그림들을 보호하기 위해 일반인의 동굴 입장을 금했습니다. 몇 년 전에 그 일은 저와 학생들에게 꽤 충격적인 일이었습니다. 우리는 그곳이 폐쇄되었다는 것을 믿지 못했습니다. 하지만 우리는 또한 이러한 고대 그림들을 보존하는 것이 더 중요하다고 믿었어요. 여러분도 동의하지 않나요?

Listening Skills
1 Lascaux is a very famous site.
2 It was actually discovered by some teenagers.
3 The French government closed the cave to the public to preserve the paintings.
4 That came as quite a surprise to my students and me.

Vocabulary Review
p.24

Ⓐ 1 delicate
2 inhabitants
3 manual
4 scratches the surface
5 motif

Ⓑ 1 Ⓐ   2 Ⓓ   3 Ⓑ   4 Ⓐ   5 Ⓐ

Ⓒ 1 Ⓑ   2 Ⓓ   3 Ⓒ   4 Ⓐ   5 Ⓓ

Ⓓ 1 race
2 significance
3 spectacular
4 prehistoric
5 damaging

Practice Test
p.26

1 Ⓑ   2 Ⓒ   3 Tassili:  1, 3 Figuig: 2, 4   4 Ⓒ

스크립트 🎧 01-19

W Professor: Let's take a look at the Sahara Desert now. There are a significant number of archaeological sites that contain rock art there. So far, we are aware of more than 2,000 sites. Some of the most famous ones are located in Morocco and Algeria. One important site in Algeria is Tassili. Actually, I was lucky enough to go there a few years ago. Much of the rock art in the caves shows large wild animals such as crocodiles. Yes, crocodiles in the Sahara. What does that suggest to you? Well, the Sahara in prehistoric times was much different from today's Sahara. We'll talk more about that in a minute though. Oh, at Tassili, some of the rock carvings also show people dancing and hunting.

A second important site in Morocco is located in the Figuig Mountains. Some of the more noted images found there show rhinos, antelopes, and felines. The felines represented are most likely lions. However, animal rock art is not the only type of art at Figuig. There are also, um, numerous geometric images, including dotted lines, parallel lines, semicircles, and rectangles. In addition, much of this art was actually carved into the rock and then painted, uh, probably with fingers. Prehistoric artists used both dark and light red when they painted.

Now, uh, I want to talk about a famous site in Chad and compare it to the two places I just talked about.

해석

W Professor: 이제 사하라 사막에 대해 살펴봅시다. 그곳에는 암각화가 보존되어 있는 고고학 유적지들이 상당히 많이 있습니다. 지금까지 우리가 아는 곳만 2,000곳이 넘습니다.

가장 유명한 곳들 중 일부는 모로코와 알제리에 위치해 있습니다. 알제리에 있는 중요한 곳 중 하나가 타실리입니다. 사실 저는 운 좋게도 몇 년 전에 그곳에 갈 수 있었습니다. 동굴들 안에 있는 많은 암각화는 크로커다일 악어와 같은 큰 야생동물들을 보여주고 있습니다. 그래요, 사하라 사막에 있는 크로커다일 악어 말입니다. 그것이 무엇을 암시할까요? 자, 선사 시대의 사하라 지역은 오늘날의 사하라 지역과는 매우 달랐습니다. 그렇지만 그것에 대해서는 잠시 후에 더 이야기를 하기로 하죠. 아, 타실리의 어떤 암각화들은 춤을 추고 사냥하는 사람들의 모습 또한 보여주고 있습니다.

모로코에 있는 두 번째로 중요한 유적지는 피기그 산악 지대에 위치해 있습니다. 그곳에서 발견된 유명한 그림 중에는 코뿔소, 영양, 고양잇과 동물들을 보여주는 것들이 있습니다. 묘사되어 있는 고양잇과 동물들은 거의 사자와 비슷합니다. 그렇지만 동물 암각화만이 피기그에 존재하는 그림의 형태는 아닙니다. 그곳에는 또한, 음, 점선, 평행선, 반원, 직사각형 등 수많은 기하학적인 그림들도 있습니다. 게다가 이러한 그림의 많은 부분이 실제로 바위에 새겨졌고 그런 다음 채색되었는데, 어, 아마도 손가락으로 채색한 것 같습니다. 선사 시대의 화가들은 채색을 할 때 어두운 빨간색과 옅은 빨간색을 모두 사용했습니다.

이제 아, 차드의 유명한 유적지에 대해 이야기한 후 그곳을 제가 방금 이야기한 두 곳과 비교해보도록 하죠.

CHAPTER 2 Office Hours

Understanding TOEFL Question Types & Listening Skills

p.30

1 Question Types ▶ Sample Question

스크립트 🎧 02-01

W Professor: Mr. Archer, this is a surprise. Come in.
M Student: Hello, Professor Chapman. Can I talk to you for a minute?
W: Sure. Grab a seat. Have you begun your paper for me yet?
M: No, not yet. Actually, I want to talk to you about our group project.
W: I see. And I detect from your voice that all is not well.
M: No, it isn't. We voted for Stephen as our group leader, but it isn't working out very well.
W: Really? How?
M: Well, he missed our first two meetings, and we're really falling behind.

해석

W Professor: 아처 군, 웬일인가요. 어서 와요.
M Student: 안녕하세요, 채프먼 교수님. 잠시 얘기 좀 할 수 있을까요?
W: 물론이죠. 자리에 앉아요. 내게 제출할 논문을 벌써 시작했나요?
M: 아뇨, 아직이요. 사실 저희 조의 프로젝트에 대해 교수님과 의논하고 싶어서요.
W: 알겠어요. 그리고 목소리를 들어보니 상황이 좋진 않은 것 같네요.
M: 네, 좋지 않아요. 저희는 스티븐을 조장으로 뽑았는데 일이 정말 잘 진행되지 않고 있어요.
W: 그래요? 어쩌다가요?
M: 그게요, 그가 처음 두 번의 회의에 빠져서 우리 조가 정말 뒤처지고 있어요.

2 Listening Skills ▶ Check-Up

1 come in
2 can I
3 grab a
4 about our

• Exercise 1 • ──────────── p.32

정답 Q1 Q2 Ⓐ

스크립트 🎧 02-03

W Student: Hi, Professor Madison. Are you free for a second?
M Professor: Um, yes, for the moment... You're, um...
W: Sandy. I'm in your world history class.
M: Oh, yes. Sandy. Right... How can I help you today?
W: I'm graduating this semester, and I was hoping you could give me some tips on finding a job.
M: A job, huh? What are you interested in?

W: That's the thing. I keep changing my mind.
M: Well, you're young. Young people do that sometimes. Do you know what?
W: What?
M: I just saw a notice on the university bulletin board this morning. The university is sponsoring a job fair this weekend, and many companies will be there.
W: Really? That's great.
M: You can talk with people working in various fields. That might help you out.
W: I'm sure it will. I had better get my résumé together. See you in class. Thanks.

해석

W Student: 안녕하세요, 매디슨 교수님. 잠깐 시간이 있으신가요?
M Professor: 음, 그래요. 잠깐이라면요… 자네는, 음…
W: 샌디라고 합니다. 교수님의 세계사 강의를 듣고 있어요.
M: 아, 그래요. 샌디. 맞아요… 오늘 무슨 일을 도와줄까요?
W: 제가 이번 학기에 졸업을 하는데, 교수님께서 제가 취직을 하는 데 조언을 좀 해 주실 수 있나 해서요.
M: 취직이란 말이죠? 어떤 것에 관심이 있나요?
W: 바로 그게 문제인데요. 생각이 계속 바뀌거든요.
M: 음, 젊잖아요. 젊은이들은 때때로 그렇죠. 그거 알아요?
W: 어떤거요?
M: 방금 오늘 아침에 학교 게시판에 올라온 한 공고를 봤어요. 학교에서 이번 주에 열리는 취업 박람회를 후원해서 많은 회사들이 그곳에 참석할 예정이에요.
W: 정말인가요? 잘됐네요.
M: 여러 다양한 분야에 종사하는 사람들과 이야기를 나눌 수 있을 거예요. 그게 도움이 될지도 몰라요.
W: 확실히 그렇겠네요. 제 이력서를 전부 정리하는 게 좋겠어요. 강의 시간에 뵙겠습니다. 감사합니다.

Listening Skills

1 how can
2 give me
3 bulletin board
4 you out

• Exercise 2 • ──────────────── p.33

정답 Q1 Ⓑ Q2 Ⓐ
스크립트 🎧 02-05

W Professor: Thanks for coming to see me, Matt. Do you know why I asked you to come?
M Student: Actually, I have no idea. What would you like to discuss?
W: As you know, our final exam is coming up. And, um, you didn't do very well on the midterm exam.
M: Yeah, I guess I didn't study enough. I hope to do better than a C this time.
W: I'm pretty sure you can.

M: Thanks.
W: But I want to tell you about my grading policy. I think it's important.
M: Yes? What is it?
W: Your tests are important to your grade, of course. However, I take other factors into account.
M: What kinds of factors?
W: Some are class participation and your presentation. Your marks for both of those are good, so you have a chance to get a high grade.
M: That's really encouraging news. Thanks so much.

해석

W Professor: 와 줘서 고마워요, 매트. 내가 왜 오라고 했는지 알고 있나요?
M Student: 사실 전혀 모르겠어요. 말씀하시고 싶은 것이 무엇인가요?
W: 알겠지만 곧 기말 시험이 있어요. 그리고, 음, 자네는 중간고사에서 성적이 그다지 좋지 못했죠.
M: 네, 공부를 충분히 하지 않았던 것 같아요. 이번에는 C 이상의 점수를 받길 바라고 있어요.
W: 분명 할 수 있을 거예요.
M: 감사합니다.
W: 하지만 자네에게 내 성적 처리 방식을 알려주고 싶어요. 그것이 중요하다고 생각해요.
M: 네? 어떻게 되나요?
W: 당연히 시험이 성적에 중요해요. 하지만 나는 다른 요인들도 고려하거든요.
M: 어떤 요인들이죠?
W: 그중에 수업 참여도와 발표가 있어요. 두 경우 모두에서 자네의 점수가 좋기 때문에 높은 성적을 받을 가능성이 있어요.
M: 정말로 힘이 나는 소식이군요. 정말 감사합니다.

Listening Skills

1 thanks for
2 study enough
3 your grade
4 high grade

• Exercise 3 • ──────────────── p.34

정답 Q1 Ⓑ Q2 Ⓒ
스크립트 🎧 02-07

W Student: Excuse me, Professor Hamilton.
M Professor: Just a minute, please . . . Okay. All finished. How can I help you?
W: Hello. Um, do you have a course catalog I can borrow?
M: A course catalog . . . ? I, uh, don't think so. Why?
W: I just want to check the course number for a psychology class.
M: That's it?
W: Yes. I need to tell my friend the number. Then, we can be in the same class.
M: I see. Well, I'm sorry, but I don't have one. I'm sure you can

pick one up at the Registrar's office.
W: Yes, I'm aware of that, but it's on the other side of campus. I thought I'd just pop in to see if you happened to have one.
M: Why don't you go to the Psychology Department office? It's in this building.
W: Is it? Oh, I feel so silly! I should've known better. Thanks, sir. I'll see you later.
M: You're welcome. Good luck.

해석

W Student: 실례합니다, 해밀턴 교수님.
M Professor: 잠시만요… 자. 다 끝났어요. 무슨 일을 도와줄까요?
W: 안녕하세요. 음, 강좌 안내책자를 가지고 계시다면 빌릴 수 있을까요?
M: 강좌 안내책자요…? 아, 가지고 있지 않은 것 같네요. 왜죠?
W: 심리학 강의의 강좌 번호만 확인해 보려고요.
M: 그게 다인가요?
W: 네. 제 친구에게 번호를 말해줘야 하거든요. 그래야 같은 강의를 들을 수 있어요.
M: 알겠어요. 음, 그런데 미안하지만 나는 갖고 있는 게 없어요. 학적과에서 분명 하나 얻을 수 있을 거예요.
W: 네, 그건 알고 있는데요, 그곳은 캠퍼스 반대편에 있어서요. 전 교수님에게 혹시 있는지 확인차 그냥 잠깐 들러 봤어요.
M: 심리학과 사무실에 가보면 어때요? 이 건물에 있어요.
W: 그런가요? 아, 저는 정말 바보 같네요! 좀 더 잘 알아봤어야 하는데. 감사합니다, 교수님. 나중에 뵐게요.
M: 천만에요. 잘 해결되길 바랄게요.

Listening Skills

1 can borrow
2 need to tell
3 you can
4 pick one up

• Exercise 4 •   p.35

정답 Q1 Ⓐ Q2 Ⓑ
스크립트 🎧 02-09

M Professor: Good afternoon, Natalie. How are you doing?
W Student: I'm all right. I wonder if you have a moment to talk.
M: What's on your mind?
W: We have the first test of the semester next week, but I'm not sure how to study for it.
M: First, have you been taking notes in class and doing the reading?
W: I try to write down everything you say in class. I'm a bit behind in the reading, but I can catch up by tomorrow.
M: In that case, I suggest reviewing your notes every day.
W: What else?
M: You should reread the material in the book. Several questions on the test will come from the book, so you need to be familiar with it.
W: Wow. Thanks for the tip. Is there anything else I can do?

M: It might not hurt to study with a friend. If you don't understand something, perhaps your friend can help explain it.
W: My roommate is in the class, so I'll see if she wants to study together. Thanks a lot, sir.

해석

M Professor: 좋은 오후예요, 나탈리. 어떻게 지내나요?
W Student: 잘 지내고 있어요. 잠시 이야기할 시간이 있으신지 궁금합니다.
M: 무슨 일인가요?
W: 다음 주에 이번 학기 첫 시험이 있는데, 어떻게 시험 공부를 해야 할지 잘 모르겠어요.
M: 먼저, 수업 중에 필기를 잘 하고 있고, 책도 읽고 있나요?
W: 수업 중에 하시는 말씀은 모두 받아 적으려고 노력하고 있어요. 읽기는 좀 뒤처지고 있지만 내일이면 따라잡을 수 있어요.
M: 그런 경우라면 필기한 것을 매일 복습하길 권해요.
W: 그 밖에는요?
M: 책에 있는 내용을 다시 읽어보는 게 좋아요. 몇몇 시험 문제들은 책에서 나오니까, 내용에 대해 잘 알고 있어야 해요.
W: 와. 조언에 감사드려요. 제가 할 수 있는 일이 또 있을까요?
M: 친구와 함께 공부를 하는 것도 나쁘지 않을 거예요. 이해가 가지 않는 것이 있으면 아마도 친구가 설명을 도와줄 수 있고요.
W: 제 룸메이트도 그 수업을 듣기 때문에 그 친구가 같이 공부하고 싶어하는지 알아볼게요. 정말 감사합니다, 교수님.

Listening Skills

1 first test
2 write down
3 catch up
4 hurt to

• Exercise 5 •   p.36

정답 Q1 Ⓐ Q2 Ⓒ
스크립트 🎧 02-11

W Professor: Yes?
M Student: Oh, hi, Professor Gilbert.
W: Jeremy Ginn. I was hoping you'd stop by sometime today.
M: Yes, I'm sorry I couldn't make it yesterday, but I got stuck in the chemistry lab.
W: That's fine. Don't worry about it.
M: I'm glad to hear that.
W: Actually, Jeremy, I have a favor to ask of you. If you agree, I will be in your debt.
M: Sure. What do you need?
W: I'm giving a quiz in my freshman anatomy class next Thursday. It's a small class with about fourteen students in it.
M: Yes . . . ?
W: Well, all of my graduate assistants are busy on that day, so I was wondering if you could proctor the quiz for me.
M: Me, a proctor? Are you serious?
W: I sure am. All I need you to do is pick up the quizzes from me in the morning and then hand them out to the class. Of course,

you need to collect them at the end of the class.
M: No problem. You can count on me.
W: I know, Jeremy. That's why I chose you. Once you collect the quizzes, just drop them in my mailbox.
M: You've got it, Professor.

해석
W Professor: 네?
M Student: 아, 안녕하세요, 길버트 교수님.
W: 제레미 진 군. 오늘은 자네가 어느 때고 한 번 들르길 바라고 있었어요.
M: 네, 어제 약속을 지키지 못해 죄송한데요, 화학 실험실에 붙어 있었거든요.
W: 괜찮아요. 그것 때문에 걱정할 건 없어요.
M: 그렇다면 다행이에요.
W: 사실, 제레미, 자네에게 부탁할 게 있어요. 괜찮다면, 신세를 좀 질게요.
M: 그럼요. 무엇이 필요하신가요?
W: 다음 주 목요일에 신입생 해부학 강의에서 간단한 시험을 낼 예정이에요. 학생이 14명 정도인 작은 수업이죠.
M: 그렇군요…?
W: 음, 그날 내 대학원생 조교들이 모두 다 바빠서, 혹시 자네가 그 시험을 대신 감독해 줄 수 있는지 알고 싶었어요.
M: 제가, 감독을요? 정말이세요?
W: 물론이죠. 아침에 내게 와서 시험 문제지를 가져가 수업 시간에 학생들에게 나눠 주기만 하면 돼요. 물론, 수업이 끝날 때 시험지를 다시 걷어야 하고요.
M: 문제없어요. 제게 맡기만 주세요.
W: 알겠어요, 제레미. 바로 그래서 자네를 선택한 거예요. 시험지를 일단 걷으면, 내 우편함에 넣기만 해줘요.
M: 알겠습니다, 교수님.

Listening Skills

1 was hoping
2 got stuck
3 was wondering
4 drop them

• **Exercise 6** • p.37

정답 Q1 Ⓓ Q2 Ⓒ
스크립트 🎧 02-13

W Student: Um, Professor Burgess? Can I speak with you for a moment, or do you have a lecture now?
M Professor: If you can make it quick, I can talk. I have to run in five minutes.
W: Okay. Well, here's the problem . . .
M: You want to drop the class. Well, the add-drop period is over, so I guess . . .
W: Oh, no. I really enjoy your class.
M: Really? I don't hear that too often.
W: Um, I was hoping you could give me some extra time in the laboratory. I need to recheck my results from class today.
M: Extra time in the lab? I think that's another first. Most students run away as fast as they can from my lab class.
W: Really. I'm being serious! Is it possible?

M: Actually, I think it's open now, but you cannot mix any chemicals unless I'm in there.
W: I won't do anything like that. I just want to go over some of my calculations.
M: That's fine. But please do not allow anyone else in. Okay?
W: No problem. It will only take me about ten minutes or so.
M: That's fine.
W: Thanks a lot, Professor Burgess.

해석
W Student: 음, 버제스 교수님? 잠시 저랑 이야기하실 수 있으신가요, 아니면 지금 수업이 있으신가요?
M Professor: 빨리 끝낼 수 있다면, 이야기할 수 있어요. 5분 후에 가야 해요.
W: 알겠습니다. 음, 문제가 있는데요…
M: 수업을 취소하고 싶군요. 음, 강의 추가와 취소 기간은 끝났어요, 내가 알기로는…
W: 아, 아니에요. 전 정말 교수님 수업이 좋아요.
M: 그래요? 그런 말은 자주 듣지 못하는데.
W: 음, 교수님께서 제가 실험실을 추가로 사용할 시간을 주실 수 있는지 알고 싶어서요. 오늘 강의에서 얻은 제 결과를 다시 확인해보고 싶어요.
M: 실험실 추가 시간이요? 이런 경우도 처음인 것 같군요. 대부분의 학생들은 내 실험 수업에서 가능한 한 빨리 도망가는데 말이죠.
W: 정말이에요. 저는 진심이에요! 가능할까요?
M: 사실, 그곳은 지금도 열려 있을 테지만, 내가 그곳에 없으면 어떤 화학물도 섞을 수 없어요.
W: 그런 건 하지 않을 거예요. 저는 단지 제 계산 결과들을 좀 검토하고 싶은 거예요.
M: 그렇다면 좋아요. 하지만 다른 사람이 들어오지 않게 해주세요. 알겠죠?
W: 물론이죠. 한 10분 정도면 될 것 같아요.
M: 그러면 좋아요.
W: 정말 감사합니다, 버제스 교수님.

Listening Skills

1 speak with
2 need to
3 I'm being
4 cannot mix

• **Exercise 7** • p.38

정답 Q1 Ⓑ Q2 Ⓒ
스크립트 🎧 02-15

W Professor: Andrew, I think you know why I asked you to see me.
M Student: Yes, ma'am. My attendance hasn't been good lately.
W: That's correct. Is there any special reason why?
M: There is, actually. I was elected president of my fraternity, and it's taking up almost all of my time.
W: I see . . . Well, I think fraternities are fine, Andrew, but academics should come first. Don't you agree?
M: Yes, ma'am.
W: The syllabus clearly states that if you miss three or more

classes, your grade will be reduced by five points. You are aware of this policy, right?
M: Yes, I am. I'm really sorry. This month, I had to attend many meetings and manage the new members. I promise to be at every class from now on.
W: That's good to hear.
M: Yes . . .
W: Andrew, I'm not going to reduce your grade; however, I'd like you to write me an essay. Please write five pages on the habits of dolphins. That should make up for the missed class time. Got it?
M: I'll have it to you by Wednesday, Professor Starling. Thank you.
W: Good. I'm glad we got this cleared up.

해석
W Professor: 앤드류, 내가 자네를 왜 보자고 했는지 알 거라고 생각해요.
M Student: 네, 교수님. 제가 최근에 출석이 좋지 않았지요.
W: 맞아요. 특별한 이유라도 있나요?
M: 그게, 사실. 제가 동호회 회장으로 선출되었는데 그 일에 제 시간의 거의 대부분을 쓰고 있어요.
W: 그렇군요… 음, 동호회 활동은 좋다고 생각해요, 앤드류, 하지만 학업이 우선이 되어야 하죠. 그렇게 생각하지 않나요?
M: 맞습니다, 교수님.
W: 강의 요강에 수업을 3회 이상 빠지게 되면 점수가 5점 감점된다고 명시되어 있어요. 이 원칙을 알고 있죠, 그렇죠?
M: 네, 알고 있습니다. 정말 죄송합니다. 이번 달엔 여러 모임에 참석하고 신입 회원들을 관리해야 했어요. 이제부터 모든 수업에 출석하겠다고 약속할게요.
W: 그렇게 이야기하니 다행이군요.
M: 네…
W: 앤드류, 점수를 깎지는 않을 거예요. 하지만 에세이를 한 편 써 오는 것이 좋겠어요. 돌고래의 습성에 대해 5쪽 분량으로 써 오세요. 그러면 빠진 수업 시간에 대해 보충할 수 있을 거예요. 알겠나요?
M: 수요일까지 제출하겠습니다, 스탈링 교수님. 감사합니다.
W: 좋아요. 우리가 이 부분에 대해 해결을 해서 다행이네요.

Listening Skills

1 asked you
2 was elected
3 should come
4 make up

• Exercise 8 • p.39

정답 Q1 Ⓑ Q2 Ⓒ
스크립트 🎧 02-17

W Professor: Hello, Brad. How are things going with you?
M Student: Hello, Professor Watson. I'm having a busy day, but everything is all right.
W: That's good news. I want to let you know about an opportunity that has just come up.
M: Yes? What's that?

W: There is a speech contest that will be held two months from now.
M: A speech contest?
W: That's right. And I think you ought to take part in it.
M: Hmm . . . I've never done this kind of thing before though. I don't know what to do.
W: It's not complicated at all. You'll be given a topic ahead of time, and you have to prepare a three-minute speech on it.
M: That doesn't sound too hard.
W: That's not all. If you get selected for the second round, you'll be given another topic about five minutes before you go up on stage to speak.
M: That's a bit harder. But it sounds interesting.
W: Oh, there are a variety of topics, but there usually isn't anything controversial.
M: Okay. You've convinced me. I think I'd like to compete in it.
W: That's great news. I'll email you a link so that you can read more about it. I'm sure you'll have a fun time, and you might even win.
M: Thanks for having confidence in me, Professor Watson.

해석
W Professor: 반가워요, 브래드. 어떻게 지내나요?
M Student: 안녕하세요, 왓슨 교수님. 바쁘기는 하지만 모두 괜찮아요.
W: 좋은 소식이군요. 방금 생긴 기회에 대해 자네에게 알려주고 싶어요.
M: 네? 그게 뭔데요?
W: 지금부터 두 달 후에 열리는 웅변 대회가 있어요.
M: 웅변 대회요?
W: 맞아요. 그리고 나는 자네가 그 대회에 참가해야 한다고 생각해요.
M: 흠… 하지만 저는 그런 걸 전에 해본 적이 없어서요. 무엇을 해야 할지 모르겠어요.
W: 전혀 복잡하지 않아요. 미리 주제가 주어질 것이고, 자네는 그에 대해 3분간의 웅변을 준비해야 해요.
M: 그렇게 어렵게 들리지는 않네요.
W: 그게 전부는 아니에요. 2차 대회에 선발되면, 무대에 올라가 말하기 약 5분 전에 또 다른 주제가 주어질 거예요.
M: 그건 좀 더 어렵겠군요. 하지만 흥미로운데요.
W: 아, 다양한 주제들이 있기는 하지만, 보통 논쟁을 일으킬 만한 것은 없어요.
M: 그렇군요. 저를 설득하셨네요. 대회에 나가보고 싶어요.
W: 정말 잘됐네요. 대회에 대해 더 많은 내용을 읽어볼 수 있도록 이메일로 링크를 보내줄게요. 분명 재미있는 시간을 보낼 거예요, 그리고 우승까지 할 수도 있고요.
M: 자신감을 주셔서 감사합니다, 왓슨 교수님.

Listening Skills

1 an opportunity
2 given another
3 bit harder
4 I'll email you

Vocabulary Review

p.40

A
1 field
2 participation
3 catalog
4 suggest
5 count on

B 1 Ⓑ   2 Ⓐ   3 Ⓒ   4 Ⓐ   5 Ⓒ

C 1 Ⓑ   2 Ⓑ   3 Ⓐ   4 Ⓑ   5 Ⓐ

D
1 review
2 opportunity
3 falling behind
4 factors
5 stage

Practice Test

p.42

1 Ⓒ   2 Ⓒ   3 Ⓑ

스크립트

W Student: Good afternoon, Professor Nelson. Can I come in for a minute?
M Professor: Well, actually, I have class at 3:00, and it's 2:45 right now . . .
W: This won't take long.
M: Okay. But make it quick, please.
W: Great. Thanks. I heard there will be an academic conference next month.
M: Right. I'm organizing it.
W: Yes, well, uh, I was hoping I could submit a paper for it.
M: Submissions are open to both undergraduate and graduate students. However . . .
W: Yes?
M: The competition will be very stiff.
W: I see.
M: This conference is one of the most prestigious in the country. Only a handful of students will be chosen to speak at it.
W: Okay.
M: Last year, we had about 200 submissions. I think we ended up choosing only five or six.
W: That is tough.
M: Yeah. Anyway, the deadline is this Friday by 5:00 PM. So you had better get busy.
W: Actually, I'm already finished. I came by here to drop it off with you.
M: Finished? Well, I'm impressed. You know, I could take a look at it for you and make some suggestions.
W: That would be wonderful.
M: That way, you will have time to make any changes I suggest.
W: Great. In that case, I'll come back here tomorrow afternoon.

해석

W Student: 안녕하세요, 넬슨 교수님. 잠시 들어가도 될까요?
M Professor: 음, 사실, 내가 3시에 수업이 있고, 지금은 2시 45분이네요…
W: 오래 걸리지는 않을 거예요.
M: 알겠어요. 그렇지만, 빨리 끝내 주세요.
W: 알겠습니다. 감사합니다. 다음 달에 학술대회가 열린다고 들었어요.
M: 맞아요. 내가 조직하고 있죠.
W: 네, 음, 아, 제가 그 학회에 논문을 제출하고 싶어서요.
M: 논문 제출은 대학생과 대학원생 모두에게 열려 있어요. 하지만…
W: 네?
M: 경쟁이 아주 치열할 거예요.
W: 그렇군요.
M: 이 학술대회는 국가에서 아주 권위 있는 대회 중 하나예요. 다섯 손가락 안에 드는 학생들만 그곳에서 발언하도록 선정될 거예요.
W: 그렇군요.
M: 작년에는 약 200편을 제출 받았어요. 결국 5편 내지 6편만 선정한 것 같고요.
W: 정말 치열하네요.
M: 그렇죠. 어쨌든 마감이 이번 주 금요일 오후 5시까지예요. 그러니까 서두르는 게 좋을 거예요.
W: 사실, 저는 이미 다 끝냈어요. 그것을 교수님께 드리려고 여기에 잠시 들른 거예요.
M: 끝냈다고요? 음, 놀랍네요. 그러면, 내가 한 번 살펴 보고 조언을 좀 해줄 수 있어요.
W: 그렇게 해주신다면 정말 좋을 것 같습니다.
M: 그렇게 하면, 내가 제안한 걸 수정할 시간도 있을 거예요.
W: 좋습니다. 그럼 제가 내일 오후에 다시 들를게요.

CHAPTER 3 Deserts and Extreme Environments

Understanding TOEFL Question Types & Listening Skills
p.46

1 Question Types ▶ Sample Question

ⓒ

스크립트 🎧 03-01

W Professor: Deserts are found in, uh, many regions of the world. They are very dry places. Dry is the key word for deserts. But how dry? Just because an area is arid, does that make it a desert? Not always. Scientists have come up with a formula that defines what deserts are. According to them, deserts are areas that receive ten or fewer inches of precipitation each year. However, please note that there are some exceptions. Some areas get more rain than that, but scientists still call them deserts.

해석

W Professor: 사막은, 어, 세계 여러 지역에서 찾아볼 수 있습니다. 사막은 매우 건조한 지역이죠. 건조하다는 것이 사막의 핵심어입니다. 하지만 얼마나 건조할까요? 어떤 지역이 건조하다는 이유만으로 사막이 될까요? 항상 그런 것은 아니에요. 과학자들은 사막을 정의하는 한 가지 공식을 제시하고 있습니다. 이들에 따르면 사막은 연 강수량이 10인치 이하인 지역이에요. 하지만 몇 가지 예외가 있다는 점도 주의하세요. 어떤 지역에서는 그보다 더 많은 비가 내리지만, 과학자들은 여전히 이러한 곳도 사막이라고 부릅니다.

2 Listening Skills ▶ Check-Up

1 They are very dry places.
2 Just because an area is arid, does that make it a desert?
3 Scientists have come up with a formula that defines what deserts are.
4 Some areas get more rain than that, but scientists still call them deserts.

• Exercise 1 •
p.48

정답 Q1 Ⓑ Q2 Ⓑ
스크립트 🎧 03-03

M Professor: Okay, let's settle down everyone. We have a lot to go over today. Oh, remember we have a quiz next week. Please don't forget.
Today, we'll start with the temperatures of most deserts. You all know that many get very hot, but can you tell me why . . . ? Let me explain. Many deserts have a big fluctuation between daytime and nighttime temperatures. For example, a desert can get very hot during the day, but that night, it might cool down almost to freezing. Why is this? Well, the answer is humidity, which is the lack of water molecules in the air. You see, water helps block sunshine from reaching the Earth's surface. Water in the air also helps insulate, that is, keep warm air close to the Earth's surface at night. With deserts, this lack of humidity allows heat to enter and escape the landscape easily. This is the reason big temperature changes occur.

해석

M Professor: 자, 모두들 자리에 앉아 조용히 해주세요. 우리는 오늘 복습할 게 많아요. 아, 다음 주에 퀴즈가 있다는 걸 명심하고요. 잊지 마세요.
오늘, 우리는 대부분 사막의 기온부터 시작할 거예요. 여러분 모두 알다시피 많은 사막이 아주 뜨겁죠, 그런데 왜 그런지 말할 수 있나요…? 설명해 줄게요. 많은 사막들이 낮과 밤의 기온 차가 크죠. 예를 들어, 사막은 낮 동안에는 아주 뜨거워질 수 있지만 그날 밤에는 살이 에일 정도로 기온이 낮아질 수 있어요. 왜 그럴까요? 음, 답은 습도에 있는데, 즉 공기 중에 물 분자가 부족하기 때문입니다. 보다시피, 물은 햇빛의 차단을 도와 햇빛이 지표면에 도달하지 못하게 합니다. 공기 중의 물은 또한 단열을 돕는데, 즉 밤에 지표면 가까이의 따뜻한 공기를 가두어 둡니다. 사막에서는 이러한 습도의 부족으로 열이 쉽게 지표에 도달하고 지표에서 빠져나가게 됩니다. 이것이 기온 변화가 크게 일어나는 원인이 됩니다.

Listening Skills

1 We have a lot to go over today.
2 Today, we'll start with the temperatures of most deserts.
3 A desert can get very hot during the day.
4 Water helps block sunshine from reaching the Earth's surface.

• Exercise 2 •
p.49

정답 Q1 Ⓑ Q2 Ⓓ
스크립트 🎧 03-05

W Professor: The coldest place on the Earth? Without a doubt, the South Pole is one of the most frigid places. It is an extremely cold environment. Think of it this way. In the middle of summer, the average temperature at the South Pole is about minus twelve degrees Fahrenheit. Cold, huh?
But that's beach weather compared to winter. Winter temperatures average—are you ready for this—minus eighty-five degrees Fahrenheit. There are a number of reasons for these cold temperatures. First, during winter, the South Pole gets zero sunlight. It's completely dark there. During summer, the sun stays low near the horizon, and with the snow cover, most of the sunlight is reflected away from the ground. Second, the South Pole is at a relatively high altitude of around 9,500 feet. This altitude is one of the reasons why the South Pole is much colder than the North Pole.

해석

W Professor: 지구상에서 가장 추운 곳은요? 의심할 여지 없이 남극이 가장 추운 곳 중 하나입니다. 그곳은 극도로 추운 환경입니다. 이렇게 생각해 봅시다. 한여름에 남극의 평균 기온은 화씨 영하 12도 정도입니다. 정말 춥죠?
하지만 그것은 겨울과 비교해 보면 해변에 가기 딱 좋은 날씨일 뿐입니다. 겨울의 평균 기온은—준비됐나요—화씨 영하 85도입니다. 이렇게 기온이 낮은 데에는 많은 이유가 있습니다. 먼저, 겨울 동안 남극에는 햇빛이 전혀 비치지 않습니다. 그곳은 완전히 어둡습니다. 여름 동안, 해는 지평선 근처에 낮게 머무르고, 눈으로 덮여 있기 때문에 대부분의 햇빛이 땅에서 반사되어 빠져나갑니다. 두 번째로, 남극은 9,500피트 정도에 이르는 비교적 높은 고도에 위치해 있습니다. 이러한 고도가 남극이 북극보다 훨씬 더 추운 이유 중 하나입니다.

Listening Skills

1 It is an extremely cold environment.
2 There are a number of reasons for these cold temperatures.
3 During summer, the sun stays low near the horizon.
4 Most of the sunlight is reflected away from the ground.

• Exercise 3 • p.50

정답 Q1 ⓒ   Q2 ⓒ
스크립트 🎧 03-07

W Professor: First, I want to congratulate everyone on your test scores. Well done, and I hope you keep it up.
Now, this morning, we'll continue our discussion on the Earth's extreme environments. One place I'd like to talk about is one you probably haven't thought of: the deep ocean. It is one of the most hostile environments to life on the planet. Cold temperatures, darkness, and immense atmospheric pressure characterize the deep ocean.
Of course, it is one of the least understood and explored areas as well because human beings simply can't survive in that type of environment. Even with special technology, it's impossible. Still, we are able to explore areas deep beneath the surface. We can use ROVs. ROV stands for remotely operated vehicle. Usually, an ROV is a small robotic vehicle installed with cameras and built to withstand great pressure. But deep-sea exploration is very expensive. That's another reason why so little of the deep ocean has been explored.

해석

W Professor: 먼저, 여러분 모두의 시험 점수에 대해 축하해주고 싶어요. 잘 했어요, 그리고 계속 잘하기를 바랄게요.
이제, 오늘 아침, 우리는 지구의 극한 환경에 대해 이야기를 계속할 예정입니다. 제가 이야기하고 싶은 한 장소는 여러분이 아마도 생각해 본 적이 없는 곳일 겁니다: 바로 심해입니다. 그곳은 지구상의 생명체에게 가장 적대적인 환경 중 하나입니다. 차가운 온도, 어둠, 그리고 엄청난 수압이 심해의 특징을 이룹니다.
물론, 인간은 이런 유형의 환경에서는 그야말로 생존할 수 없기 때문에, 그곳은 가장 이해하기 어렵고 탐험하기 힘든 곳 중 하나이기도 합니다. 아무리 특별한 기술을 가지고도, 그것은 불가능합니다. 그렇지만 우리는 해수면 아래 깊은 영역들을 탐험할 수는 있습니다. 우리는 ROV를 사용할 수 있습니다. ROV란 자동조정장치를 의미합니다. 보통 ROV는 카메라가 장착된 작은 로봇 종류의 운송 수단으로, 높은 압력을 견딜 수 있도록 설계되었습니다. 그러나 심해 탐험은 비용이 아주 많이 듭니다. 심해의 극히 일부분만이 조사되고 있는 또 다른 이유입니다.

Listening Skills

1 It is one of the most hostile environments to life on the planet.
2 Even with special technology, it's impossible.
3 We are able to explore areas deep beneath the surface.
4 Deep-sea exploration is very expensive.

• Exercise 4 • p.51

정답 Q1 Ⓐ   Q2 ⓒ
스크립트 🎧 03-09

M Professor: Imagine a place so dry that parts of it haven't received any rain in more than 400 years. Yes, that place really exists. It's the Atacama Desert, and it's located in Chile in South America.
Interestingly, the desert is located next to the Pacific Ocean. The ocean is the reason so little rain falls there. There is a cold-water current alongside Chile. As a result, there's cold air at the surface while there's warm air higher up. This means that very little rain falls. However, fog is one feature of parts of the desert. The desert, by the way, is not very hot. Depending on the season, the temperature can be anywhere between zero and thirty degrees Celsius.
Here's something interesting about the desert. Because it is so dry there, the conditions in the Atacama Desert are similar to those on Mars. NASA, the American space organization, has conducted numerous tests there. For example, the rovers currently on Mars were tested in the Atacama Desert to see how they would react to conditions there.

해석

M Professor: 너무 건조해서 일부 지역의 경우 400년 이상 비가 내리지 않는 곳을 상상해 보세요. 네, 그런 곳이 실제로 존재합니다. 바로 아타카마 사막인데, 이곳은 남아메리카의 칠레에 위치해 있습니다.
흥미롭게도 이 사막은 태평양 옆에 위치해 있어요. 그곳에 비가 그토록 거의 내리지 않는 이유는 이 바다 때문입니다. 칠레를 따라 차가운 해류가 흐릅니다. 그 결과 지표면에는 차가운 공기가 존재하고, 보다 높은 곳에는 따뜻한 공기가 존재합니다. 이는 비가 정말 거의 내리지 않는다는 점을 의미합니다. 하지만 그 사막의 일부 지역에서 나타나는 한 가지 특징은 바로 안개입니다. 그건 그렇고, 이 사막은 그다지 덥지 않아요. 계절에 따라 다르지만, 기온이 섭씨 0도에서 30도 사이죠.
이 사막에 대해 흥미로운 점을 알려드릴게요. 그곳은 너무나 건조하기 때문에, 아타카마 사막의 환경은 화성의 환경과 유사합니다. 나사 즉, 미항공우주국은 그곳에서 수많은 시험을 실시해 왔습니다. 예를 들어 현재 화성에 있는 탐사선들은, 그곳의 환경에 탐사선들이 어떻게 반응하는지를 알아내기 위해, 아타카마 사막에서 시험을 거쳤습니다.

Listening Skills

1 The ocean is the reason so little rain falls there.
2 However, fog is one feature of parts of the desert.
3 Here's something interesting about the desert.
4 NASA, the American space organization, has conducted

numerous tests there.

Exercise 5
p.52

정답 Q1 ⓒ Q2 ⓑ
스크립트 🎧 03-11

M Professor: Yellowstone National Park in the northwest part of the United States is a hotbed of extreme environments. First of all, much of the region is full of volcanic activity. In fact, most of the park is located above a supervolcano, one of the largest and most volatile types of volcanoes. It hasn't erupted in more than 600,000 years, but below the surface are hot gases and an enormous magma pool.

Now, the Yellowstone Caldera, which is the name of the crater at the top of the volcano, is not dead. In fact, it's still active. Well, I suppose it's actually more dormant. After all, it hasn't erupted for so long. Nevertheless, hot rocks are very active beneath the surface. They release steam and gas through vents or geysers throughout the park. Some of the gases are highly toxic, so they're dangerous to animals and humans if they get too close. Many of the geysers contain extremely hot water. It's often more than 200 degrees Fahrenheit. So don't get too close to any geysers if you ever visit the park.

해석

M Professor: 미국 북서부 지역의 옐로스톤 국립공원은 극한 환경의 온상입니다. 먼저, 이 지역의 많은 곳에서 화산 활동이 활발합니다. 실제로 공원 대부분이, 가장 크고 가장 불안정한 화산 유형 중 하나인, 초화산 위에 위치해 있습니다. 60만년이 넘도록 분출이 일어나지 않았지만, 지표면 아래에는 뜨거운 가스와 거대한 마그마 웅덩이가 존재합니다.

자, 옐로스톤의 칼데라는, 그러니까 칼데라는 화산 꼭대기에 있는 분화구의 명칭인데, 영원히 활동을 멈춘 것이 아니에요. 사실 그것은 아직까지도 활동 중입니다. 음, 실제로는 휴면에 가까운 상태라고 해야겠네요. 어쨌거나, 매우 오랫동안 분출이 일어나지 않았어요. 그럼에도 불구하고 지표면 아래에는 뜨거운 암석들이 매우 활발히 활동하고 있습니다. 이들은 공원 곳곳에 있는 분출공이나 간헐천을 통해 증기와 가스를 뿜어내죠. 가스 중에는 매우 유독한 것도 있어서 만약 동물이나 인간이 너무 가까이 다가가는 경우 위험합니다. 많은 간헐천이 매우 뜨거운 물을 함유하고 있어요. 화씨 200도 이상인 경우가 많죠. 그러니 이 공원을 방문한다면 간헐천 근처에는 너무 가까이 가지 마세요.

Listening Skills

1. First of all, much of the region is full of volcanic activity.
2. It hasn't erupted in more than 600,000 years.
3. Below the surface are hot gases and an enormous magma pool.
4. Some of the gases are highly toxic.

Exercise 6
p.53

정답 Q1 ⓑ Q2 ⓓ
스크립트 🎧 03-13

W Professor: As you should know, there are both hot and cold deserts. Antarctica is a good example of a cold desert, and the Sahara in North Africa is a hot desert.

I'd like to discuss the effects these hostile environments can have on human beings. Let's begin with hot deserts. High heat and a lack of humidity as well as a lack of water are not a healthy combination for humans. Our bodies will sweat a lot in an attempt to keep our body temperature down. However, after even a few hours of not drinking enough water, a number of conditions can quickly occur. Of course, dehydration is a big threat in hot deserts. A more extreme one is heatstroke, and after a few punishing days, death.

In cold deserts, dehydration can be a factor. Sure, you could melt snow or ice for water, but without a source of heat, you'll be in big trouble. Another problem that humans face in cold deserts after long exposure is hypothermia. This happens when the body cannot retain heat and becomes too cold.

해석

W Professor: 여러분이 아는 대로, 열대 사막과 냉대 사막이 모두 존재합니다. 남극대륙은 냉대 사막의 좋은 예이고, 북아프리카의 사하라 사막은 열대 사막입니다.

저는 이와 같은 극한의 환경이 인간에게 끼칠 수 있는 영향에 대해 이야기해 보고자 합니다. 먼저 열대 사막부터 시작해 봅시다. 물 부족뿐 아니라 높은 열기와 습도의 부족은 인간에게 건강한 조합이 아닙니다. 우리의 몸은 체온을 낮추기 위해서 많은 양의 땀을 흘릴 것입니다. 그러나 물을 충분히 마시지 않은 채 몇 시간이라도 지나버리면, 여러 가지 상황이 급속도로 발생할 수 있습니다. 물론 뜨거운 사막에서는 탈수가 큰 위협이 됩니다. 그보다 더 극단적인 것은 열사병으로, 며칠 동안 고통에 시달리다가 죽습니다.

냉대 사막에서는 탈수가 요인이 될 수 있습니다. 물론, 눈이나 얼음을 녹여 물을 얻을 수 있겠지만, 열을 가할 요소가 없다면 큰일입니다. 냉대 사막에서 오랫동안 노출될 때 인간이 직면하는 또 다른 문제는 저체온증입니다. 이것은 몸이 열을 유지하지 못해 몸이 너무 차가워질 때 발생합니다.

Listening Skills

1. Let's begin with hot deserts.
2. Our bodies will sweat a lot in an attempt to keep our body temperature down.
3. In cold deserts, dehydration can be a factor.
4. This happens when the body cannot retain heat.

Exercise 7
p.54

정답 Q1 ⓓ Q2 ⓐ
스크립트 🎧 03-15

W Professor: In Asia, the Tibetan Plateau in western China is one of the most inhospitable places for people to live. Actually, the southern region isn't too bad. It has grasslands, and the temperatures and the altitude are manageable for human beings.

However, in the north and the northeast, it is a very different situation. Moving to the north, the plateau increases in elevation, and the air gets much colder and drier. In the northwest part of the plateau is Changtang Province. It's <u>the</u> <u>most</u> <u>remote</u> <u>area</u> of Tibet. <u>What</u> <u>makes</u> <u>it</u> <u>so</u> <u>remote</u>? Well, the average altitude is <u>more</u> <u>than</u> <u>sixteen</u> <u>thousand</u> <u>feet</u>. That's one reason. Another reason, as you can guess, <u>is</u> <u>the</u> <u>temperature</u>. Annually, the temperature averages <u>around</u> <u>minus</u> <u>four</u> <u>degrees</u> Celsius. <u>In</u> <u>winter</u>, it is absolutely frigid as the temperature averages <u>about</u> <u>forty</u> <u>degrees</u> <u>below</u> <u>zero</u> Celsius. Chilly, huh? It is <u>difficult</u> <u>for</u> <u>anything</u>, especially humans, <u>to</u> <u>live</u> <u>in</u> <u>this</u> <u>region</u>. It should <u>come</u> <u>as</u> <u>no</u> <u>surprise</u> that it is <u>the</u> <u>least</u> <u>populated</u> <u>region</u> in all of Asia. Only Antarctica, and perhaps Greenland <u>have</u> <u>fewer</u> <u>people</u>.

해석
W Professor: 아시아에서, 중국 서부 지역의 티베트 고원은 사람들이 살기에 가장 혹독한 지역 중 하나입니다. 사실 그곳의 남부 지역은 그다지 나쁘지 않습니다. 초원이 있고, 기온과 고도가 사람이 살기에 그럭저럭 괜찮습니다.
하지만 북부와 북동부는 상황이 매우 다릅니다. 북쪽으로 갈수록 고원의 고도가 높아지고, 공기가 더 차갑고 더 건조해지죠. 티베트 고원의 북서부 지역에는 창탕 고원이 있습니다. 티베트에서 가장 고립된 지역이죠. 무엇 때문에 그처럼 고립되었을까요? 음, 평균 고도가 1만 6천 피트가 넘습니다. 그것이 한 가지 이유입니다. 또 다른 이유는, 짐작하겠지만, 온도 때문입니다. 매년 평균 기온이 섭씨 영하 4도 정도예요. 겨울에는 평균 기온이 대략 섭씨 영하 40도일 정도로 엄청나게 춥습니다. 정말 춥죠, 그렇죠? 이 지역에서는 어떤 것이든, 특히 인간이, 살기가 힘들어요. 이곳이 아시아 전체에서 사람이 가장 적게 사는 지역이라는 점은 전혀 놀랍지 않습니다. 그보다 사람이 더 적은 곳은 오로지 남극과, 그리고 아마도 그린란드 정도일 거예요.

Listening Skills
1 Actually, <u>the</u> southern region <u>isn't</u> too bad.
2 <u>In</u> <u>the</u> northwest part <u>of</u> <u>the</u> plateau is Changtang Province.
3 Another reason, <u>as</u> <u>you</u> <u>can</u> guess, <u>is</u> <u>the</u> temperature.
4 <u>In</u> winter, <u>it</u> is absolutely frigid <u>as</u> <u>the</u> temperature averages <u>about</u> forty degrees <u>below</u> zero Celsius.

• **Exercise 8** • p.55

정답 Q1 Ⓑ Q2 Ⓐ
스크립트  03-17

M Professor: North Africa is the winner <u>when</u> <u>it</u> <u>comes</u> <u>to</u> <u>having</u> <u>the</u> <u>largest</u> <u>hot</u> <u>desert</u> in the world. <u>The</u> <u>name</u> <u>of</u> <u>this</u> <u>desert</u> <u>is</u> the Sahara, and it <u>covers</u> <u>more</u> <u>than</u> <u>two</u> <u>million</u> <u>square</u> <u>miles</u>. Yes, I said million, class. It occupies most of <u>the</u> <u>entire</u> <u>region</u> <u>of</u> <u>northern</u> <u>Africa</u>.
However, the Sahara <u>hasn't</u> <u>always</u> <u>been</u> <u>in</u> <u>bad</u> <u>shape</u>. An ice age long ago <u>brought</u> <u>water</u> <u>to</u> <u>the</u> <u>region</u>, but once it ended, the Sahara <u>dried</u> <u>out</u> <u>quickly</u>. In addition, monsoon rains <u>affected</u> <u>both</u> the southern <u>and</u> northern regions of the Sahara, but that <u>happened</u> <u>at</u> <u>different</u> <u>times</u>. Not times of the year. I'm talking about <u>different</u> <u>periods</u> <u>in</u> <u>history</u>.
Experts believe that the monsoons <u>eventually</u> <u>shifted</u> <u>to</u> <u>the</u> <u>southern</u> Sahara, and they <u>still</u> <u>affect</u> <u>that</u> <u>area</u> today. Let me <u>put</u> <u>it</u> <u>this</u> <u>way</u>. Most of the Sahara is very dry, but <u>the</u> <u>southern</u> region receives a bit <u>more</u> <u>rainfall</u>, which still <u>isn't</u> <u>much</u>, than the north. Another funny thing about the Sahara is that <u>when</u> <u>it</u> <u>does</u> <u>rain</u>, <u>a</u> <u>lot</u> <u>falls</u>. We call these torrential rains, and they can <u>last</u> <u>for</u> <u>days</u> or even <u>weeks</u>.

해석
M Professor: 세계에서 가장 큰 열대 사막이 있는 곳으로 치자면 북아프리카가 승자입니다. 이 사막의 이름은 사하라 사막으로, 그곳은 200만 평방마일 이상에 이릅니다. 맞아요, 제가 100만 단위를 말했죠, 여러분. 그 사막은 북아프리카 전체 지역의 대부분을 차지합니다.
그러나 사하라 사막의 상태가 항상 좋지 않았던 것은 아닙니다. 오래전 한 빙하기 때에는 이 지역에 물이 공급되었으나, 그 기간이 끝나자 사하라 지대는 급격하게 메말랐습니다. 게다가 계절풍에 따른 비가 사하라 지대의 남부와 북부 지방 모두에 영향을 끼쳤지만, 이 일은 각각 다른 시기에 발생했습니다. 1년 동안의 시기가 아닙니다. 역사적으로 다른 시기를 이야기하는 것입니다.
전문가들은 계절풍이 결국에는 사하라 남부 지역 쪽으로 방향을 바꾸면서 오늘날까지도 이 지역에 영향을 끼치고 있다고 생각합니다. 이렇게 설명해 보죠. 대부분의 사하라 지역이 매우 건조하긴 하지만, 북부 지방보다는 남부 지방에, 많지는 않더라도 약간 더 많은 비가 내립니다. 사하라 사막에 대해 또 다른 흥미로운 점은 비가 정말로 오기라도 하면, 엄청나게 많이 내린다는 것입니다. 우리는 이것을 폭우라고 부르는데, 몇 날 며칠, 심지어는 몇 주 동안 계속해서 내리기도 합니다.

Listening Skills
1 It occupies <u>most</u> <u>of</u> <u>the</u> entire region <u>of</u> northern Africa.
2 <u>However</u>, <u>the</u> Sahara <u>hasn't</u> always <u>been</u> <u>in</u> bad shape.
3 Experts believe <u>that</u> <u>the</u> monsoons eventually shifted <u>to</u> <u>the</u> southern Sahara.
4 <u>The</u> southern region receives <u>a</u> bit more rainfall.

Vocabulary Review p.56

Ⓐ 1 crater
  2 sweat
  3 inhospitable
  4 shape
  5 exposure

Ⓑ 1 Ⓑ 2 Ⓒ 3 Ⓐ 4 Ⓒ 5 Ⓒ

Ⓒ 1 Ⓐ 2 Ⓒ 3 Ⓐ 4 Ⓒ 5 Ⓓ

Ⓓ 1 fog
  2 insulated
  3 rover
  4 hostile
  5 frigid

Practice Test p.58

1 Ⓑ 2 Ⓐ 3 Ⓐ 4 Painted Desert: ①, ④
Petrified Forest: ②, ③

스크립트 🎧 03-19

M Professor: One of my favorite places is the Painted Desert in northern Arizona. It's absolutely beautiful. The landscape of mountains and hills is made up of brightly colored minerals. The layers, which we call strata, in the mountains are very distinct and defined. Reds, oranges, yellows, and other earth tones have been carved by natural erosion over thousands and thousands of years. Wind and rain are two major factors which have shaped this desert region. Of course, sunrise and sunset are the best times to take in the brilliant colors of the Painted Desert.

One curious area lying within parts of the Painted Desert is the Petrified Forest. It is full of petrified, you know, fossilized, wood, trees, and even dinosaur bones and skeletons. Most of the petrified items were buried in ancient riverbeds and were petrified by volcanic ash. Ash and sand helped petrify trees and wood as well as leaves and other items located throughout the forest.

The Petrified Forest also contains some of the oldest known dinosaur fossils in North America. One fascinating fossil found there is the phytosaur. This was a huge reptile that was somewhat similar to an alligator or crocodile. It once roamed the area. But that's not all. There are also fossils of invertebrates such as shellfish and snails in the forest.

해석

M Professor: 제가 가장 좋아하는 곳 중 하나는 애리조나주 북부에 위치한 오색 사막입니다. 그곳은 정말로 아름답습니다. 산과 언덕의 풍광이 밝은 색의 광물들로 이루어져 있습니다. 우리가 지층이라고 부르는 산의 여러 층들이 매우 뚜렷하고 선명합니다. 수천 년에 걸친 자연 풍화 작용으로 빨간색, 주황색, 노란색, 그리고 그 외 흙빛의 색들이 새겨져 있습니다. 바람과 비가 이러한 사막 지역을 형성한 두 가지 주요한 요인입니다. 물론, 일출과 일몰이 오색 사막의 찬란한 색들을 감상하기에 가장 좋은 때입니다.

오색 사막의 일부 지역에 자리하고 있는 독특한 한 곳은 화석림입니다. 이곳은 석화된, 그러니까 화석화된 목재, 나무, 심지어는 공룡의 뼈와 잔해로 가득합니다. 화석들의 대부분은 고대의 강 바닥에 묻혀졌고 화산재로 인해 석화되었습니다. 재와 모래가, 숲 전체에 걸쳐 분포해 있는 나뭇잎과 기타 요소들은 물론, 나무와 목재를 석화시키는 데 일조한 것이죠.

화석림에는 또한 북아메리카에서 가장 오래된 것으로 알려진 공룡 화석들의 일부가 있습니다. 그곳에서 발견된 놀라운 화석으로는 피토사우루스가 있습니다. 이것은 앨리게이터 악어나 크로커다일 악어와 다소 비슷한 거대 파충류였습니다. 한때 그 지역을 돌아다녔죠. 하지만 이것이 전부는 아닙니다. 숲에는 조개류와 달팽이 같은 무척추동물들의 화석도 있습니다.

CHAPTER 4 Service Encounters

Understanding TOEFL Question Types & Listening Skills
p.62

1 Question Types ▶ Sample Question

스크립트 🎧 04-01

M Student: Excuse me. I need to register for a class.
W Registrar's Office Employee: Sure. Which one is it?
M: The class is History 26. It's being taught by Professor Cole.
W: Hold on a moment. Let me check on its availability.
M: Sure.
W: I'm sorry, but that class is currently full.
M: Full? Oh, no. That's bad news.
W: Yes, it's full, but I can put you on the waiting list. You would be first if you do that.
M: What are the chances of my getting into the class?
W: In most classes, at least a couple of students drop out each semester.
M: That's good to hear. Then go ahead and sign me up, please.
W: All right. May I see your student ID?

해석

M Student: 실례합니다. 수강 신청을 해야 해요.
W Registrar's Office Employee: 그래요. 어떤 수업인가요?
M: 역사학 26 수업이에요. 콜 교수님께서 가르치고 계시죠.
W: 잠시만요. 가능한지 확인해 볼게요.
M: 네.
W: 유감이지만 그 수업은 현재 인원이 다 찼어요.
M: 다 찼다고요? 아, 이런. 나쁜 소식이군요.
W: 네, 다 찼지만, 대기자 명단에 이름을 올려줄 수 있어요. 그렇게 하면 첫 번째 대기자가 될 거예요.
M: 수업에 들어갈 수 있는 가능성이 어느 정도일까요?
W: 대부분의 수업에서 학기마다 최소한 두세 명의 학생들은 수강을 취소해요.
M: 반가운 소리군요. 그렇다면 어서 제 이름을 올려주세요.
W: 알겠어요. 학생증을 볼 수 있을까요?

2 Listening Skills ▶ Check-Up

1 I need to / register for a class.
2 It's being taught / by Professor Cole.
3 Let me check / on its availability.
4 Then go ahead / and sign me up, / please.

• Exercise 1 • p.64

정답
스크립트

W Student: Hello. Could you make a quick photocopy for me?

M Librarian: You need to use the photocopiers on the second floor.
W: Oh, come on, please. It'll take you two seconds.
M: I would, but my manager is standing right there.
W: Oh, I see. Well, thanks . . .
M: Wait a minute.
W: What?
M: Do you have a copy card?
W: Doesn't the copier take change or bills or a credit card?
M: Not anymore. You have to purchase a copy card. You can put credit on the card and then put it in the copier.
W: Where can I buy a copy card?
M: From me.
W: Okay. I'll take one with five dollars' worth of credit on it.
M: Okay. Here's your card, and here's five in change.
W: Great. Thanks a lot. Second floor, right?
M: That's correct.
W: See you later.
M: What a minute. You forgot your purse. Here you are . . .
W: Oh, thanks.

해석

W Student: 안녕하세요. 빨리 복사 좀 해주실 수 있나요?
M Librarian: 2층에 있는 복사기를 사용하셔야 해요.
W: 아, 그러지 마시고 부탁 좀 드릴게요. 잠깐이면 될 거예요.
M: 그러고 싶지만 저기 제 상사가 서 계시거든요.
W: 아, 알겠어요. 그러면, 감사합니다…
M: 잠깐만요.
W: 네?
M: 복사 카드가 있나요?
W: 복사기에 잔돈이나 지폐, 신용카드 사용이 안 되나 보죠?
M: 더 이상은 안돼요. 복사 카드를 사야 해요. 카드에 충전을 한 다음 복사기에 넣어 사용할 수 있어요.
W: 어디에서 복사 카드를 살 수 있나요?
M: 저한테서요.
W: 알겠어요. 5달러만큼 충전한 카드를 살게요.
M: 알겠습니다. 여기 카드가 있고요, 이건 잔돈으로 5달러요.
W: 좋네요. 정말 감사합니다. 2층 맞죠?
M: 맞아요.
W: 또 뵐게요.
M: 잠시만요. 지갑을 잊으셨네요. 여기요…
W: 아, 감사합니다.

Listening Skills

1 It'll take you / two seconds.
2 Do you have / a copy card?
3 Here's your card, / and here's five / in change.
4 You forgot / your purse.

• Exercise 2 • ──────────────── p.65

정답 Q1 ⓓ   Q2 ⓒ

스크립트 04-05
W Housing Office Employee: Hi. Can I help you?
M Student: Yes, I'm interested in university housing.
W: You have a number of options. Do you prefer on- or off-campus housing?
M: On campus. The off-campus housing is too far for me to walk, and I don't like buses.
W: You don't like buses? Okay. Then do you have a preference between an on-campus apartment or a dormitory?
M: Are there any studio apartments available? I prefer to live alone. Roommates really complicate things.
W: I hear you. There sure are.
M: How soon can I move into the studio?
W: Actually, there are a couple of units open now. You just need to make a deposit, and then it's all yours.
M: Great. Where do I sign?
W: Let me get the paperwork together, and we'll go over it together. Okay?
M: Sounds good. Let's do it.

해석

W Housing Office Employee: 안녕하세요. 도와 드릴까요?
M Student: 네, 대학 숙소에 대해 관심이 있어요.
W: 여러 선택권이 있어요. 교내 숙소가 좋으세요, 아니면 외부 숙소가 좋으세요?
M: 교내 숙소요. 외부 숙소는 제가 걸어 다니기에는 너무 멀고, 버스는 좋아하지 않아요.
W: 버스를 좋아하지 않는다고요? 알겠어요. 그러면 교내 아파트나 기숙사 중 선호하는 것이 있나요?
M: 스튜디오형 아파트도 있나요? 전 혼자 사는 게 더 좋아요. 룸메이트는 정말이지 일을 복잡하게 만들어요.
W: 이해해요. 물론 있어요.
M: 제가 얼마나 빨리 스튜디오로 이사할 수 있을까요?
W: 사실 지금 비어 있는 곳이 두세 곳 있어요. 보증금만 내면 학생 마음대로 할 수 있어요.
M: 좋아요. 어디에 서명하면 되죠?
W: 제가 서류를 모두 정리한 다음 함께 검토해 볼게요. 어때요?
M: 좋아요. 그렇게 하죠.

Listening Skills

1 I'm interested in / university housing.
2 Are there / any studio apartments available?
3 Actually, / there are a couple of units / open now.
4 You just need to make a deposit, / and then it's all yours.

• Exercise 3 • ──────────────── p.66

정답 Q1 Ⓐ   Q2 Ⓐ
스크립트 04-07

M Registrar's Office Employee: Uh, number twenty-two is next, please . . .
W Student: Hello. Um . . . I'm not sure if I'm in the right place.

M: Okay. This window handles class changes.
W: Oh, good. I'd like to change one of my classes to the pass-fail option.
M: Okay. Student number, please.
W: 2-1-5-7-8-8.
M: Hmm . . . It looks like you can't take any more pass-fail classes this semester. You're only allowed one per semester.
W: I know. So I'd like to do this. I want to drop my biology class completely from my schedule. Then, I'd like to change my Japanese class to pass-fail. Can I do that?
M: You sure can. Biology 414 . . . dropped . . . Change Japanese II to pass-fail. Okay. You're all set. Anything else?
W: Oh, one more thing. When is the deadline to pay tuition? Next Friday, right?
M: Yes, but you can get a one-month extension if you need it.
W: Oh, good. Thanks.

해석

M Registrar's Office Employee: 아, 다음 22번이요…
W Student: 안녕하세요. 음… 제가 제대로 왔는지 잘 모르겠네요.
M: 네. 이 창구는 강의 변경을 담당해요.
W: 아, 잘됐네요. 제 강의 중 하나를 통과-낙제 과목으로 바꾸고 싶어요.
M: 알겠습니다. 학번을 말씀해 주세요.
W: 2-1-5-7-8-8입니다.
M: 음… 학생은 이번 학기에 통과-낙제 과목 수업을 더 이상 들을 수 없는 것 같은데요. 한 학기에 한 과목만 가능해요.
W: 알고 있어요. 그래서 이렇게 하고 싶어요. 제 시간표에서 생물 수업을 완전히 취소하고 싶어요. 그러고 나서 일본어 수업을 통과-낙제 과목으로 바꾸고 싶어요. 그렇게 할 수 있나요?
M: 물론 할 수 있어요. 생물학 414 강의를… 빼고… 일본어 II 수업을 통과-낙제 과목으로 바꾸기. 됐어요. 다 됐네요. 또 다른 건요?
W: 아, 하나 더 있어요. 수업료 납부 기한이 언제죠? 다음 주 금요일 맞나요?
M: 네, 하지만 필요하면 한 달 연장이 가능해요.
W: 아, 좋네요. 감사합니다.

Listening Skills

1 This window / handles class changes.
2 You're only allowed one / per semester.
3 When is the deadline / to pay tuition?
4 You can get a one-month extension / if you need it.

• Exercise 4 • ─────────────── p.67

정답 Q1 Ⓓ   Q2 Ⓐ
스크립트 🎧 04-09

W Student: Mr. Jefferson, could I have a quick word with you?
M Cafeteria Manager: Sure, Stephanie. What do you want to talk about?
W: It's about my shift here this Thursday evening.
M: What about it?
W: Is it possible to change shifts with someone else?
M: For the rest of the semester? I don't think that's ideal.

W: Oh, I don't mean for the rest of the semester. I'm talking about this Thursday only.
M: What's going on?
W: I've got a group presentation to give on Friday, and the group wants to practice all evening on Thursday.
M: Hmm . . . Well, school is the reason that you're here.
W: Thank you so much for understanding.
M: However, you need to find a person willing to work as your replacement. If you don't do that, you'll have to come to work.
W: I don't really know any of the other student employees here. Who do you think I should speak with?
M: David is always looking for extra hours.
W: Which one is David?
M: He's standing over by the sink. Why don't you have a chat with him now?

해석

W Student: 제퍼슨 매니저님, 잠깐 이야기를 나눌 수 있을까요?
M Cafeteria Manager: 그럼요, 스테파니. 무슨 이야기를 하고 싶나요?
W: 이번 주 목요일 저녁에 여기서 할 제 근무에 대한 거예요.
M: 어떤 거죠?
W: 다른 사람과 근무를 바꿀 수 있을까요?
M: 나머지 학기 동안이요? 좋지 않은 것 같은데요.
W: 아, 나머지 학기 동안을 말씀드리는 게 아니에요. 이번 주 목요일만 말씀드리는 거예요.
M: 무슨 일이 있나요?
W: 금요일에 할 조별 발표가 있는데, 조원들이 목요일 저녁 내내 연습하길 원해요.
M: 흠… 어쨌든, 학업 때문에 스테파니가 여기에 있는 거니까요.
W: 이해해 주셔서 정말 감사합니다.
M: 하지만 스테파니를 대신해서 일할 사람을 찾아야 해요. 그렇게 하지 않으면 와서 일을 해야 할 거예요.
W: 저는 이곳에서 일하는 다른 학생들 중에 잘 아는 사람이 없어요. 제가 누구와 이야기해야 할까요?
M: 데이비드가 늘 추가 근무를 찾고 있죠.
W: 누가 데이비드인가요?
M: 저쪽 싱크대 옆에 서 있는 사람이에요. 지금 그와 이야기를 해보는 게 어때요?

Listening Skills

1 Mr. Jefferson, / could I have a quick word / with you?
2 I don't think / that's ideal.
3 Thank you so much / for understanding.
4 He's standing / over by the sink.

• Exercise 5 • ─────────────── p.68

정답 Q1 Ⓒ   Q2 Ⓐ
스크립트 🎧 04-11

W Student: Good morning. What's all of this for? A celebrity photo shoot?
M Student Affairs Office Assistant: Um, actually, we're starting to

take graduation photos this morning. You know, for graduating students . . . Cap and gown. That kind of thing.
W: Oh, really? Nobody told me. This is my last semester.
M: Have you applied to graduate?
W: Yes.
M: Were you approved?
W: Of course.
M: Then you should be on my list. What's your name?
W: Heather Hampton.
M: Hampton, Hampton . . . Yes, here you are. Would you like to have your graduation pictures taken?
W: I sure would, but I don't have a cap or a gown.
M: Nobody does. We have some different ones for you to wear just for the pictures.
W: Great. How much does it cost?
M: There's no fee. Your picture will automatically be put in the yearbook, and the university will send you a notice via regular or email . . .
W: Okay.
M: Once you preview your picture, you can choose to order prints or not on the request form.
W: I see. It won't take long, will it? I have class in fifteen minutes.
M: No, not long at all. Here, have a seat . . .

해석
W Student: 안녕하세요. 이게 다 뭔가요? 유명인이 사진을 찍나요?
M Student Affairs Office Assistant: 음, 사실 오늘 아침부터 졸업 사진을 찍거든요. 알다시피, 졸업생들을 위한… 학사모와 가운이에요. 뭐 그런 거요.
W: 아, 정말요? 아무도 저에게 말해주지 않았어요. 이번이 제 마지막 학기예요.
M: 졸업 신청은 했나요?
W: 네.
M: 승인이 되었나요?
W: 물론이에요.
M: 그렇다면 제가 가지고 있는 명단에 있을 거예요. 이름이 뭐죠?
W: 헤더 햄튼입니다.
M: 햄튼, 햄튼… 네, 여기 있네요. 졸업 사진을 찍으시겠어요?
W: 물론이죠, 하지만 학사모와 가운은 없어요.
M: 아무도 가지고 있지 않죠. 사진 찍을 때만 입는 다양한 옷들이 여러 벌 마련되어 있어요.
W: 좋네요. 얼마죠?
M: 비용은 없어요. 사진이 자동적으로 졸업 앨범에 들어가고 대학에서 서면이나 이메일로 학생에게 안내문을 보낼 거예요…
W: 알겠어요.
M: 일단 사진을 미리 보고, 신청서에 인화를 신청할지 선택하면 돼요.
W: 알겠습니다. 오래 걸리진 않아요, 그렇죠? 15분 후에 수업이 있어요.
M: 네, 전혀 오래 걸리지 않아요. 여기 앉으세요…

Listening Skills

1. Have you applied / to graduate?
2. Then / you should be / on my list.
3. There's / no fee.
4. I have class / in fifteen minutes.

• Exercise 6 •

p.69

정답 Q1 Ⓓ   Q2 Ⓐ
스크립트 🎧 04-13

M Student: Hello. I'm interested in running for student council.
W Student Government Office Assistant: Only full-time students can do that. You're full time, right?
M: What exactly does full time mean?
W: You must take at least twelve hours this semester.
M: Oh, I'm taking five classes for a total of fifteen hours.
W: Wonderful. The other criterion is that you must have a professor's written and signed nomination.
M: I have that, too.
W: May I see it, please? Okay, um, this looks fine. Actually, I had Dr. Jensen last year. He's great.
M: Yeah, he's my director for my undergraduate thesis.
W: What position on the student council would you like to run for?
M: Secretary.
W: Do you have your résumé with you?
M: Here you go. You can keep that copy.
W: Thanks. All of the information—your address, email, and phone number—is current?
M: Yes, it is.
W: Perfect. Then could I please have you write your signature and the date here on this line?
M: There you go.
W: Okay. We'll notify you via email in two or three days. It's just a formality.
M: Sounds good. Thanks a lot.

해석
M Student: 안녕하세요. 학생회에 후보 등록을 하고 싶은데요.
W Student Government Office Assistant: 전일제 학생이어야 그렇게 할 수 있어요. 전일제로 수업을 듣는 거 맞죠?
M: 전일제가 정확하게 어떤 의미인가요?
W: 이번 학기에 적어도 12시간은 수업을 들어야 해요.
M: 아, 저는 5개 수업을 총 15시간 동안 들어요.
W: 좋아요. 또 다른 요건으로 교수님 한 분이 써 주시고 서명하신 추천서가 있어야 해요.
M: 그것도 가지고 있어요.
W: 보여 주시겠어요? 좋아요, 음, 좋네요. 사실은 저도 작년에 젠슨 박사님이 지도 교수님이셨어요. 좋은 분이시죠.
M: 네, 교수님은 제 학부 논문 지도 교수님이세요.
W: 학생회의 어떤 직책에 후보 등록을 하고 싶죠?
M: 총무요.
W: 이력서를 가지고 있나요?
M: 여기 있어요. 그 사본을 가지고 계셔도 돼요.
W: 고마워요. 모든 정보, 그러니까 주소, 이메일, 전화번호가 현재 정보인가요?
M: 네, 맞아요.
W: 좋아요. 그러면 여기 이 줄 위에 서명하고 날짜를 써 주시겠어요?
M: 여기 있습니다.
W: 됐습니다. 2~3일 후에 이메일로 통지해 줄 거예요. 형식적인 절차일 뿐이죠.

M: 좋습니다. 정말 감사합니다.

> **Listening Skills**

1 What exactly / does full time mean?
2 May I see it, / please?
3 You can keep / that copy.
4 It's just a / formality.

• **Exercise 7** • ──────────────── p.70

정답 Q1 Ⓐ Q2 Ⓒ
스크립트 🎧 04-15

W Student: Excuse me. I wonder if I could get some help with my housing situation.
M Housing Office Employee: What exactly is the problem?
W: I would like to move to a new dorm room. Is that possible?
M: The date for moving passed a couple of days ago.
W: Oh, that's too bad.
M: Why don't you tell me why you want to move? Maybe I can help.
W: It's my roommate. She and I simply don't get along well.
M: In what way?
W: I go to bed early, but she stays up very late. She's very loud and always has friends over.
M: Have you asked her to stop doing that?
W: Yes, I have, but she never listens to me. My grades are dropping because of my horrible living situation.
M: Hmm . . . We could probably allow you to change dorm rooms.
W: You could? That would be wonderful.
M: I have to speak with my boss. I can't make any promises though.
W: As long as you try, I'll appreciate it.
M: Let me talk to my boss. I'll be back in a couple of minutes.

해석

W Student: 실례합니다. 제 기숙사 상황에 대해 도움을 좀 얻을 수 있을지 궁금해서요.
M Housing Office Employee: 정확히 어떤 문제가 있나요?
W: 기숙사 방을 옮기고 싶어요. 가능할까요?
M: 방을 옮길 수 있는 날짜는 이틀 전에 지났어요.
W: 아, 어쩌죠.
M: 왜 옮기고 싶은지 얘기를 해 볼래요? 제가 도움을 줄 수도 있어요.
W: 제 룸메이트 때문이에요. 그녀와 저는 그야말로 잘 맞지가 않아요.
M: 어떤 점에서요?
W: 저는 일찍 자는 반면에 그녀는 매우 늦게까지 잠을 안 자요. 매우 시끄럽고 항상 친구들을 데리고 와요.
M: 그러지 말라고 요청해 봤나요?
W: 네, 그랬지만, 제 말을 전혀 듣지 않아요. 생활 환경이 엉망진창이라 성적이 떨어지고 있고요.
M: 흠… 아마도 기숙사 방을 바꿔 줄 수도 있을 것 같네요.
W: 그렇게 해주실 수 있으세요? 그러면 정말 좋을 것 같아요.

M: 제 상사와 이야기를 해야 해요. 그렇지만 장담은 못해요.
W: 노력만 해주셔도 감사해요.
M: 상사와 이야기를 해보죠. 잠시 후에 돌아올게요.

> **Listening Skills**

1 What exactly / is the problem?
2 Maybe / I can help.
3 Have you asked her / to stop doing that?
4 I have to speak / with my boss.

• **Exercise 8** • ──────────────── p.71

정답 Q1 Ⓐ Q2 Ⓒ
스크립트 🎧 04-17

W University Fitness Center Employee: Hello. Can I see your faculty or university employee ID, please?
M Student: Um . . . what do you mean? Isn't the gym for everybody? Faculty and students?
W: Oh, you must be a freshman. They never remember to tell you guys during orientation, do they? I'll have to remind them again.
M: Could you fill me in, please?
W: This is the faculty-only fitness center. Actually, university employees can work out here, too.
M: Then where is the student fitness center?
W: You're pretty close. It's in the basement of this building. You can just take the elevator right over there.
M: Thanks. By the way, can students work in the fitness centers?
W: Sure. Are you a certified trainer?
M: Oh, no. I'm asking for my friend.
W: Well, if your friend is certified, there's a good chance. I think there's an opening in the student center.
M: Wonderful. I'll tell her.
W: Yeah, here's an application. Just tell her to fill it out and to bring it in sometime soon.
M: I will. Thanks for your help.
W: Have a good workout.

해석

W University Fitness Center Employee: 안녕하세요. 교수진 혹은 교직원 신분증을 보여 주시겠어요?
M Student: 음… 무슨 말씀이세요? 모두 쓸 수 있는 체육관이 아닌가요? 교수진과 학생들이요?
W: 아, 신입생인가 보군요. 오리엔테이션에서 신입 학생들에게 말해주는 걸 잊었나 봐요, 그렇죠? 다시 한 번 알려줘야겠어요.
M: 자세히 좀 알려주시겠어요?
W: 이곳은 교수진 전용 피트니스 센터에요. 사실 교직원들도 이곳에서 운동할 수 있고요.
M: 그러면 학생용 피트니스 센터는 어디죠?
W: 아주 가까이에 있어요. 이 건물 지하에 있죠. 저쪽에서 바로 엘리베이터를 타면 돼요.

M: 감사합니다. 그런데요, 학생들이 피트니스 센터에서 일을 할 수도 있나요?
W: 그럼요. 트레이너 자격증이 있나요?
M: 아, 아니에요. 친구 때문에 여쭤보는 거예요.
W: 음, 만약 친구가 자격증이 있다면, 좋은 기회가 있어요. 학생 피트니스 센터에 빈 자리가 있다고 알고 있거든요.
M: 잘됐군요. 그녀에게 말해줘야겠어요.
W: 그래요, 여기 지원서요. 그 친구에게 이 지원서를 작성해서 조만간 가져오라고 말해주세요.
M: 그럴게요. 도움 주셔서 감사합니다.
W: 그럼 운동 잘 하세요.

Listening Skills

1 I'll have to / remind them again.
2 This is the faculty-only / fitness center.
3 I think / there's an opening / in the student center.
4 Yeah, / here's an application.

Vocabulary Review   p.72

A
1 situation
2 certified
3 run
4 automatically
5 shift

B 1 Ⓑ   2 Ⓐ   3 Ⓓ   4 Ⓓ   5 Ⓒ

C 1 Ⓐ   2 Ⓐ   3 Ⓐ   4 Ⓒ   5 Ⓒ

D
1 willing
2 orientation
3 promise
4 formality
5 criterion

Practice Test   p.74

1 Ⓑ   2 Ⓒ   3 Ⓓ

스크립트 🎧 04-19

M Student: Hello. Where do I go to learn about clubs at the school?
W Student Activities Office Employee: We had a big event yesterday. Is that what you're talking about?
M: It was yesterday? I thought it was today.
W: There were lots of advertisements all around campus. Didn't you see them?
M: I guess I must have gotten the dates confused.
W: Anyway, clubs are still accepting new members. So you have time to join one or two of them if you are interested.
M: That's great news. What kinds of clubs are there?

W: Here's a list of clubs.
M: Hmm . . . Do you know which ones are popular?
W: The movie club is big with lots of students. So are the cycling club and the jogging club.
M: Those last two clubs aren't really for me. Are there any clubs that are more academic in nature?
W: How about the chess club? It has a few members. There's also a computer programming club.
M: Those sound pretty interesting. I might check out both of them.
W: Is there anything else you need to know?
M: I really like learning about rocks. Is there a geology club?
W: I'm afraid that there isn't, but there is a paleontology club. Its members discuss dinosaurs and fossils. Sometimes they even go out searching for fossils.
M: Woah, that sounds awesome. It's just the kind of thing I'm interested in.
W: You're in luck. The club is having its first meeting of the year this evening at six thirty.
M: Where's it going to be?
W: It's going to be in room 203 in Carmichael Hall. According to the information I have, the club is looking for more members. Good luck.

해석

M Student: 안녕하세요. 교내 동아리에 대해 알려면 어디로 가야 하나요?
W Student Activities Office Employee: 어제 큰 행사가 있었죠. 그것에 대해 말하는 건가요?
M: 어제였다고요? 전 오늘이라고 생각했어요.
W: 교내 전체에 광고를 많이 했어요. 보지 못했나요?
M: 제가 날짜를 헷갈린 게 틀림없는 것 같네요.
W: 어쨌든 동아리들이 아직 신입 회원들을 받고 있어요. 그러니까 관심이 있다면 그중 한두 곳에 가입할 수 있는 시간은 있어요.
M: 좋은 소식이군요. 어떤 종류의 동아리들이 있나요?
W: 여기 동아리 목록이 있어요.
M: 흠… 어떤 곳이 인기가 많은지 아시나요?
W: 영화 동아리가 크고 학생들이 많아요. 자전거 동아리와 달리기 동아리도 마찬가지고요.
M: 그 마지막 두 동아리는 정말로 저와 맞지 않아요. 좀 더 학구적인 성격의 동아리가 있을까요?
W: 체스 동아리는 어때요? 회원 수가 많지 않아요. 컴퓨터 프로그래밍 동아리도 있고요.
M: 상당히 재미있어 보이네요. 두 곳 모두 확인해 봐야겠어요.
W: 또 알아야 할 게 있나요?
M: 저는 정말로 암석에 대해 배우고 싶어요. 지질학 동아리가 있을까요?
W: 안타깝게도 없지만, 화석학 동아리는 있어요. 회원들이 공룡과 화석에 대해 토론을 하죠. 가끔씩 화석을 찾으러 야외로 나가기도 하고요.
M: 와, 멋진걸요. 제가 관심 있는 딱 그런 종류예요.
W: 운이 좋네요. 그 동아리는 오늘 저녁 6시 30분에 올해 첫 모임을 가질 예정이에요.
M: 어디에서 모이죠?
W: 카마이클 홀 203호에서 모임이 있을 거예요. 제가 가지고 있는 정보에 따르면 그 동아리는 회원을 더 모집 중이에요. 행운을 빌어요.

CHAPTER 5 Office Hours

Understanding TOEFL Question Types & Listening Skills   p.78

1 Question Types ▶ Sample Question

Ⓑ

스크립트 🎧 05-01

M Professor: Samantha, please have a seat.
W Student: Good morning, Dr. Givens.
M: Samantha, the reason I called you in is to discuss your thesis.
W: Did you like it?
M: Kind of. I like your idea, but the thesis is too broad and general.
W: I see. I was afraid of that.
M: It isn't a big issue. Here's your paper. I've made a few suggestions there at the bottom in blue. That'll help you out.
W: Thanks so much, Dr. Givens.
M: My pleasure, Sam. Once you revise it, bring it back in. Okay?
W: Sure. Is next week okay with you?
M: That's fine with me.
W: Thanks a lot.

해석

M Professor: 사만다, 앉아요.
W Student: 안녕하세요, 기븐스 교수님.
M: 사만다, 자네를 부른 이유는 자네의 논문에 대해 이야기하기 위해서예요.
W: 제 논문이 마음에 드셨나요?
M: 그런 편이죠. 자네의 아이디어는 좋은데 논문이 너무 광범위하고 평이해요.
W: 알겠습니다. 그 부분에 대해 걱정은 했어요.
M: 큰 문제는 아니에요. 여기 자네의 논문이에요. 거기 아래에 파란색으로 제안 사항 몇 가지를 써 두었어요. 도움이 될 거예요.
W: 정말 감사합니다, 기븐스 교수님.
M: 천만에요, 사만다. 일단 수정해서 다시 가져와요. 알겠죠?
W: 알겠습니다. 다음 주면 괜찮으세요?
M: 괜찮아요.
W: 정말 감사합니다.

2 Listening Skills ▶ Check-Up

Student: Good morning, Dr. Givens.
Professor: Samantha, the reason I called you in is to discuss your thesis.
Student: Did you like it?
Professor: Kind of. I like your idea, but the thesis is too broad and general.

• Exercise 1 •   p.80

정답 Q1 Ⓑ   Q2 Ⓑ
스크립트 🎧 05-03

W Professor: Come in, Lance. Did you talk to everyone?
M Student: Yes, I did.
W: So what's the verdict?
M: The majority of the students want to go to White Beach for the field trip.
W: Really? That's interesting. I thought they would prefer to visit the aquarium.
M: Me, too. I actually voted for the aquarium. The final vote was twenty-two for White Beach and five for the aquarium.
W: Hmm . . . You told them that each student must pay 75 dollars for the trip, right? I mean to White Beach.
M: I did, and I told them the trip to the aquarium would be free. Still, as I said, most of them prefer White Beach.
W: Isn't that curious? Well, then it's settled. We'll journey to White Beach next Saturday to do some exploration.
M: I guess so.
W: Okay. Lance, can you do me a favor and collect the fee from everyone? Tell them they should pay you by next Thursday. If they don't pay the fee, they can't go. Okay?
M: You're the boss, Professor Shamrock.

해석

W Professor: 들어와요, 랜스. 모두와 이야기를 했나요?
M Student: 네, 했어요.
W: 그럼 어떻게 결정되었나요?
M: 대다수 학생들이 화이트 비치로 견학가기를 원해요.
W: 정말이요? 흥미롭네요. 다들 수족관에 가고 싶어 할 거라고 생각했는데요.
M: 저도 그랬어요. 사실 저는 수족관에 투표했거든요. 최종 투표 결과 화이트 비치가 22표, 수족관이 5표가 나왔어요.
W: 흠… 학생들에게 견학 경비로 1인당 75달러를 내야 한다고 말했죠, 그렇죠? 화이트 비치에 갈 경우에 말이에요.
M: 했어요. 그리고 수족관으로 가는 견학은 무료일 거라고도 말했어요. 그래도, 말씀드린 대로 대부분이 화이트 비치를 더 좋아해요.
W: 신기하지 않나요? 자, 그럼 결정된 거네요. 우리는 다음 주 토요일에 화이트 비치로 탐험을 하러 떠날 거예요.
M: 그럴 것 같아요.
W: 좋아요. 랜스, 경비를 전부 걷는 걸 부탁해도 될까요? 학생들에게 다음 주 목요일까지 자네에게 경비를 내야 한다고 말해주세요. 경비를 내지 않으면 갈 수 없어요. 알겠죠?
M: 그대로 전하겠습니다, 샴록 교수님

Listening Skills

Professor: So what's the verdict?
Student: The majority of the students want to go to White Beach for the field trip.
Professor: Really? That's interesting. I thought they would prefer to visit the aquarium.
Student: Me, too. I actually voted for the aquarium.

• **Exercise 2** • ───────────────────── p.81

정답 Q1 ⒝ Q2 ⒝

스크립트 🎧 05-05

W Student: Hi, Professor Gibson. May I come in, or are you on your way out?
M Professor: Sure, I've got a few minutes.
W: Thanks. Do you mind if I sit down?
M: Not at all. Go ahead.
W: I'm a bit lost when it comes to the final examination.
M: I see. How so?
W: Um, what exactly will it cover?
M: Were you in class for the review yesterday?
W: No, sir.
M: You didn't take the time to attend the review? So tell me why I should take my own time to explain everything again.
W: To tell the truth, I was in a minor car accident yesterday.
M: Oh, my. Are you okay? I didn't mean to sound like I was blaming you.
W: That's okay. And yes, I'm fine. Thanks.
M: Right. Then, um, let me explain the breakdown of the test for you. Do you have a pen and paper handy?

해석

W Student: 안녕하세요, 깁슨 교수님. 들어가도 될까요, 아니면 나가시는 길인가요?
M Professor: 그럼요, 잠깐 시간이 있어요.
W: 감사합니다. 앉아도 될까요?
M: 물론이죠. 앉아요.
W: 기말고사 관련해서 제가 좀 헷갈리는 부분이 있어요.
M: 그렇군요. 어떤 점이죠?
W: 음, 기말고사 범위가 정확히 어떻게 되나요?
M: 어제 복습 강의를 들었나요?
W: 아뇨, 교수님.
M: 복습 강의에 참석할 시간을 내지 않았군요? 그러면 내가 왜 내 시간을 들여 그 모든 것을 다시 설명을 해야 하는지 말해봐요.
W: 사실은, 어제 경미한 차 사고가 있었습니다.
M: 아, 이런. 괜찮나요? 자네를 꾸중하는 것처럼 들렸다면 그런 의도는 아니었어요.
W: 괜찮습니다. 그리고 네, 저는 괜찮아요. 감사합니다.
M: 알겠어요. 그러면, 음, 시험에 대해 요약해 설명해 줄게요. 펜과 종이를 가지고 있나요?

Listening Skills

Student: Thanks. Do you mind if I sit down?
Professor: Not at all. Go ahead.
Student: I'm a bit lost when it comes to the final examination.
Professor: I see. How so?

• **Exercise 3** • ───────────────────── p.82

정답 Q1 ⒜ Q2 ⒝

스크립트 🎧 05-07

M Professor: Good morning, Karen. What brings you here?
W Student: Good morning, Professor Cartwright.
M: You look like you lost your favorite pet or something. What's going on?
W: I just don't get it, sir.
M: Get what?
W: It's so unfair.
M: Um, what are you talking about, Karen?
W: I just checked my grades online, and I received a D in your class! Did I bomb the final or what because I thought I did really well?
M: Hold on now. Calm down. We'll get to the bottom of this. First, you had one of the best scores in the class on the final. Second, your final grade was outstanding.
W: It was?
M: Yes, I distinctly remember how well you did.
W: So what happened?
M: There must have been a computer glitch. It happens sometimes. I'll tell you what I'll do this minute. I'll call the Registrar's office to see what is going on.
W: Gee, thanks, sir. You're a huge help.

해석

M Professor: 좋은 아침이에요, 카렌. 무슨 일이죠?
W Student: 안녕하세요, 카트라이트 교수님.
M: 아끼는 반려 동물이나 뭐 그런 거라도 잃어버린 표정이네요. 무슨 일이죠?
W: 저는 정말이지 이해가 되질 않아요, 교수님.
M: 어떤 게 말이죠?
W: 너무 불공평해요.
M: 음, 어떤 걸 말하는 거예요, 카렌?
W: 방금 온라인으로 성적을 확인해 보았는데, 제가 교수님 수업에서 D를 받았어요! 제가 기말 시험을 완전히 망친 걸까요, 아니면 무엇 때문에 저는 제가 정말 잘했다고 생각했을까요?
M: 잠깐만요. 진정해요. 이 부분에 대해 처음부터 살펴 볼게요. 먼저, 자네는 기말 시험에 대해 반에서 가장 좋은 점수에 드는 점수를 받았어요. 둘째로, 자네의 총 점수는 우수했어요.
W: 그랬나요?
M: 맞아요, 자네가 얼마나 잘했는지 내가 확실히 기억해요.
W: 그러면 어떻게 된 일이죠?
M: 분명히 컴퓨터 오류가 있었을 거예요. 가끔 그런 일이 생기죠. 바로 지금 내가 뭘 할지 말해 줄게요. 학적과에 전화를 해서 어떻게 된 일인지 알아볼 거예요.
W: 휴, 감사합니다, 교수님. 큰 도움이 되네요.

Listening Skills

Professor: Good morning, Karen. What brings you here?
Student: Good morning, Professor Cartwright.
Professor: You look like you lost your favorite pet or something. What's going on?
Student: I just don't get it, sir.

• **Exercise 4** • p.83

정답 Q1 ⓒ Q2 ⓑ

스크립트 🎧 05-09

W Professor: Come in.
M Student: Do you have a moment, Professor Stevens? I need to chat with you about something.
W: All right, Mr. Chambers, but make it quick. I've got a meeting with the dean at noon.
M: The dean, huh? Sounds important.
W: Believe me. It is. So what's up?
M: I'm thinking about doing a double major.
W: You're going to do what?
M: Go for a double major.
W: Hold on a second. Are you sure about that? Do you know how much work and time that will involve?
M: Well, I thought I did. So you don't think it's a good idea?
W: For students who can handle it, I think it's great, but I'm not sure you're one of those students.
M: Biting off more than I can chew, huh?
W: Look. You're a good student, but a double major could ruin your grades. I just don't think you're ready for that.
M: Thanks for being honest with me.

해석

W Professor: 들어와요.
M Student: 잠시 시간 되세요, 스티븐스 교수님? 교수님께 드릴 말씀이 있어서요.
W: 알겠어요, 챔버스 군, 그렇지만 빨리 끝내 주세요. 정오에 학장님과 회의가 있어요.
M: 학장님과요? 중요한 일인 것 같네요.
W: 맞아요. 중요한 일이죠. 그래서 무슨 일인가요?
M: 저는 복수전공을 할까 생각 중이에요.
W: 무엇을 한다고요?
M: 복수전공을 하려고요.
W: 잠깐만요. 정말인가요? 그게 얼마나 많은 노력과 시간을 필요로 하는지 알고 있나요?
M: 음, 알고 있다고 생각했어요. 그러면 교수님은 그게 좋은 생각이 아니라고 생각하시는 거죠?
W: 그걸 관리할 수 있는 학생들의 경우엔 좋다고 생각하지만, 자네가 그런 학생들 중 한 명이라고 확신할 수가 없군요.
M: 제가 과한 욕심을 부리고 있다는 말씀이시죠?
W: 자. 자네는 좋은 학생이지만 복수전공을 하면 성적이 엄청 떨어질 수 있어요. 자네가 그 부분에 대해 준비가 되어 있다고 생각되지 않을 뿐이에요.
M: 솔직하게 말씀해 주셔서 감사합니다.

Listening Skills

Student: The dean, huh? Sounds important.
Professor: Believe me. It is. So what's up?
Student: I'm thinking about doing a double major.
Professor: You're going to do what?

• **Exercise 5** • p.84

정답 Q1 ⓑ Q2 ⓒ

스크립트 🎧 05-11

W Student: Professor Chambers, could I speak with you, please?
M Professor: Of course. Um . . . I'm afraid I don't know your name. Are you in my class?
W: No, sir, but I'm thinking about taking your class next semester. My name is Amber Marston.
M: It's a pleasure to meet you, Amber. Which of my classes are you interested in?
W: It's the class on medieval English literature. I was wondering if you could tell me about it.
M: Sure. Basically, we're going to read some of the most important works in English from the Middle Ages.
W: Does that include Chaucer?
M: It sure does. We'll also read poems such as *Pearl* and *Sir Gawain and the Green Knight*. We'll read a few different works about King Arthur, too.
W: Are we going to read them in modern English or in Middle English?
M: Middle English.
W: Oh, I don't know if I can handle that.
M: Don't be worried. It's actually fun to learn to read. I've been teaching this class for fifteen years. In my experience, students learn to read Middle English fairly quickly.
W: That's great to hear. I'll definitely sign up for the class in that case.
M: I'm looking forward to seeing you in class in the fall.

해석

W Student: 체임버스 교수님, 교수님과 이야기를 나눌 수 있을까요?
M Professor: 물론이죠. 음… 미안하지만 자네의 이름을 모르겠네요. 내 수업을 듣나요?
W: 아니에요, 교수님, 하지만 다음 학기에 교수님 수업을 들을 생각이에요. 제 이름은 앰버 마스턴입니다.
M: 만나서 반가워요, 앰버. 내 수업 중 어떤 것에 관심이 있나요?
W: 중세 영문학 수업이요. 그 수업에 대해 이야기해주실 수 있는지 궁금했어요.
M: 그럼요. 기본적으로 우리는 중세 시대에 영어로 쓰여진 가장 중요한 작품들 중 몇 편을 읽게 될 거예요.
W: 거기에 초서가 포함되나요?
M: 물론이죠. 또한 *진주*는 물론 *가웨인 경과 녹색의 기사*와 같은 시도 읽을 거예요. 아서왕에 관한 여러 가지 작품들도 몇 편 읽을 것이고요.
W: 현대 영어로 읽나요, 아니면 중세 영어로 읽나요?
M: 중세 영어요.
W: 아, 제가 그걸 감당할 수 있을지 모르겠어요.
M: 걱정하지 말아요. 실제로 읽는 법을 배우면 재미있어요. 나는 이 수업을 15년 동안 강의해 왔어요. 내 경험상, 학생들은 중세 영어를 읽는 법을 상당히 빨리 배우죠.
W: 그렇다면 다행이에요. 그런 경우라면 꼭 수업에 등록할게요.
M: 가을에 수업에서 만나길 기대하고 있을게요.

Listening Skills

Student: Professor Chambers, could I speak with you, please?
Professor: Of course. Um . . . I'm afraid I don't know your name. Are you in my class?
Student: No, sir, but I'm thinking about taking your class next semester. My name is Amber Marston.
Professor: It's a pleasure to meet you, Amber. Which of my classes are you interested in?

• Exercise 6 • p.85

정답 Q1 Ⓑ Q2 Ⓐ

스크립트 🎧 05-13

M Student: Professor Watson, may I come in?
W Professor: Yes. Hi, Brandon.
M: I came in to say goodbye, ma'am.
W: Yes, I heard that you were transferring schools.
M: Yeah.
W: We're all sorry to see you go, Brandon. I hope it works out for you.
M: Me, too. I want you to know I really enjoyed your lectures, and I appreciate all of your pep talks during the past few months.
W: You're very welcome. Is there anything I can do to help you out?
M: I want to continue as a finance major at the other university, but it is really competitive to get in to the program.
W: I'm sure it is. It's one of the top programs in the country. I actually have a couple of friends in the department. Did you know that it is my alma mater?
M: I didn't know that. In that case, would you mind writing a letter to the department head on my behalf? It might help me get in.
W: I'll do better than that, Brandon. I'll give her a call this evening and give her my highest recommendation for you. How does that sound?
M: That's very kind of you.

해석

M Student: 왓슨 교수님, 들어가도 될까요?
W Professor: 그래요. 어서 와요, 브랜든.
M: 작별 인사를 드리려고 왔어요, 교수님.
W: 그래요, 자네가 학교를 옮긴다고 들었어요.
M: 네.
W: 자네가 떠난다니 우리 모두 아쉬워요, 브랜든. 그곳이 자네와 잘 맞길 바랄게요.
M: 저도 그래요. 제가 정말로 교수님의 강의를 좋아했다는 걸 알아주시면 좋겠어요, 그리고 지난 몇 달 동안 교수님이 해 주신 모든 격려 말씀에 감사드려요.
W: 천만에요. 내가 도와줄 일이 있을까요?
M: 저는 그쪽 대학에서 재무를 계속 전공하고 싶은데, 그 프로그램에 들어가려면 경쟁이 정말 치열해요.
W: 확실히 그럴 거예요. 국가에서 가장 우수한 프로그램 중 하나잖아요. 사실 그 학과에 내 친구들이 몇 명 있어요. 그 학교가 내 모교라는 건 알고 있었나요?
M: 그건 몰랐어요. 그렇다면 그곳 학과장님께 저를 위해서 편지를 써 주실 수 있으세요? 그러면 들어가는 데 도움이 될 것 같아요.
W: 그것보다 더 좋은 방법이 있어요, 브랜든. 오늘 저녁에 내가 그녀에게 전화를 해서 자네를 정말 추천한다고 알려 줄게요. 어떤가요?
M: 마음 써 주셔서 정말 감사합니다.

Listening Skills

Student: I came in to say goodbye, ma'am.
Professor: Yes, I heard that you were transferring schools.
Student: Yeah.
Professor: We're all sorry to see you go, Brandon.

• Exercise 7 • p.86

정답 Q1 Ⓑ Q2 Ⓓ

스크립트 🎧 05-15

M Professor: Hey, Jamie. Are you still looking for a part-time job?
W Student: Yes, I am. Why?
M: I think I might have one for you, but the hours are a bit odd.
W: Could you tell me about the job?
M: You would be assisting a colleague of mine, Dr. Holloway in the Religion Department.
W: So far, so good.
M: You'd be doing research, typing documents, and maybe doing some editing for him. Those kinds of things . . .
W: Yes . . .
M: But, well, how can I put this . . . ? Dr. Holloway is a bit eccentric.
W: How so?
M: He does most of his work very early in the morning.
W: How early?
M: Four AM, Jamie. He believes that's when his mind is at its best. You would assist him from four to seven in the morning three times a week.
W: Four? Are you kidding? Is the pay pretty good?
M: I'm glad you asked. Yes, I think it is very attractive at 40 dollars per hour.
W: Forty an hour, huh? Well, that's a pretty good incentive.
M: Give it some thought, Jamie, and please let me know by Friday. Okay?
W: I will. Thanks!

해석

M Professor: 안녕, 제이미. 아직 시간제 일자리 찾고 있나요?
W Student: 네, 맞아요. 왜요?
M: 자네에게 맞는 일이 있는 것 같은데, 근무 시간이 약간 애매해요.
W: 어떤 일인지 말씀해 주시겠어요?
M: 내 동료인, 종교학과의 할로웨이 교수님을 보조하게 될 거예요.
W: 지금까지는, 정말 좋은데요.
M: 그 교수님을 도와 조사도 하고, 문서도 입력하고, 몇 가지 편집 일들도 할지도 몰라요. 그런 종류의 일들 말이죠…
W: 네…

M: 하지만, 음, 이걸 어떻게 설명해야 할지…? 할로웨이 교수님은 약간 괴짜예요.
W: 어떻게요?
M: 그 교수님은 대부분의 업무를 아주 이른 아침에 하세요.
W: 얼마나 이른데요?
M: 새벽 4시요, 제이미. 그 교수님은 정신 상태가 가장 좋을 때가 바로 그때라고 생각하거든요. 일주일에 세 번 아침 4시부터 7시까지 보조하게 될 거예요.
W: 4시요? 농담하시는 거죠? 보수는 꽤 괜찮은가요?
M: 물어봐 줘서 다행이네요. 맞아요, 시간당 40달러면 꽤 괜찮다고 생각해요.
W: 시간당 40달러라고요? 음, 그 정도면 꽤 의욕이 생기는데요.
M: 생각해 봐요, 제이미, 그리고 금요일까지 내게 알려줘요. 알겠죠?
W: 그럴게요. 감사합니다!

Listening Skills

Professor: But, well, <u>how</u> can I put this . . . ? Dr. <u>Holloway</u> is a bit <u>eccentric</u>.
Student: How <u>so</u>?
Professor: He does <u>most</u> of his <u>work</u> very <u>early</u> in the <u>morning</u>.
Student: How <u>early</u>?

• Exercise 8 •   p.87

정답 Q1 Ⓐ Q2 Ⓑ
스크립트 🎧 05-17

W Professor: Derrick, come in and have a seat . . . Coffee?
M Student: No thanks, ma'am.
W: Not a coffee drinker, huh? Anyway, thanks for <u>coming</u> <u>in</u> <u>on</u> <u>short</u> <u>notice</u>.
M: Sure, Professor Walker. <u>Is</u> <u>anything</u> <u>wrong</u>?
W: Just <u>the</u> <u>opposite</u>. I have <u>a</u> <u>great</u> <u>opportunity</u> <u>for</u> <u>you</u>.
M: Really? What is it?
W: The university <u>is</u> <u>hosting</u> <u>an</u> <u>academic</u> <u>conference</u> in our department next week, and I'd like you <u>to</u> <u>present</u> <u>one</u> <u>of</u> <u>your</u> <u>papers</u>.
M: Wow. That is <u>a</u> <u>great</u> <u>honor</u>. Thank you.
W: So do you <u>accept</u> <u>this</u> <u>offer</u>? It will be <u>a</u> <u>great</u> <u>experience</u> and <u>a</u> <u>great</u> <u>addition</u> to your résumé. <u>Are</u> <u>you</u> <u>in</u>?
M: Of course. I <u>can't</u> <u>pass</u> <u>up</u> this kind of an opportunity.
W: You're right. You can't. You'll meet <u>lots</u> <u>of</u> <u>highly</u> <u>respected</u> <u>scholars</u> in the field. <u>Who</u> <u>knows</u>? Perhaps someone will <u>take</u> <u>an</u> <u>interest</u> <u>in</u> <u>you</u> and <u>offer</u> <u>you</u> <u>a</u> <u>scholarship</u>.
M: <u>I'm</u> <u>speechless</u>, Professor.
W: You <u>deserve</u> <u>it</u>. <u>How</u> <u>about</u> <u>if</u> <u>we</u> <u>practice</u> beginning tomorrow morning? Does that sound good?
M: All right, Professor. I'll <u>be</u> <u>here</u> at nine in the morning.

해석

W Professor: 데릭, 들어와서 앉아요… 커피 줄까요?
M Student: 아뇨, 괜찮습니다, 교수님.
W: 커피를 마시지 않는군요? 어쨌든, 급한 공지에 와 줘서 고마워요.
M: 물론이죠, 워커 교수님. 잘못된 일이 있는 건가요?
W: 그 반대예요. 자네에게 좋은 기회가 있어요.
M: 정말이요? 그게 뭐죠?

W: 다음 주에 학교에서 우리 과와 관련된 학회를 주최할 예정인데, 자네가 쓴 논문 중 하나를 자네가 발표하면 좋겠어요.
M: 와. 정말 영광이네요. 감사합니다.
W: 그러면 이 제안을 수락하는 건가요? 좋은 경험이 되면서 이력서에 추가로 넣기도 좋을 거예요. 할 거죠?
M: 물론이에요. 이런 기회를 지나칠 수 없죠.
W: 맞아요. 그럴 수 없죠. 그 분야에서 가장 존경받는 학자들을 많이 만나게 될 거예요. 누가 알겠어요? 어떤 분이 자네에게 관심을 보이고 장학금을 제안할지도요.
M: 뭐라고 말씀드려야 할지 모르겠네요, 교수님.
W: 자네는 그럴 자격이 있어요. 내일 아침부터 연습해 보는 게 어때요? 괜찮나요?
M: 좋습니다, 교수님. 아침 9시에 여기로 올게요.

Listening Skills

Student: <u>Sure</u>, Professor Walker. Is anything <u>wrong</u>?
Professor: <u>Just</u> the <u>opposite</u>. I have a <u>great</u> opportunity for you.
Student: <u>Really</u>? What is <u>it</u>?
Professor: The university is <u>hosting</u> an academic <u>conference</u> in our department next <u>week</u>.

Vocabulary Review   p.88

A
1 medieval
2 getting in
3 eccentric
4 respected
5 definitely

B 1 Ⓒ 2 Ⓐ 3 Ⓓ 4 Ⓒ 5 Ⓐ

C 1 Ⓓ 2 Ⓑ 3 Ⓒ 4 Ⓐ 5 Ⓑ

D
1 aquarium
2 alma mater
3 passed up
4 short notice
5 colleagues

Practice Test   p.90

1 Ⓐ 2 Ⓓ 3 Ⓑ

스크립트 🎧 05-19

M Professor: Jamie, come in, please.
W Student: Hello, Dr. Mears. That test today <u>was</u> <u>pretty</u> <u>hard</u>.
M: I know. But don't worry. The next one <u>will</u> <u>be</u> <u>easier</u>.
W: I sure <u>hope</u> <u>so</u>. Anyway, I <u>have</u> <u>a</u> <u>question</u> <u>for</u> <u>you</u>.
M: Sure. Go ahead.
W: I'm trying to decide <u>if</u> <u>I</u> <u>should</u> <u>take</u> <u>classes</u> during the summer session.
M: I see. <u>Have</u> <u>you</u> <u>stayed</u> <u>here</u> during a summer or winter

session before?
W: No, I haven't.
M: Well, you've got to take one sometime, right?
W: That's what I hear.
M: Then why are you trying to make up your mind? You should just do it.
W: Well, I heard that summer classes are more difficult than those during the regular term.
M: I wouldn't say they're more difficult. More information is packed into a shorter time period. You'll also have the same class just about every day.
W: Right.
M: But you'll only take one or two classes as opposed to four or five like you do in fall and spring.
W: Is there a big difference between the summer and winter sessions?
M: The courses are the same, but the weather isn't. The weather is freezing here in the winter. It's rather unpleasant.
W: Yeah, I didn't think about that.
M: Oh, wait. I made a mistake about the courses. I believe there's a greater variety of courses offered during summer.
W: I didn't know that. Then I think I'll stay for summer. Thanks, sir.

해석

M Professor: 제이미, 어서 들어와요.
W Student: 안녕하세요, 미어스 교수님. 오늘 그 시험은 정말 어려웠어요.
M: 알고 있어요. 하지만 걱정 말아요. 다음 시험은 더 쉬울 거예요.
W: 정말 그렇다면 좋겠습니다. 어쨌든, 질문이 한 가지 있어요.
M: 그럼요. 말해 봐요.
W: 제가 여름 학기에 수업을 들어야 할지 고민 중이에요.
M: 그렇군요. 전에는 여름이나 겨울 학기 동안 이곳에서 지낸 적이 있나요?
W: 아니요, 없어요.
M: 음, 언젠가는 한 번은 들어야 하죠, 그렇죠?
W: 그렇게 들었어요.
M: 그러면 왜 결정을 못해서 고민 중인 거죠? 그냥 해요.
W: 음, 정규 학기보다 여름 학기 수업이 더 어렵다고 들었어요.
M: 더 어렵다고 말할 수는 없을 것 같아요. 더 짧은 기간 안에 더 많은 정보가 압축되어 있는 거죠. 또 거의 매일 같은 수업을 들을 거예요.
W: 그렇군요.
M: 하지만 가을과 봄학기에 하듯이 4~5개가 아니라 1~2개의 강의만 듣게 될 거예요.
W: 여름 학기와 겨울 학기 사이에 큰 차이점이 있나요?
M: 과정은 똑같지만, 날씨가 다르죠. 겨울에 이곳은 정말 추워요. 그렇게 쾌적하진 않죠.
W: 그렇군요, 그건 생각하지 못했어요.
M: 아, 잠깐만요. 과정에 대해 착각한 게 있네요. 여름에 더 다양한 과정이 제공되는 것 같아요.
W: 그건 몰랐어요. 그렇다면 여름에 있는 편이 좋겠어요. 감사합니다, 교수님.

CHAPTER 6 Infectious Diseases

Understanding TOEFL Question Types & Listening Skills p.94

1 Question Types ▶ Sample Question

Ⓑ

스크립트 🎧 06-01

M Professor: Achoo. Sorry, everyone, but it looks like I have caught a cold. It's kind of ironic because the common cold is something I plan to discuss today. Generally, adults catch colds between one and four times a year, but children get them more often. They might be sick twice as many times each year. Moreover, the most common symptoms of a cold are a sore throat, sneezing, and fatigue. Coughing is another one. Additionally, body aches, a fever, and even the chills might accompany a cold. Medication can help with the symptoms of a cold, but it can't actually cure it. You basically just have to wait until your body recovers.

해석

M Professor: 에취. 모두들 미안하지만, 제가 감기에 걸린 것 같군요. 공교롭게도 오늘 제가 논의하려는 것이 감기예요. 일반적으로 성인들은 일년에 한 번에서 네 번 정도 감기에 걸리지만, 아이들은 감기에 더 자주 걸립니다. 아이들은 매년 2배는 더 걸릴 수 있죠. 또한 감기의 가장 일반적인 증상으로는 목 아픔, 재채기, 피로감을 들 수 있습니다. 기침도 포함되죠. 그에 더해 몸살, 고열, 심지어는 오한이 감기에 동반될 수 있습니다. 약은 감기의 증상 완화에 도움이 될 수는 있지만, 실제로 감기를 치료하지는 못합니다. 기본적으로 몸의 회복될 때까지 기다릴 수밖에 없죠.

2 Listening Skills ▶ Check-Up

1 Moreover, the most common symptoms of a cold are a sore throat, sneezing, and fatigue.
2 Additionally, body aches, a fever, and even the chills might accompany a cold.

• Exercise 1 • p.96

정답 Q1 Ⓑ Q2 Ⓐ
스크립트 🎧 06-03

M Professor: Rabies is a deadly viral infection. If it's not treated immediately, it will prove to be fatal. So stay clear of animals, especially dogs, bats, raccoons, and skunks that are acting funny.
Now, I don't mean funny as in humorous or playful. On the contrary, I'm talking about animals that act and look insane with a crazy look in their eyes. Another clue is that the animals have lots of saliva around their mouths.
Actually, rabies is spread by saliva. It usually spreads due to a bite by an infected animal, but a person can sometimes get it just via contact with an open wound on the body. Scary, huh? Fortunately, all is not lost. In most countries, a vaccine has been

used to protect pets against rabies since the late nineteenth century. There's a vaccine for people as well. Consequently, rabies is very rare in most developed countries. However, it still pops up every once in a while, so always be extremely careful around certain animals.

해석
M Professor: 광견병은 치명적인 바이러스 감염병입니다. 즉시 치료하지 않으면 치명적으로 판명될 것입니다. 그러므로 동물들, 특히 개, 박쥐, 너구리, 그리고 스컹크가 우스꽝스럽게 행동할 때는 가까이 가지 마세요.
자, 우스꽝스럽다는 것은 재미있거나 혹은 장난치는 것을 의미하는 게 아닙니다. 그 반대로, 눈에 광기를 지니면서 미친 것처럼 행동하고 그렇게 보이는 동물을 이야기하는 것입니다. 그 동물들이 입 주변으로 침을 많이 흘리는 것도 또 다른 단서가 됩니다.
실제로 광견병은 침에 의해 전염됩니다. 보통 감염된 동물에게 물리면 전염이 되지만, 때로는 몸에 노출된 상처와 접촉하는 것만으로도 사람이 감염될 수 있습니다. 무섭죠, 그렇죠? 다행히, 전혀 희망이 없는 것은 아닙니다. 대부분의 국가에서 19세기 후반부터 반려 동물을 광견병으로부터 보호하기 위해 백신이 사용되고 있습니다. 사람을 위한 백신도 있습니다. 그 결과 대부분의 선진 국가에서는 광견병이 매우 드뭅니다. 그러나 아직도 이따금 한 번씩 발생하고 있기 때문에, 항상 특정 동물 주변에서는 정말 조심하도록 하세요.

Listening Skills

1 So stay clear of animals that are acting funny.
2 On the contrary, I'm talking about animals that act and look insane.

• **Exercise 2** • p.97

정답 Q1 ⓒ Q2 ⓓ
스크립트 🎧 06-05

W Professor: Good afternoon, class. I'm sure many of you had chickenpox when you were children. Yes, I see a lot of heads nodding out there. It wasn't fun, was it? Well, let's discuss it some, shall we?
First, it is caused by a virus and is highly contagious. That's why you had to stay home from school and keep away from other kids when you had it. It can be spread by touching the sores on the skin or by coughing and sneezing. Next, symptoms in the form of small, circular spots begin to appear on the body. They're extremely itchy, but it isn't good to scratch them because they can create scars.
Ultimately, chickenpox cannot be cured by any medications. It must run its course, which takes about a week or so. However, the good news is that you'll probably never get it again because the body develops lifelong immunity against the virus.

해석
W Professor: 안녕하세요, 여러분. 여러분 중 많은 분들이 어릴 때 수두를 앓았을 거예요. 그래요, 고개를 많이 끄덕이는 모습이 보이네요. 재미있는 일은 아니었죠, 그렇죠? 음, 그것에 대해 좀 이야기해 볼까요?
먼저, 수두는 바이러스가 원인이고 전염성이 매우 강합니다. 그 때문에 여러분은 수두에 걸렸을 때 학교에 가지 않고 집에 있으면서 다른 아이들과 떨어져 지내야 했어요. 수두는 피부에 난 종기를 만지거나, 기침과 재채기로 전염될 수 있습니다. 그 다음에는, 작고 둥근 반점 형태의 증상이 몸에 나타나기 시작합니다. 그것은 매우 간지럽지만 상처를 남길 수 있기 때문에 긁으면 좋지 않습니다.
본질적으로 수두는 어떤 약물로도 치료할 수 없습니다. 약 일주일 정도 걸리는 그 과정을 지나야만 합니다. 그러나 좋은 소식은 여러분이 아마도 다시는 수두에 걸리지 않을 거라는 점인데, 왜냐하면 신체에 그 바이러스에 대한 면역력이 평생 동안 지속되기 때문입니다.

Listening Skills

1 Ultimately, chickenpox cannot be cured by any medications.
2 However, the good news is that you'll probably never get it again.

• **Exercise 3** • p.98

정답 Q1 ⓒ Q2 ⓑ
스크립트 🎧 06-07

M Professor: So far, what we call vaccines are the most effective way to protect humans against infectious diseases and viruses. Let me explain in basic terms what a vaccine is.
A vaccine is most often an inoculation. That is, it's a shot. It's an injection or a series of injections into a person's body. The inoculation contains some form of the virus to be protected against. Usually, it is a weakened or even dead form of the virus. Afterward, the body begins producing its own antibodies against the given virus.
Antibodies are the human body's natural defenses against diseases. They are usually found in the form of proteins and blood cells. Because of antibodies, our bodies can ward off viruses and infectious diseases more easily. The first vaccine was created by Edward Jenner in 1756. It was a vaccine for smallpox. Since 1979, there hasn't been a single reported case of smallpox in a human being. Now, that's good medicine. Don't you agree?

해석
M Professor: 아직까지는, 우리가 백신이라고 부르는 것들이 감염병과 바이러스로부터 인류를 보호하는 가장 효과적인 방법입니다. 백신이 무엇인지 기본적인 용어부터 설명하겠습니다.
백신은 대부분이 예방 접종인 경우가 많습니다. 즉, 주사입니다. 신체에 한 번 혹은 여러 번 주사합니다. 예방 접종에는 막아야 할 바이러스의 어떤 형태가 포함되어 있습니다. 보통은, 바이러스의 약화된 형태 혹은 심지어는 죽은 형태입니다. 이후에, 몸은 주입된 바이러스에 대항하여 고유한 항체를 형성하기 시작합니다.
항체는 질병에 대항하는 신체의 자연적 방어 체계입니다. 항체는 주로 단백질과 혈액 세포의 형태로 발견됩니다. 항체로 인하여 우리의 몸은 바이러스와 감염병을 더 쉽게 물리칠 수 있습니다. 최초의 백신은 1756년에 에드워드 제너에 의해 만들어졌습니다. 그것은 천연두 백신이었습니다. 1979년 이후로, 사람에게 천연두가 발생한 사례는 단 한 차례도 보고된 적이 없습니다. 우수한 치료제인 것이죠. 그렇지 않나요?

Listening Skills

1 <u>So</u> <u>far</u>, what we call vaccines are the most effective way to protect humans against infectious diseases.
2 <u>Let</u> <u>me</u> <u>explain</u> in basic terms what a vaccine is.

• Exercise 4 • — p.99

정답 Q1 Ⓐ Q2 Ⓑ
스크립트 🎧 06-09

W Professor: Maybe you are all aware of <u>the</u> <u>many</u> <u>devastating</u> <u>viruses</u> <u>in</u> <u>human</u> <u>history</u>. Of course, currently, AIDS is one of <u>the</u> <u>most</u> <u>tragic</u> and <u>deadliest</u>. However, <u>there</u> <u>have</u> <u>been</u> <u>worse</u> <u>ones</u>.
The statistics are not concrete or conclusive, but <u>back</u> <u>in</u> <u>the</u> <u>early</u> <u>twentieth</u> <u>century</u>, there was the Spanish flu. <u>It</u> <u>might</u> <u>have</u> <u>killed</u> <u>more</u> <u>people</u> than most other diseases in history. Some experts estimate that <u>it</u> <u>killed</u> <u>around</u> <u>fifty</u> <u>million</u> <u>people</u> while others think it was more likely <u>double</u> <u>that</u> <u>number</u>.
<u>One</u> <u>of</u> <u>the</u> <u>reasons</u> the Spanish flu was <u>so</u> <u>devastating</u> <u>was</u> that it was a pandemic. This means that <u>it</u> <u>was</u> <u>a</u> <u>global</u> <u>disease</u> and that <u>no</u> <u>one</u> <u>was</u> <u>safe</u> from it. <u>For</u> <u>instance</u>, unlike other flu outbreaks, it was <u>extremely</u> <u>contagious</u>. <u>Furthermore</u>, it <u>attacked</u> <u>everyone</u> <u>from</u> the young, strong, and healthy <u>to</u> the old and weak. <u>In</u> <u>addition</u>, <u>the</u> <u>symptoms</u> <u>were</u> <u>extreme</u> for a flu virus, causing even more deaths. <u>Finally</u>, around June 1920, the Spanish flu <u>went</u> <u>away</u> <u>as</u> <u>mysteriously</u> <u>as</u> it arrived.

해석

W Professor: 아마도 여러분 모두는 인류 역사에 존재했던 많은 파괴적인 바이러스들에 관해 잘 알고 있을 것입니다. 물론, 최근에는 AIDS가 가장 비극적이고 치명적인 바이러스 중 하나입니다. 그러나 더 심각한 것들이 존재해 왔습니다.
그 통계가 구체적이거나 확실하지는 않지만, 20세기 초로 거슬러 올라가면 스페인 독감이 존재했습니다. 이것은 역사상 대부분의 다른 질병보다도 더 많은 사람들을 사망에 이르게 했을 것입니다. 어떤 전문가들은 이 때문에 약 5천만 명의 사람들이 사망했다고 추산하는 반면, 또 다른 이들은 그 수치가 두 배 이상이었을 가능성이 있다고 생각합니다.
스페인 독감이 그렇게 파괴적이었던 이유 중 하나는 그것이 대유행병이었기 때문입니다. 이는 그것이 전 세계적인 질병이었고 아무도 그것으로부터 안전하지 못했다는 것을 의미합니다. 예를 들어, 다른 독감 유행과는 다르게 그것은 굉장히 전염성이 강했습니다. 게다가 젊고, 튼튼하고, 건강한 사람부터 나이 들고, 약한 사람에 이르기까지 모든 사람들을 공격했습니다. 그뿐 아니라, 그 증상이 독감 바이러스라고 하기에는 극도로 심각해서 훨씬 더 많은 사망자를 초래했습니다. 마침내 1920년 6월 무렵, 스페인 독감은 그것이 찾아왔을 때와 똑같이 불가사의하게 사라졌습니다.

Listening Skills

1 <u>Of</u> <u>course</u>, currently, AIDS is one of the most tragic and deadliest.
2 <u>For</u> <u>instance</u>, unlike other flu outbreaks, it was extremely contagious.

• Exercise 5 • — p.100

정답 Q1 Ⓐ Q2 Ⓐ
스크립트 🎧 06-11

M Professor: Today, I'd like to begin by discussing the West Nile Virus, or WNV. First, I'll discuss <u>what</u> <u>it</u> <u>is</u> and <u>how</u> <u>it</u> <u>is</u> <u>spread</u>. Then, I'll <u>get</u> <u>into</u> <u>some</u> <u>of</u> <u>the</u> <u>symptoms</u> if time allows. How does that sound for a plan?
The West Nile Virus is often a serious, seasonal virus in North America that <u>happens</u> <u>each</u> <u>year</u> <u>between</u> <u>summer</u> <u>and</u> <u>fall</u>. Although some people think <u>it</u> <u>is</u> <u>spread</u> <u>from</u> <u>person</u> <u>to</u> <u>person</u>, they are incorrect. On the contrary, it <u>is</u> <u>mainly</u> <u>spread</u> <u>by</u> mosquitoes. Mosquitoes become infected <u>when</u> <u>they</u> <u>feed</u> <u>on</u> infected birds and <u>pass</u> <u>it</u> <u>on</u> <u>to</u> <u>humans</u>. <u>Therefore</u>, touching dead birds is <u>a</u> <u>potential</u> <u>problem</u> <u>for</u> <u>people</u>. Just remember, class, to <u>watch</u> <u>out</u> <u>for</u> <u>dead</u> <u>birds</u> and mosquitoes.
Now, uh, a West Nile Virus infection can <u>lead</u> <u>to</u> <u>certain</u> <u>symptoms</u>. <u>However</u>, the majority of infected people <u>have</u> <u>no</u> <u>symptoms</u>. That's right. You heard me correctly. Experts estimate that <u>nearly</u> <u>eighty</u> <u>percent</u> <u>of</u> <u>people</u> infected with WNV <u>experience</u> <u>nothing</u>. They have <u>no</u> <u>distress</u> <u>at</u> <u>all</u>. However, <u>nearly</u> <u>all</u> <u>of</u> <u>the</u> <u>other</u> <u>twenty</u> <u>percent</u> <u>experience</u> <u>symptoms</u> such as nausea, fever, vomiting, and body aches.

해석

M Professor: 오늘은, 웨스트 나일 바이러스, 즉 WNV에 대해 이야기하며 시작할까 합니다. 먼저, 그것이 무엇이고 어떻게 확산되는지 이야기해 보겠습니다. 그러고 나서 시간이 된다면 몇 가지 증상들로 넘어가도록 하겠습니다. 제 계획이 어떤가요?
웨스트 나일 바이러스는 주로 여름과 가을 사이에 북아메리카에서 매년 발생하는 심각한 계절성 바이러스입니다. 어떤 사람들은 이것이 사람과 사람 간에 전염된다고 생각하지만, 그렇지 않습니다. 그 반대로, 그것은 주로 모기에 의해 전염됩니다. 감염된 새들의 피를 모기가 빨아 먹으면서 모기가 감염되고, 사람에게 그것을 옮깁니다. 그러므로 죽은 새를 만지면 사람에게 잠재적으로 위험합니다. 여러분, 죽은 새는 물론 모기를 조심해야 한다는 점을 꼭 기억하세요.
자, 아, 웨스트 나일 바이러스 감염병은 특정한 증상을 일으킬 수 있습니다. 그러나 감염된 사람들 대부분이 아무런 증상을 보이지 않습니다. 그렇습니다. 제 말을 제대로 들으셨죠. 전문가들은 WNV에 감염된 거의 80퍼센트의 사람들이 아무런 증상도 경험하지 않는다고 추정합니다. 고통을 전혀 겪지 않는 거죠. 하지만 나머지 20퍼센트에 해당하는 거의 모든 사람들이 메스꺼움과 발열, 구토, 몸살과 같은 증상을 겪습니다.

Listening Skills

1 <u>Today</u>, I'd like to begin by discussing the West Nile Virus.
2 <u>First</u>, I'll discuss what it is and how it is spread.
3 <u>Then</u>, I'll get into some of the symptoms if time allows.

• Exercise 6 • — p.101

정답 Q1 Ⓒ Q2 Ⓑ
스크립트 🎧 06-13

W Professor: Let's talk about <u>childhood</u> <u>illnesses</u> <u>today</u>. There are some diseases that <u>children</u> <u>get</u> <u>more</u> <u>than</u> <u>adults</u>. <u>One</u> <u>of</u>

them is chickenpox. But we've already covered it. Another is measles. Let me tell you about it.

Measles is a very common childhood illness that's caused by a virus. Nowadays, most children get vaccinated for it when they're young. However, this doesn't happen everywhere in the world. As a result, around 200,000 children die from measles each year. That's a really high number I hope comes down soon. What about the symptoms? Well, the symptoms appear around ten to fourteen days after a child gets infected. Lots of them resemble symptoms of the common cold. So children may have a fever, a runny nose, and a sore throat. But they might also get tiny white spots with blue centers in their mouths. A skin rash with large blotches is also common. Usually, the rash appears on the face first and then spreads elsewhere.

The rash normally lasts around seven days. The other symptoms might last for ten days. Children with measles almost always get better, but, uh, not all of them do.

해석

W Professor: 오늘은 아동기 질환에 대해 이야기해 보죠. 성인보다 아이들이 더 많이 걸리는 몇 가지 질병들이 있습니다. 그중 하나가 수두입니다. 하지만 우리는 이미 수두에 대해 다룬 적이 있어요. 또 다른 질병으로는 홍역이 있습니다. 이것에 대해 이야기해 보겠습니다.

홍역은 바이러스에 의해 발생하는 매우 흔한 아동기 질환입니다. 오늘날 대부분의 아이들은 어렸을 때 홍역 백신을 맞죠. 하지만 전 세계 모든 곳에서 일어나는 일은 아닙니다. 그 결과, 매년 20만명 정도의 아이들이 홍역으로 사망합니다. 이는 정말로 높은 수치로, 저는 곧 줄어들기를 바랍니다. 증상은 어떨까요? 음, 아이가 홍역에 걸리면 약 10일에서 14일 후에 증상이 나타납니다. 그중 다수는 일반적인 감기 증상과 비슷합니다. 그래서 아이들에게 발열, 콧물, 목 통증 증상이 나타날 있습니다. 하지만 또한 입 안에 가운데가 파란, 작고 흰 반점이 나타날 수도 있습니다. 커다란 반점과 함께 나타나는 피부 발진 또한 일반적이지요. 보통 발진은 얼굴에 먼저 나타나고 그 후에 다른 곳으로 퍼집니다.

발진은 보통 7일 정도 지속됩니다. 다른 증상들은 10일 동안 지속될 수 있습니다. 홍역에 걸린 아이들은 거의 항상 회복되지만, 아, 모두가 그런 것은 아닙니다.

Listening Skills

1 Nowadays, most children get vaccinated for it when they're young.
2 However, this doesn't happen everywhere in the world.
3 Usually, the rash appears on the face first and then spreads elsewhere.

• Exercise 7 • — p.102

정답 Q1 Ⓒ   Q2 Ⓐ
스크립트 🎧 06-15

M Professor: Yellow fever is another viral infection, and, unfortunately, it's on the rise. I say unfortunately, but I should say sadly because there's an inexpensive vaccine out there that's ninety-five-percent effective. If only more people would get the vaccine, they wouldn't have to suffer from this disease.

First, let me give you some background. Yellow fever is the most prevalent in the Americas and Africa. I would say that the main danger is in Central America. Still, without protection, people are at risk in many regions around the world. That's especially true for travelers. So you definitely want to get the vaccine for yellow fever if you have any trips to these regions planned.

Now, why is it called yellow fever? The answer can be found in the symptoms. Some unfortunate people develop serious problems with the liver and some other organs in the body. The liver, by the way, helps process waste. Sometimes a person's skin turns yellow if that individual has yellow fever. This means that person's body cannot get rid of or filter waste properly.

해석

M Professor: 황열병은 또 다른 바이러스 감염병으로, 안타깝게도 증가하고 있습니다. 안타깝다기보다는 슬프다고 말을 해야 하는데, 그 이유는 95퍼센트의 효과를 보이는 저렴한 백신이 나와 있기 때문입니다. 더 많은 사람들이 백신을 맞기만 하면 이 질병으로 고생할 필요가 없을 것입니다.

먼저 몇 가지 배경을 알려드리죠. 황열병은 아메리카 대륙과 아프리카에 가장 널리 퍼져 있습니다. 주요 위험은 중앙 아메리카에 존재한다고 말하고 싶군요. 하지만 보호를 받지 못한 채, 전 세계 여러 지역의 사람들이 위험에 처해 있습니다. 특히 여행객들이 그렇습니다. 그러니 이러한 지역에 대한 여행을 계획 중이라면 분명 황열병 백신을 맞고 싶을 것입니다.

자, 왜 황열병이라고 불릴까요? 그 답은 증상에서 찾을 수 있어요. 일부 운이 나쁜 사람들은 간과 기타 신체 기관에 심각한 문제를 겪습니다. 그건 그렇고 간은 노폐물 처리를 돕습니다. 때때로 사람이 황열병에 걸리면 피부가 노랗게 변합니다. 이것은 그 사람의 신체가 노폐물을 제대로 처리하거나 걸러낼 수 없다는 것을 의미합니다.

Listening Skills

1 First, let me give you some background.
2 Still, without protection, people are at risk in many regions around the world.
3 Now, why is it called yellow fever?

• Exercise 8 • — p.103

정답 Q1 Ⓐ   Q2 Ⓑ
스크립트 🎧 06-17

W Professor: I'm sure that everyone here has heard about smallpox. You probably know that it killed millions of people in the 1500s. This happened when Europeans visited the New World. They brought smallpox with them. Native Americans had no immunity to this disease. So they died in huge numbers. In some cases, entire villages were wiped out by smallpox. But what exactly is it? Let me tell you.

Smallpox is caused by a virus. It has been around for thousands of years. Basically, a person with smallpox gets a rash over his or her entire body. It especially affects the face, the arms, and the legs. Smallpox is extremely deadly. In the past, it killed at least three out of every ten people it infected. Scientists estimate it has killed up to half a billion people throughout history.

Fortunately, a vaccine for it was discovered. Edward Jenner came up with this vaccine. Since then, incidents of smallpox declined steadily. Today, smallpox has been eradicated from the world. It can only be found in laboratories. Hopefully, it never escapes because it could kill millions of people if it did.

해석

W Professor: 여기 모든 분들이 천연두에 대해 분명히 들어보셨을 거예요. 그로 인해 1500년대에 수백만 명의 사람들이 사망했다는 점을 알고 계실지도 모르고요. 유럽인들이 신대륙에 갔을 때 일어났던 일입니다. 그들과 함께 천연두가 유입되었습니다. 아메리카 원주민들은 이 질병에 대한 면역력을 가지고 있지 않았습니다. 그래서 수많은 사람들이 목숨을 잃었습니다. 어떤 경우에는 천연두로 인해 마을 전체가 사라졌습니다. 그런데 천연두는 정확히 무엇일까요? 제가 말해 드리죠.

천연두는 바이러스에 의해 발생합니다. 그것은 수천 년 동안 존재해 왔습니다. 기본적으로, 사람이 천연두에 걸리면 몸 전체에 발진이 일어납니다. 특히 얼굴과 팔다리에 영향을 미치죠. 천연두는 매우 치명적입니다. 과거에는 천연두에 감염된 사람은 10명 중 최소 3명꼴로 목숨을 잃었습니다. 과학자들은 역사적으로 5억 명에 가까운 사람들이 목숨을 잃었던 것으로 추산하고 있습니다.

다행히도 이에 대한 백신이 발견되었습니다. 에드워드 제너가 이러한 백신을 만들었죠. 그 이후로 천연두에 걸리는 일이 꾸준히 감소했습니다. 오늘날 천연두는 세상에서 완전히 사라졌습니다. 실험실에서만 찾아볼 수 있죠. 그것이 밖으로 나오는 경우 수백만 명의 사람들의 목숨을 앗아갈 수 있기 때문에 결코 그런 일이 없기를 바랍니다.

Listening Skills

1 Basically, a person with smallpox gets a rash over his entire body.
2 Fortunately, a vaccine for it was discovered.
3 Hopefully, it never escapes because it could kill millions of people if it did.

Vocabulary Review   p.104

A
1 feed
2 ironic
3 risk
4 waste
5 recover

B 1 Ⓐ 2 Ⓓ 3 Ⓑ 4 Ⓐ 5 Ⓓ

C 1 Ⓐ 2 Ⓑ 3 Ⓓ 4 Ⓐ 5 Ⓐ

D
1 viral
2 wiped out
3 inoculations
4 contagious
5 on the rise

Practice Test   p.106

1 Ⓑ   2 Ⓒ   3 Ⓐ   4 Ⓑ

스크립트 🎧 06-19

W Professor: In the mid-1300s, a horrible plague hit Europe. It lasted for several years from 1347 to 1351. During that time, millions of Europeans died. Some people believe up to half of all Europeans died from this plague. The entire continent was devastated. The plague was called the Black Death. It was caused by the bubonic plague.

The bubonic plague is an infectious disease caused by bacteria. It can be spread by fleas. That's what happened to Europe. Fleas got infected on it and lived on rats. Rats would then go into cities and towns, where the fleas would infect people by biting them. One symptom of the bubonic plague is swelling. People's bodies would swell under their arms, behind their ears, and in other places. The swollen areas were black or purple in color. This is why people called it the Black Death. There were other symptoms, but the swelling was the most painful.

The bubonic plague was very deadly. Between thirty and ninety percent of people who get it nowadays die without any treatment. In the Middle Ages, so many people died that it basically shut down society. The bubonic plague still exists today. Fortunately, there are vaccines for it. It can also be treated by various antibiotics. So if there are breakouts in the future, most people should be all right.

해석

W Professor: 1300년대 중반에 끔찍한 전염병이 유럽을 강타했습니다. 이는 1347년부터 1351년까지 여러 해 동안 지속되었습니다. 이 기간 동안 수백만 명의 유럽인들이 목숨을 잃었습니다. 유럽 전체 인구의 절반 가까이가 이 전염병으로 사망했다고 믿는 사람들도 있죠. 대륙 전체가 폐허가 되었습니다. 이 전염병은 흑사병이라고 불렸습니다. 그것은 림프절 페스트에 의해 발생했습니다.

림프절 페스트는 박테리아에 의해 발생하는 감염병입니다. 이는 벼룩에 의해 전파될 수 있습니다. 그것이 바로 유럽에서 일어났던 일입니다. 림프절 페스트에 감염된 벼룩들이 쥐에 붙어 살았습니다. 그런 다음 쥐들이 도시와 마을로 유입되어, 그곳에서 벼룩이 사람들을 물어 감염시켰을 것입니다. 림프절 페스트의 한 가지 증상은 종창입니다. 팔 아래, 귀 뒤쪽, 그리고 기타 신체 부위들이 부풀어 올랐을 것입니다. 부푼 부위는 검거나 보랏빛이었습니다. 이 때문에 사람들은 그것을 흑사병이라고 불렀습니다. 다른 증상들도 있었지만, 종창이 가장 고통스러운 것이었습니다.

림프절 페스트는 매우 치명적이었습니다. 오늘날에도 이에 감염되는 30퍼센트에서 90퍼센트 사이의 사람들이 치료를 받지 않으면 사망합니다. 중세 시대에는 너무 많은 사람들이 사망해서 기본적으로 사회가 마비되었습니다. 림프절 페스트는 오늘날에도 존재합니다. 다행히 이에 대한 백신이 존재합니다. 또한 다양한 항생제로 치료될 수 있습니다. 따라서 훗날 발생하더라도 대부분의 사람들이 괜찮을 것입니다.

CHAPTER 7 Photography

Understanding TOEFL Question Types & Listening Skills
p.110

1 Question Types ▶ Sample Question

스크립트 🎧 07-01

W Professor: Today, I'd like to focus on the two main components of the camera: the lens and the aperture. I think most of you already know about the lens. Its main function is to focus the subject as an image inside the camera. The lens adjusts forward and backward to create a sharp, clear image of what a person is taking a picture of. Next is the aperture. It is typically a circular, adjustable hole inside the lens, and it regulates the amount of light entering the lens. Together, the lens and the aperture control the brightness of the image.

해석
W Professor: 오늘은, 카메라의 두 가지 중요한 구성 요소인 렌즈와 조리개에 초점을 맞추도록 하겠습니다. 여러분 대부분이 이미 렌즈에 대해서는 알고 있으리라 생각합니다. 렌즈의 주요 기능은 카메라 내부에 상(像)으로 생기는 피사체에 초점을 맞추는 것입니다. 렌즈를 앞뒤로 조절함으로써 사람이 사진을 찍는 대상의 뚜렷하고 선명한 상이 만들어집니다. 다음은 조리개입니다. 조리개는 기본적으로 렌즈의 안쪽에 있는 원형의 구멍으로 조절이 가능하며 렌즈로 들어오는 빛의 양을 조절합니다. 렌즈와 조리개는 모두 상의 선명도를 제어합니다.

2 Listening Skills ▶ Check-Up

1 (focus) – pocus
2 rinse – (lens)
3 (picture) – fixture
4 right – (light)

• Exercise 1 •
p.112

정답 Q1 A   Q2 Film Cameras: ③, ④ Digital Cameras: ①, ②

스크립트 🎧 07-03

M Professor: Well, I guess the big question many of you are asking is which is better, film cameras or digital cameras. That's a difficult question to answer.
Let me start with black and white pictures. There is no question that a film camera is better than a digital for black and white photography. It creates a more detailed image while a digital camera loses a lot. Another advantage of film is that it has a higher resolution than the megapixels of a digital camera. Sure, as technology advances, this could change, but currently, film lends more detail than digital.
Let's move on to the advantages of digital cameras. First, is an obvious one: convenience. Digital cameras can store tons of more pictures than film ever can. You also have the option of immediate viewing, and then you can get rid of the ones you don't like. With a film camera, you are stuck with every image as if it were set in stone.

해석
M Professor: 음, 저는 많은 분들이 정말 많이 물어보시는 질문이 필름 카메라와 디지털 카메라 중 어느 것이 더 나은지에 관한 것이라고 생각합니다. 그것은 대답하기가 어려운 질문입니다.
흑백 사진으로 시작해 보겠습니다. 흑백 사진을 찍을 때 디지털 카메라보다는 필름 카메라가 더 낫다는 점에는 의문의 여지가 없습니다. 필름 카메라는 이미지를 좀 더 상세하게 만드는 반면 디지털 카메라는 많은 것을 놓칩니다. 필름의 또 다른 장점은 디지털 카메라가 가진 몇백만 화소의 해상도보다 더 높은 해상도를 가지고 있다는 점입니다. 물론, 기술이 발전하면서, 이것은 바뀔 수 있지만, 현재로서는 필름이 디지털보다 더 세부적인 묘사를 제공해줍니다.
디지털 카메라의 장점으로 넘어가 봅시다. 먼저, 분명한 것은 바로 편의성입니다. 디지털 카메라는 엄청나게 많은 양의 사진을 저장할 수 있는데, 필름이 지금까지 저장할 수 있는 양보다도 많습니다. 또한 즉석에서 바로 볼 수 있는 기능이 있고, 그러면 마음에 들지 않는 사진들을 삭제할 수 있습니다. 필름 카메라를 사용하면 모든 이미지가 돌에 새겨진 것처럼 확정되어 여러분은 그 모든 이미지를 어쩔 수 없이 갖게 됩니다.

Listening Skills

1 fig – (big)
2 firm – (film)
3 flack – (black)
4 (while) – white

• Exercise 2 •
p.113

정답 Q1 C   Q2 Pre-Kodak: ①, ④ Post-Kodak: ②, ③

스크립트 🎧 07-05

W Professor: Everyone, please take a seat. Now, uh, I'd like to pick up where we left off the last time with the history of modern photography.
You all remember that photography pre-1880s was not for everyone. Only the rich could afford to buy cameras and film and then have the film developed. Thankfully, during the late nineteenth century, a company called Eastman Kodak changed everything.
George Eastman was, of course, the founder of the company, and he is responsible for making the world of photography available to just about everyone. He created a box camera with film on the inside that could hold about 100 images. It was easy to use and required no special skills or instruction. A person would simply point the camera and shoot. Simple, huh? Yes, it was just like the disposable cameras of today. After using all of the film a person would send the camera to the Kodak Company. Then, the pictures would be developed and returned to the person who took them.

해석
W Professor: 여러분, 모두들 자리에 앉아 주세요. 자, 아, 우리가 지난 시간에 현대 사진의 역사를 공부하다 남겨 놓은 부분부터 시작하도록 할게요.
1880년대 이전에는 사진이 모두를 위한 것이 아니었다는 걸 모두들 기억하고 있죠. 부자들만이 카메라와 필름을 사고 그 필름을 현상할 여유가 있었어요. 고맙게도 19세기 후반에 이스트먼 코닥이라고 하는 한 회사가 모든 것을 바꿔 놓았죠.
조지 이스트먼은 물론 그 회사의 창업자였으며, 사진이라는 세계를 거의 모든 이들이 이용할 수 있게 만든 장본인입니다. 그는 안에 필름이 들어 있는 상자형 카메라를 만들었는데, 그 카메라는 거의 100장의 이미지를 담을 수 있었어요. 그 카메라는 사용하기가 쉬웠고 특별한 기술이나 설명이 전혀 필요하지 않았죠. 그저 카메라를 맞추고 찍으면 됐습니다. 간단하잖아요, 그렇죠? 맞아요, 그것은 오늘날의 일회용 카메라와 정말 비슷했습니다. 필름을 다 쓰고 나면 개인이 코닥 회사에 카메라를 보내곤 했습니다. 그러면 사진을 현상해 그것을 찍은 사람에게 돌려 보내곤 했습니다.

Listening Skills

1 (seat) – sheet   2 (all) – are
3 (for) – poor   4 (it) – eat

• Exercise 3 •   p.114

정답 Q1 B   Q2 UV Filters: 1   Polarizer Filters: 2, 3, 4

스크립트 ∩ 07-07

W Professor: There are many ways to improve upon the pictures you take. Of course, technique, camera quality, film quality, and lighting are all important in photography. But let's not stop there. Let's step back for a minute. What else? I'll give you a hint. It starts with an F . . . That's right . . . Filters. Please be sure to use them when you take pictures. They'll make a world of difference.
Filters are plastic or glass discs which are usually screwed onto a lens to manipulate the qualities of images. They're pretty cheap, so that makes them appealing. Anyway, there are two kinds of filters I want to discuss. They are UV filters and polarizer filters. UV filters basically protect lenses from scratches and dirt. Some photographers claim they can also reduce the annoying purple coloring that sometimes appears in digital images. Polarizer filters are good for enhancing contrasts, for example, between clouds and the sky. They are also useful because they can reduce reflections from glass or water surfaces, creating more depth.

해석
W Professor: 여러분이 찍는 사진들을 개선시킬 수 있는 많은 방법들이 있습니다. 물론 기술, 카메라의 질, 필름의 질, 조명이 모두 사진술에 있어 중요합니다. 그렇지만 거기서 멈추지 맙시다. 잠시 한 걸음 물러나 생각해 봅시다. 또 뭐가 있을까요? 제가 힌트를 줄게요. F로 시작합니다… 맞아요… 바로 필터입니다. 사진을 찍을 때 꼭 필터를 사용해 보세요. 필터는 다른 세계를 만들어 줄 것입니다.
필터는 플라스틱이나 유리로 된 납작한 원판으로, 주로 렌즈 위에 나사로 고정되어 있으며 이미지의 질을 조정합니다. 필터는 꽤 저렴하기 때문에 그 또한 매력적인 요소입니다. 어쨌든 저는 두 가지 종류의 필터에 대해 이야기하고 싶습니다. 바로 UV 필터와 편광 필터입니다. UV 필터는 기본적으로 긁힘과 먼지로부터 렌즈를 보호합니다. 어떤 사진가들은 UV 필터가 이따금 디지털 이미지에 나타나는 성가신 보랏빛 색채도 감소시킬 수 있다고 주장합니다. 편광 필터는 예를 들어 구름과 하늘 사이와 같이, 대비를 강화시키는 데 좋습니다. 또한 유리나 물 표면에 생기는 반사광을 감소시켜 심도를 더해 줄 수 있어 유용합니다.

Listening Skills

1 staff – (step)   2 (cheap) – cheat
3 crowds – (clouds)   4 (glass) – grass

• Exercise 4 •   p.115

정답 Q1 D   Q2 Underwater Photography: 1, 4
Land Photography: 2, 3

스크립트 ∩ 07-09

W Professor: All of you are pretty comfortable taking pictures now, right? Well, at least more than at the beginning of the semester. I sure hope so. Now, at this point, I would like to mix it up a little by giving you a new assignment. How does that sound? On your desks is some special equipment for underwater photography. Aren't you all excited? We're going to take some shots underwater and compare them to the pictures that we've taken on land. Don't worry. You don't have to be a great swimmer or really a swimmer at all. We'll be in the shallow end of the university pool.
Okay. The biggest difference between underwater and regular photography is color. Water absorbs sunlight, and we lose a lot of color in our vision when we're under the water. Another is clarity. On land, we can be far from our subjects, but underwater, you've got to get really close to your subject.

해석
W Professor: 여러분 모두는 이제 사진을 찍는 게 꽤 편하잖아요, 그렇죠? 음, 적어도 학기 초반보다는 더 그럴 거예요. 확실히 그렇길 바랍니다. 이제, 이 시점에서, 저는 여러분에게 새로운 과제를 줌으로써 약간 변형시켜 보려고 해요. 어때요? 여러분의 책상 위에는 수중 사진을 위한 몇 가지 특수 장비들이 있습니다. 모두들 신나지 않나요? 우리는 수중에서 사진을 몇 장 찍고 그것을 우리가 지면 위에서 찍은 사진들과 비교해 볼 거예요. 걱정 마세요. 수영을 잘해야 한다거나 혹은 진짜 수영을 할 필요는 없습니다. 우리는 교내 수영장 끝 쪽의 얕은 곳에 있을 거예요.
좋아요. 수중 사진과 일반 사진 사이의 가장 큰 차이점은 색입니다. 물은 햇빛을 흡수하고, 우리가 물속에 있을 때 시야에서 많은 색을 잃습니다. 또 다른 점은 선명도입니다. 땅 위에서는 피사체로부터 멀리 떨어져도 되지만, 물속에서는 피사체에 정말 가까이 다가가야 합니다.

Listening Skills

1 (shot) – chop   2 (we'll) – we're
3 fool – (pool)   4 (vision) – mission

• Exercise 5 •   p.116

정답 Q1 C   Q2 Ansel Adams: 1, 3   Annie Leibovitz: 2, 4

스크립트 ∩ 07-11

M Professor: This morning, we will be discussing two highly influential photographers: Ansel Adams and Annie Leibovitz. Ansel Adams was a landscape photographer, and he, more often than not, worked with black and white photography. The American West was his canvas, and from it, he created haunting black and white contrasts of deserts, mountain peaks, and woodlands. He did absolutely brilliant work. If you haven't yet seen any of his work, go online and check it out. You will be stunned by the pictures that Adams took.

Leibovitz, in contrast, is mostly noted for her portraits of famous people. She shot photos of celebrities such as actors and singers. Her photography is very intimate and revealing of her subjects. It was quite striking photography. One of her first jobs was with the music magazine, *Rolling Stone*. Her most famous photo is arguably the one she took of John Lennon and Yoko Ono on the morning of December 8, 1980. Sadly, Leibovitz became the last person to photograph Lennon professionally. Okay. I didn't mean to ruin the mood in class, but on a lighter note, I'll now discuss a couple more modern photographers.

해석
M Professor: 오늘 아침, 우리는 두 명의 아주 영향력 있는 사진작가들에 대해 이야기할 것입니다. 바로 앤설 애덤스와 애니 레보비츠입니다. 앤설 애덤스는 풍경 사진작가였고, 그렇지 않은 경우도 있었지만, 대개는 흑백 사진으로 작업을 했습니다. 미국의 서부 지역이 그의 캔버스였고 그곳에서 그는 사막, 산봉우리, 삼림 지대의 잊혀지지 않는 흑백 대비를 창조했습니다. 그는 정말 눈부신 업적을 이루었습니다. 여러분이 아직 그의 작품을 보지 못했다면 온라인에서 확인해 보세요. 애덤스가 찍은 사진들을 보면 넋을 잃을 것입니다.
그에 반해, 레보비츠는 주로 유명한 사람들의 인물 사진으로 유명합니다. 그녀는 배우와 가수와 같은 유명인들의 사진을 찍었습니다. 그녀의 사진은 그녀가 찍는 인물의 친밀하면서도 흥미로운 면들을 잘 드러냅니다. 대단히 눈에 띄는 사진 기술이었죠. 음악 잡지, 롤링 스톤과 함께 한 것이 그녀의 첫 작업들 중 하나였습니다. 그녀의 가장 유명한 사진은 거의 틀림없이, 1980년 12월 8일 아침에 존 레논과 오노 요코를 찍은 사진입니다. 슬프게도, 레보비츠는 레논의 사진을 직업적으로 찍은 마지막 사람이 되었습니다. 자. 수업 분위기를 망칠 의도는 아니었는데, 좀 더 가벼운 분위기로, 이제 두세 명의 현대 사진작가들에 대해 좀 더 이야기해 보겠습니다.

Listening Skills

1 (west) – vest 2 (from) – plumb
3 (subjects) – objects 4 (couple) – cup of

• **Exercise 6** • ────────────── p.117

정답 Q1 Ⓓ Q2 3 - 1 - 4 - 5 - 2
스크립트 ∩ 07-13

W Professor: Last on the agenda today is a brief review of how film is developed. And, yes, there's an important reason for this: We're having a quiz on it next Thursday.
If you don't already have a solid understanding of this, please listen carefully and take notes. First, the film is removed from the camera and placed on a reel. Now, this occurs where . . . ? That's right. It is done in total and complete darkness, preferably in a darkroom. The key here is no safety lights. There should be none at all because it will ruin the film.
Next, the reel of film is placed in a daylight processing tank. This is a special light-proof canister. Again, no light should enter the canister to allow for proper developing. Then, water is added to the tank to soak the film for a couple of minutes, and after that, developer must be added. When the developer is in the tank, the tank needs to be shaken. After the developer works on the film, the film can be removed and dried. At this point, the film should be ready to view and make prints.

해석
W Professor: 필름이 인화되는 방식에 대한 간략한 복습이 오늘 강의 계획의 마지막 부분입니다. 그리고, 맞아요, 이렇게 하는 중요한 이유가 있죠. 다음 주 목요일에 그것에 대해 간단한 시험을 볼 거예요.
여러분이 이것에 대해 아직 확실하게 이해하고 있지 않다면 주의 깊게 듣고 필기하도록 하세요. 먼저, 카메라에서 필름을 빼서 필름통에 넣습니다. 자, 이 작업은 어디에서 이루어질까요…? 맞아요. 이 작업은 완전히 깜깜한 어둠 속에서, 가급적 암실에서 이루어집니다. 여기에서 중요한 것은 안전한 빛은 없다는 것입니다. 빛은 필름을 손상시키기 때문에 안전한 빛이란 전혀 존재하지 않습니다.
다음으로, 필름통을 일광 처리 수조 안에 넣습니다. 이것은 특수 차광 통입니다. 다시 말하지만, 적절한 인화가 이루어지기 위해서는 어떠한 빛도 통 안에 들어가서는 안 됩니다. 그런 다음, 통에 물을 넣어 몇 분간 필름을 담궈 두고 그 후에 현상액을 넣어야 합니다. 현상액을 통 안에 넣으면 통을 반드시 흔들어 주어야 합니다. 현상액이 필름에 작용하고 나면 필름을 꺼내 말려도 됩니다. 이 시점에서, 필름을 보고 인화할 준비가 된 것입니다.

Listening Skills

1 (reason) – season 2 votes – (notes)
3 (reel) – feel 4 (view) – few

• **Exercise 7** • ────────────── p.118

정답 Q1 Ⓒ Q2 Wide-Angle Lenses: ③
Telephoto Lenses: ①, ②, ④
스크립트 ∩ 07-15

M Professor: There are four common types of camera lenses. Hang on for a second . . . Did I just say four? I meant three. Sorry. There are three common types of lenses. They are standard, wide-angle, and telephoto lenses.
Right now, I'd like to limit my discussion to wide-angle and telephoto lenses, but let me talk about standard lenses first. You see, the power of each kind of lens is measured in millimeters. Pros like myself call this the focal length. That's the focal length of the lens. So a standard lens for a 35mm camera is typically 50mm. Um, is everyone able to follow me okay? Very good.
Okay, let's move on to wide-angle lenses. They are good for depth and especially for taking landscape pictures. Finally, um, telephoto lenses are great for sports shots because they reduce depth and are good at focusing on specific subjects.

해석
M Professor: 카메라 렌즈에는 일반적으로 네 가지 종류가 있습니다. 잠시만요… 제가 방금 네 가지라고 말했나요? 세 가지를 의미한 거였어요. 미안해요. 일반적으로 세 가지 종류의 렌즈가 있어요. 바로 표준 렌즈, 광각 렌즈, 그리고

망원 렌즈입니다.
지금은 광각 렌즈와 망원 렌즈로 제한해서 이야기를 하고 싶지만, 우선 표준 렌즈에 대해서 이야기할게요. 알겠지만, 각각의 종류에 따라 렌즈가 가지는 굴절력은 밀리미터 단위로 측정됩니다. 저와 같은 전문 사진작가는 이것을 초점 거리라고 부릅니다. 그것이 렌즈가 가지는 초점의 길이입니다. 그래서 35밀리미터 카메라의 표준 렌즈는 보통 50밀리미터입니다. 음, 모두 저를 잘 따라올 수 있나요? 아주 좋아요.
그렇다면, 광각 렌즈로 넘어가 봅시다. 광각 렌즈는 심도가 좋아서 특히 풍경 사진을 찍기에 좋습니다. 마지막으로, 음, 망원 렌즈는 심도를 줄이고 세밀한 피사체에 초점을 맞추는 데 좋기 때문에 스포츠 사진에 적합합니다.

Listening Skills

1 (angle) – anger   2 (telephoto) – telephone
3 life – (like)   4 (first) – thirst

• Exercise 8 • ───────────── p.119

정답 **Q1** Ⓑ **Q2** Before the Great Depression: ①, ③
During and After the Great Depression: ②, ④

스크립트 ∩ 07-17

M Professor: One of the greatest photographers in the 1900s was Dorothea Lange. Some of you have probably heard of her. She became famous during the Great Depression in the 1930s. However, she was taking pictures long before then.
After finishing high school, Lange became interested in photography. She studied it at Columbia University and worked for some photographers as an apprentice. In the 1920s, she traveled around the southwestern part of the country. She took many photographs of Native Americans.
Then, in the 1930s, the Great Depression came. She started taking pictures of poor laborers. She took a job with the government and began traveling around the country. Her photographs showed the sad conditions of people in rural areas. There were also usually captions beneath her pictures. Most of the time, they were quotations from the people she had photographed. Lange took her most famous photograph during the depression. It was called *Migrant Mother*. Later, during World War II, she took many photographs of Japanese immigrants in detention camps. She also visited other countries to take pictures. Let's look at some of her most famous pictures now.

해석

M Professor: 1900년대에 가장 뛰어난 사진작가 중 한 사람은 도로시아 랭이었습니다. 여러분 중에는 아마도 그녀에 대해 들어본 사람이 있을 것입니다. 그녀는 1930년대 대공황 시기에 유명해졌습니다. 하지만 그녀는 훨씬 이전부터 사진을 찍고 있었죠.
랭은 고등학교 졸업 후 사진에 대해 관심을 갖게 되었습니다. 그녀는 콜롬비아 대학에서 공부를 했고, 몇몇 사진작가 밑에서 견습생으로 일했습니다. 1920년대에 그녀는 미국의 남서부 지방을 여행했습니다. 그녀는 아메리카 원주민들의 사진을 많이 찍었죠.
이후 1930년대에 대공황이 찾아왔습니다. 그녀는 가난한 노동자들의 사진을 찍기 시작했어요. 그녀는 정부에서 일자리를 받아 전국을 돌아다니기 시작했죠. 그녀의 사진들은 시골 지역에 사는 사람들의 슬픈 상황들을 보여주었습니다. 또한 그녀의 사진 아랫부분에는 보통 자막이 있었습니다. 대부분의 경우, 그녀가 찍은 사람들이 말한 것을 옮겨 적은 것이었습니다. 랭은 대공황 시기에 그녀의 가장 유명한 사진을 찍었습니다. 바로 *이민자 어머니*라는 사진이었죠. 이후 제2차 세계 대전 동안에는 임시 수용소에 있던 일본인 이민자들의 사진을 많이 찍었습니다. 그녀는 또한 사진을 찍기 위해 다른 나라들을 방문하기도 했습니다. 이제 그녀의 가장 유명한 사진들 중 몇 장을 함께 살펴 봅시다.

Listening Skills

1 (greatest) – latest   2 wrong - (long)
3 capture – (caption)   4 prevention – (detention)

Vocabulary Review   p.120

A 1 agenda
      2 angles
      3 Depression
      4 point
      5 technique

B 1 Ⓒ   2 Ⓐ   3 Ⓑ   4 Ⓒ   5 Ⓓ

C 1 Ⓑ   2 Ⓐ   3 Ⓓ   4 Ⓐ   5 Ⓐ

D 1 detention
      2 founder
      3 shallow
      4 component
      5 light–proof

Practice Test   p.122

1 Ⓑ   2 Ⓑ   3 Ⓒ   4 Ⓐ

스크립트 ∩ 07-19

M Professor: Today, if you have a mobile phone, you have a digital camera. People everywhere have access to cameras. But camera technology isn't very old. In fact, people have only been able to create images from cameras since the 1800s.
The first type of photography that was invented was called the daguerreotype. That's spelled D-A-G-U-E-R-R-E-O-T-Y-P-E, uh, just so you know. Who invented it? A man named Louis-Jacques-Mandé Daguerre created it with some help from Nicéphore Niépce. They did their work in the 1830s and perfected the process in the year 1839.
The two men experimented with various chemicals. Here's what they did. They coated a copper plate with silver iodide. Then, they exposed the plate to light by using a camera. Then, they used some other chemicals to create a permanent image on the plate. Unfortunately, there were no negatives like modern cameras. So each image made with a daguerreotype was an original. Still, many pictures taken with it were beautiful.

The daguerreotype became extremely popular very quickly. Just a few years later, there were numerous studios that produced images in big cities. Portraits were especially popular with people. Before the daguerreotype, the only way to capture a person's image was by drawing or painting it. The daguerreotype didn't last very long though. Improvements in technology happened, and better and cheaper ways to take pictures were invented starting at the end of the 1850s.

해석

M Professor: 오늘날에는 휴대전화를 갖고 있으면 디지털 카메라를 가지고 있는 셈이죠. 어디에서든 사람들은 카메라를 사용할 수 있습니다. 하지만 카메라 기술은 그다지 오래된 것이 아니에요. 실제로 1800년대 이후에야 카메라로 이미지를 만들어낼 수 있었습니다.

최초로 발명된 사진술은 은판사진술이라고 불리는 형태였습니다. 철자는, D-A-G-U-E-R-R-E-O-T-Y-P-E인데, 아, 참고로 말해드리는 겁니다. 누가 이것을 발명했을까요? 루이 자크 망데 다게르라는 사람이 니세포르 니에프스의 도움을 받아 만들었습니다. 이들은 1830년대에 이 연구를 했고 1839년에 그 과정을 완성했습니다.

이 두 사람은 다양한 화학물질로 실험을 했습니다. 다음이 그들이 한 일입니다. 그들은 구리로 된 판에 요오드화은을 발랐습니다. 그런 다음에 카메라를 사용해서 이 판을 빛에 노출시켰습니다. 그러고 나서 몇 가지 다른 화학물질들을 이용해 판에 영구적인 이미지를 만들어냈습니다. 안타깝게도 현대의 카메라와 같은 원화는 존재하지 않았어요. 그래서 은판사진술로 만들어진 이미지는 하나뿐이었습니다. 그럼에도 불구하고 이를 이용해 찍은 많은 사진들이 아름다웠습니다.

은판사진술은 매우 빠른 속도로 큰 인기를 얻게 되었습니다. 불과 몇 년 후, 이미지를 만들어내는 스튜디오들이 대도시에 많이 생겨났습니다. 특히 인물 사진의 인기가 높았어요. 은판사진술 전에는 사람의 이미지를 포착하는 유일한 방법이 선이나 색으로 그림을 그리는 것이었습니다. 하지만 은판사진술은 그다지 오래 가지 않았습니다. 기술의 발전이 이루어졌고, 1850년대 후반부터는 더 우수하고 저렴한 사진 촬영법들이 발명되었습니다.

CHAPTER 8

Inventions

Understanding TOEFL Question Types & Listening Skills

p.126

1 Question Types ▶ Sample Question

스크립트 🎧 08-01

W Professor: I think many of you will agree with me on this one. The wheel was perhaps the single most important invention in human history. When was it first developed? Well, that's hard to pinpoint although many experts believe it dates back to about 4000 B.C. in Mesopotamia. But the earliest wheel was most likely a pottery wheel, not one used for transportation. There is evidence of the first wheeled vehicle being used around 500 years later in 3500 B.C. This was a simple wagon used in Western Europe. Still later, the chariot was definitely present in China sometime between 2000 and 1200 B.C.

해석

W Professor: 저는 많은 분들이 이것에 대해 제 말에 동의할 거라고 생각합니다. 바퀴는 아마 인류 역사상 단 하나의 가장 중요한 발명품이었을 것입니다. 바퀴는 언제 처음 개발되었을까요? 글쎄요, 많은 전문가들이 기원전 약 4000년경 메소포타미아에서 기원한다고 생각하고 있지만 정확히 정하기는 어렵습니다. 그러나 가장 초기의 바퀴는 도자기로 만든 바퀴였을 가능성이 높기 때문에 이동수단으로 쓰인 것은 아니었습니다. 그로부터 약 500년 후인 기원전 3500년경에 바퀴를 단 최초의 이동수단이 사용된 증거가 있습니다. 이것은 서유럽에서 사용된, 단순한 형태의 마차였습니다. 훨씬 이후인, 기원전 2000년에서 1200년 사이의 어느 시기에 중국에는 확실히 전차가 존재했습니다.

2 Listening Skills ▶ Check-Up

1 It dates back to about 4000 B.C. in Mesopotamia.
2 There is evidence of the first wheeled vehicle being used around 500 years later in 3500 B.C.
3 Still later, the chariot was definitely present in China sometime between 2000 and 1200 B.C.

• Exercise 1 • ─────────────── p.128

정답 Q1 Q2

스크립트 🎧 08-03

M Professor: Around 50,000 to 60,000 years ago, humans began venturing out onto the seas. Small craft similar to canoes were probably the first ones they used. However, these watercrafts could only go very short distances. Still, they helped people explore islands and other lands.

Much later, there is evidence that the Egyptians had ships around 2500 B.C. You see, uh, an entire ship was entombed in one of the pyramids at Giza. Then, about 1,000 years later, the Egyptians were regularly building ships between eighty and

ninety feet in length with great skill.
But that wasn't all. The Egyptians also incorporated masts and sails onto their ships. Still later, around 700 B.C., we know the Chinese began assembling navies. They constructed large barge-like vessels with numerous levels or decks. Around 1100 A.D., China's first official navy came about during the Song Dynasty.

해석

M Professor: 약 5만 년에서 6만 년 전에 인류는 바다로 모험을 떠나기 시작했습니다. 인류가 최초로 사용한 배는 아마도 카누와 비슷한 작은 배였을 것입니다. 그러나 이러한 배들은 아주 짧은 거리만 이동할 수 있었습니다. 그렇더라도, 이 덕분에 사람들은 섬들과 다른 육지들을 탐험할 수 있었습니다.
한참 후인 기원전 약 2500년경에 이집트인들이 배를 가지고 있었다는 증거가 있습니다. 그러니까, 아, 완전한 배 한 척이 기자의 피라미드들 중 한 곳에 안치되어 있었습니다. 그러고 나서 약 1,000년 후에 이집트인들은 훌륭한 기술력을 가지고 길이가 80피트에서 90피트 사이의 배를 정기적으로 축조하고 있었습니다.
그러나 그것이 전부가 아니었습니다. 이집트인들은 또한 배에 돛대와 돛을 달았습니다. 한참 후인 기원전 약 700년경에는 중국인들이 해군을 조직하기 시작했다고 알려져 있습니다. 그들은 여러 층, 즉 갑판이 있는, 바지선과 같이 커다란 배를 만들었습니다. 서기 1100년경에는 중국의 공식적인 해군이 송나라 왕조 때 최초로 출현했습니다.

Listening Skills

1 Around 50,000 to 60,000 years ago, humans began venturing out onto the seas.
2 The Egyptians were regularly building ships between eighty and ninety feet in length with great skill.
3 Still later, around 700 B.C., we know the Chinese began assembling navies.

• **Exercise 2** • p.129

정답 Q1 Ⓐ Q2 Ⓒ
스크립트 🎧 08-05

W Professor: One of the most important inventions in history is right here in my hand. Take a look. Do you know what it is . . . ? Anyone . . . ? It's a compass. We use it to determine directions.
Why was it such an important invention? In the past, sailing on ships was very dangerous. Most ships never sailed out of sight of land. Why? If they lost sight of land, they might never return home. Sure, some sailors were able to navigate by using the stars. But they couldn't do that when it was cloudy. They also couldn't do that during the day.
So . . . the compass was invented. Nobody knows for sure exactly when. We know it was invented in China sometime between 200 B.C. and 200 A.D. It used a lodestone. That's a type of iron ore, which is magnetic. As a result, the compass always pointed to the north. However, the Chinese didn't use it to navigate the seas for many years. They started doing that between the years 1000 and 1200. In the West, the compass was first used around 1190. Let me show you some pictures of ancient compasses now.

해석

W Professor: 역사상 가장 중요한 발명품 중 하나가 바로 여기 제 손 안에 있습니다. 보세요. 무엇인지 아시나요…? 아는 사람이 있나요…? 바로 나침반이에요. 우리는 방향을 알기 위해 나침반을 사용하죠.
이것이 왜 그처럼 중요한 발명품이었을까요? 과거에는 배로 항해를 하는 일이 매우 위험했습니다. 대부분의 배들은 육지가 보이지 않은 곳까지 결코 항해하지 않았습니다. 왜일까요? 육지가 보이지 않는 경우, 결코 집으로 돌아갈 수가 없을 것입니다. 물론, 어떤 선원들은 별을 이용해 길을 찾을 수 있었어요. 하지만 흐린 날에는 그럴 수가 없었죠. 또한 낮에도 마찬가지였고요.
그래서… 나침반이 발명되었습니다. 정확히 언제인지는 아무도 확실히 알지 못합니다. 기원전 200년에서 서기 200년 사이의 어느 시점에 중국에서 발명되었다고 알려져 있죠. 자철석을 이용한 것이었습니다. 이는 자성을 가지고 있는 철광석의 일종이죠. 그 결과 나침반은 항상 북쪽을 가리켰습니다. 하지만 중국인들은 오랜 시간 동안 이를 이용해 바다를 항해하지 않았어요. 1000년과 1200년 사이에 그렇게 하기 시작했죠. 서양에서는 1190년 무렵에 나침반이 처음으로 사용되었습니다. 이제 매우 오래된 나침반의 사진을 몇 장 보여드리죠.

Listening Skills

1 We know it was invented in China sometime between 200 B.C. and 200 A.D.
2 They started doing that between the years 1000 and 1200.
3 In the West, the compass was first used around 1190.

• **Exercise 3** • p.130

정답 Q1 Ⓑ Q2 Ⓐ
스크립트 🎧 08-07

M Professor: It's mostly likely true that gunpowder was first developed by the Chinese. They did this sometime during the ninth century. Guns were invented a couple of hundred years later in the 1100s. The oldest gun ever found dates back to 1288 by the way. But let me get back to gunpowder.
Ancient Chinese texts prove that the Chinese were working with mixtures of substances to create explosions. The actual recipe for an early gunpowder mixture from one of these texts is in your book on page 454. The recipe was 48.4% saltpeter, 25.6% sulfur, and 21% other nonessential ingredients. From this mixture, the Chinese made fire bombs that they used during battles.
Ah, what is saltpeter? It is a natural resource of nitrogen, which we all know can be highly explosive. Now, uh, by doing more experiments with saltpeter, the Chinese eventually developed bombs, and special arrows that could explode on impact. Around the twelfth century, the Chinese managed to invent metal-encased grenades as well.

해석

M Professor: 화약이 중국인들에 의해 처음 개발되었다는 점은 사실일 가능성이 높습니다. 9세기의 어느 시점에 이 일이 이루어졌습니다. 총은 200여년 후인 1100년대에 발명되었습니다. 덧붙이자면 지금까지 발견된 가장 오래된

총은 1288년으로 거슬러 올라갑니다. 하지만 화약으로 되돌아가 봅시다. 고대 중국의 문헌들을 통해, 중국인들이 폭발을 일으키는 물질들을 혼합하는 작업을 하고 있었다는 점이 증명됩니다. 이러한 문헌 중 하나에 나오는 초기 화약 혼합물의 실제 제조법이 교재 454쪽에 있습니다. 그 제조법은 초석 48.4퍼센트와, 유황 25.6퍼센트, 그리고 기타 꼭 필요하지는 않은 재료 21퍼센트로 되어 있었습니다. 이러한 혼합물로 중국인들은 전쟁 중에 사용한 소이탄을 만들었습니다.

아, 초석이 무엇일까요? 초석이란 질소의 천연 원천인데, 우리 모두 알다시피 이것은 폭발력이 아주 강할 수 있습니다. 자, 아, 초석으로 더 많은 실험을 함으로써 중국인들은 결국 폭탄은 물론 충돌 시 폭발할 수 있는 특별한 화살을 개발했습니다. 약 12세기경, 중국인들은 금속으로 감싼 수류탄도 발명하게 되었습니다.

Listening Skills

1 They did this sometime during the <u>ninth</u> century.
2 The oldest gun ever found dates back to <u>1288</u>.
3 The recipe was <u>48.4</u>% saltpeter, <u>25.6</u>% sulfur, and <u>21</u>% other nonessential ingredients.

• Exercise 4 • p.131

정답 Q1 ⓒ   Q2 ⓑ
스크립트 ∩ 08-09

W Professor: He could just about do it all. I'm <u>talking about the one and only</u> Leonardo da Vinci. He was <u>a painter</u>, sculptor, musician, <u>writer</u>, scientist, <u>and many other things</u>. What I'd like <u>to focus on</u> today, though, is Leonardo <u>the inventor</u>.

He was <u>way ahead of his time</u>. He was <u>fascinated with flight</u>. Yes, flight. He studied the flight of birds, and he <u>incorporated</u> that <u>into a number of designs for various flying machines</u>. He even designed a helicopter as well as a hang glider.

Now, some of his designs <u>were practical</u> while <u>others were not so great</u>. By the way, Leonardo lived in the 1500s. So <u>keep that in mind</u>, please. Leonardo was also <u>a bridge designer</u>. In 1502, he <u>came up with a design</u> for a bridge <u>more than 720 feet long</u> for the Ottomans. However, the Ottomans <u>didn't accept his design</u>. They thought his bridge was <u>too fanciful</u>. They considered <u>it impossible to make</u>. However, he did <u>have other designs</u> that were able to <u>get off the drawing board</u>.

해석

W Professor: 그는 거의 모든 것을 할 수 있었습니다. 유일무이한 레오나르도 다 빈치에 대해 말하고 있는 것입니다. 그는 화가이자 조각가였고, 음악가이자 작가, 과학자인 동시에 많이 다른 일들에도 뛰어났습니다. 하지만 제가 오늘 주목하고 싶은 것은 발명가 레오나르도입니다.

그는 시대를 크게 앞선 인물이었습니다. 그는 비행에 매료되어 있었죠. 네, 비행이요. 그는 새들의 비행을 연구해서, 다양한 비행 기계들을 다수 설계하는 데 이를 접목했습니다. 그는 심지어 행글라이더는 물론 헬리콥터도 설계했죠.

자, 그의 설계 중 일부는 실용적이었던 반면에 그렇게 대단하지 않은 것들도 있었습니다. 어쨌든 레오나르도는 1500년대에 살았잖아요. 그러니까 이 점을 명심해 주세요. 레오나르도는 또한 교량 설계자였습니다. 1502년, 그는 오스만 제국을 위해 720피트가 넘는 길이의 교량의 설계를 생각해 냈습니다. 하지만 오스만 제국은 그의 설계를 받아들이지 않았어요. 그의 교량이 너무 비현실적이라고 생각했죠. 그것을 만들기가 불가능하다고 여겼습니다. 하지만 그는 정말로 실행 가능한 다른 설계들도 가지고 있었습니다.

Listening Skills

1 Leonardo lived in the <u>1500s</u>.
2 In <u>1502</u>, he came up with a design for a bridge more than <u>720</u> feet long.

• Exercise 5 • p.132

정답 Q1 ⓒ   Q2 ⓐ
스크립트 ∩ 08-11

W Professor: Okay. Let's get started. I'd like you to <u>follow my lecture by looking at</u> your textbooks today. Please turn to page ninety-six and look at the top of the page. You'll notice that two men <u>were</u> primarily <u>responsible for the invention of the telephone</u>.

Yes, I know that <u>most of you learned that</u> Alexander Graham Bell <u>invented it</u>. <u>His first telephone patent was given</u> in 1876. Its patent number is 174,465. However, you all are certainly <u>familiar with</u> Thomas Edison. We know him for <u>inventing the light bulb</u>, but he did <u>much more than that</u>. He also <u>held some important patents</u> concerning telephone technology. In 1877, Edison was <u>granted a patent for the invention</u> of the carbon microphone, <u>a crucial component in all telephones</u> until the 1980s. It was U.S. patent number 474,230. Please make note of that.

Now, <u>another important date</u> for you <u>to remember</u> is March 10, 1876. And yes, I do expect you to remember <u>any dates that I mention</u>. Anyway, this was the day that <u>the first successful transmission</u> of speech by telephone <u>was recorded</u>. It was <u>between Bell and his assistant</u>, a man named Watson.

해석

W Professor: 좋아요. 시작해 봅시다. 오늘은 여러분들이 교재를 보면서 제 강의를 따라오면 좋을 것 같군요. 96쪽을 펴고 그 페이지의 맨 위쪽을 봐주세요. 전화의 발명에 크게 기여했던 두 사람이 보일 겁니다.

네, 여러분 대부분이 알렉산더 그레이엄 벨이 전화를 발명했다고 배운 것으로 알고 있어요. 그의 첫 번째 전화기는 1876년에 특허를 받았습니다. 특허 번호는 174,465이고요. 하지만 여러분 모두는 분명 토머스 에디슨도 잘 알고 있죠. 우리는 그를 전구를 발명한 사람으로 알고 있지만, 그는 그보다 훨씬 더 많은 일을 했습니다. 에디슨 또한 전화 기술과 관련된 몇 가지 중요한 특허들을 보유했어요. 1877년에 에디슨은 1980년대까지 모든 전화기에 들어 있던 중요한 부품인 탄소 마이크로폰을 발명하여 특허를 획득했습니다. 미국 특허 번호는 474,230이었죠. 이것을 필기해 두세요.

자, 여러분이 기억해야 할 또 다른 중요한 날짜는 1876년 3월 10일입니다. 그리고 맞아요, 제가 말하는 모든 날짜를 기억하기를 바랍니다. 어쨌거나 이 날은 전화를 이용해 최초로 음성 전송에 성공한 날로 기록되었습니다. 벨과, 왓슨이라는 이름의 그의 조수 사이의 통화였죠.

Listening Skills

1 Its patent number is <u>174,465</u>.
2 In <u>1877</u>, Edison was granted a patent for the invention of the carbon microphone.

3 It was U.S. patent number 474,230.

• Exercise 6 • p.133

정답 Q1 Ⓐ Q2 Ⓒ

스크립트 🎧 08-13

M Professor: Let me make something clear. The Wright brothers, Orville and Wilbur Wright, were not the first to build and fly an early type of aircraft. What they did do, however, was make the first controlled, engine-powered continuous flight. Sure, other inventors had built aircraft, but they did not fly successfully. Basically, these inventors couldn't control their flying machines. The big moment happened at Kitty Hawk, North Carolina, on December 17, 1903. The name of the plane was the *Wright Flyer I*, and it had a wingspan of forty feet. The engine weighed 170 pounds and had twelve horsepower. The total weight of the plane was 625 pounds.

The first true flight was achieved by Orville, who covered about 120 feet in twelve seconds. The Wrights made two more flights after that. The longest covered about 200 feet, and their average altitude was about ten feet. But these first three flights were just test runs. The last flight of the day was the most important one. Wilbur flew the plane 852 feet down the sand dunes. With that, powered flight had been achieved.

해석

M Professor: 분명히 해 둘 게 있습니다. 바로 라이트 형제 즉, 오빌 라이트와 윌버 라이트는 초기 형태의 항공기를 만들어 날아 오른 최초의 인물들은 아니었습니다. 하지만 그들이 해낸 것은 최초로 조종이 가능하며, 엔진의 힘으로 작동되는 비행기로 지속적인 비행을 했다는 점입니다. 물론, 다른 발명가들도 항공기를 만들었지만, 그들은 비행에 성공하지 못했습니다. 기본적으로 이 발명가들은 자신들이 만든 비행 기계들을 조종하지 못했습니다.

그 위대한 순간은 1903년 12월 17일, 노스캐롤라이나주 키티호크에서 일어났습니다. 그 비행기의 이름은 *라이트 플라이어 1*호였고, 그것은 40피트의 날개폭을 가지고 있었습니다. 엔진의 무게는 170파운드였으며 12마력을 지녔습니다. 비행기의 전체 무게는 625파운드였습니다.

최초의 진짜 비행은 오빌에 의해 이루어졌는데, 그는 약 120피트 정도를 12초 동안 이동했습니다. 라이트 형제는 그 이후 2번 더 비행했습니다. 가장 긴 비행의 경우 약 200피트를 이동했으며 평균 고도는 약 10피트였습니다. 그러나 처음의 이 3번의 비행은 그저 시험 비행이었을 뿐입니다. 그날의 마지막 비행이 가장 중요한 것이었습니다. 윌버는 모래언덕 아래로 852피트를 비행기로 날아 내려갔습니다. 그로써, 동력 비행이 성공을 거두었습니다.

Listening Skills

1 The engine weighed 170 pounds and had twelve horsepower.
2 The total weight of the plane was 625 pounds.
3 Wilbur flew the plane 852 feet down the sand dunes.

• Exercise 7 • p.134

정답 Q1 Ⓑ Q2 Ⓓ

스크립트 🎧 08-15

M Professor: I want to talk about Coca-Cola, the fizzy cola drink found in virtually every corner of the world. It all started in Georgia in the southern United States by a man by the name of John Pemberton. He came up with the recipe for Coke in 1885 or 1886.

The first sales were in, believe it or not, a pharmacy in 1886. A glass of Coke sold for five cents. At that time, soda fountains were popular in the U.S., and there were often soda fountains located in pharmacies. Back then, people believed carbonated beverages were healthy, and Pemberton looked to take advantage of this.

He claimed that Coca-Cola was pretty much a wonder drug. He advertised it as a cure for problems such as addictions and headaches. Anyway, the first bottled Coke came out in March of 1894, and it was put in cans much later in 1955. Today, of course, the company is enormous. It has more than 79,000 employees, and its global revenues amounted to more than thirty-eight billion dollars in 2021. Staggering, isn't it?

해석

M Professor: 저는 사실상 세계 구석구석 어디에서나 발견되는 탄산수 콜라 음료인 코카콜라에 대해 이야기하고 싶습니다. 그 모든 것이 존 펨버턴이라는 이름의 한 사람에 의해 미국 남부에 있는 조지아주에서 시작되었습니다. 그는 1885년 내지 1886년에 콜라의 제조법을 생각해 냈습니다.

첫 판매는, 믿기 힘들겠지만, 1886년에 한 약국에서 이루어졌습니다. 콜라 한 잔이 5센트에 팔렸습니다. 그 당시에 소다수 판매점이 미국에서 인기 있었고, 소다수 판매점들은 종종 약국 안에 위치해 있었습니다. 그때 당시에는 사람들이 탄산음료가 몸에 좋다고 믿었고, 펨버턴은 이것으로 이득을 얻길 기대했죠. 그는 코카콜라가 거의 신비의 약과 다름 없다고 주장했습니다. 그는 그것을 중독과 두통과 같은 질병에 대한 치료제라고 광고했죠. 어쨌든, 최초의 병 콜라는 1894년 3월에 출시되었고, 그보다 훨씬 뒤인 1955년에 캔에 담겼습니다. 오늘날, 물론 그 회사는 거대합니다. 7만 9천 명 이상의 직원들이 있으며 2021년 기준 전 세계 수입은 380억 달러 이상에 육박했습니다. 정말 엄청나지 않나요?

Listening Skills

1 He came up with the recipe for Coke in 1885 or 1886.
2 The first bottled Coke came out in March of 1894, and it was put in cans much later in 1955.
3 Its global revenues amounted to more than thirty-eight billion dollars in 2021.

• Exercise 8 • p.135

정답 Q1 Ⓓ Q2 Ⓑ

스크립트 🎧 08-17

W Professor: Let's talk about a small yet incredibly important invention. It's the nail. Yes, that's right. The nail. I'm talking about that thing you use to connect two pieces of wood to each other. Who invented the nail? Most experts agree that the Romans did that more than 2,000 years ago. The Romans were outstanding builders, so it should come as no surprise that they

Answer Key 39

made the first nails. You're probably wondering how people made buildings with wood in the past, aren't you? It's simple. They cut boards so that they interlocked with one another. Using nails was a much faster and easier way.

For centuries, people made nails by hand. Basically, a blacksmith had to heat up a piece of iron. Then, he hammered it until he created a single nail. Again, that was a very long and difficult process. Fortunately, in the 1790s, nail-making machines were invented. These were able to mass-produce large numbers of nails. Another improvement was making nails from steel rather than iron. This started in the mid-1800s and continued throughout the early 1900s.

해석

W Professor: 크기는 작지만 정말 중요한 발명품에 대해 이야기해 보죠. 바로 못입니다. 네, 맞아요. 못이요. 두 개의 나무 조각을 서로 연결할 때 사용하는 물건에 대해 말하는 것입니다. 누가 못을 발명했을까요? 대부분의 전문가들은 2,000년도 더 전에 로마인들이 못을 발명했다는 데 동의하고 있습니다. 로마인들은 뛰어난 건축가들이었기 때문에 그들이 최초의 못을 만들었다는 점은 그리 놀라운 일이 아닐 것입니다. 아마도 여러분들은 과거에 어떻게 나무로 건물을 지었는지 궁금할 수도 있겠군요, 그렇지 않나요? 간단해요. 판재를 잘라서 서로 이어 붙였습니다. 못을 사용하는 것은 훨씬 더 빠르고 더 쉬운 방법이었죠.

수 세기 동안 사람들은 손으로 못을 만들었습니다. 기본적으로, 대장장이가 쇳조각에 열을 가해야 했어요. 그런 다음에는 하나의 못이 만들어질 때까지 망치질을 했죠. 다시 말해, 그것은 매우 오래 걸리고 어려운 과정이었습니다. 다행히 1790년대에 못을 생산하는 기계가 발명되었습니다. 이 덕분에 많은 수의 못을 대량 생산할 수 있었죠. 또 다른 발전은 철이 아니라 강철로 못을 만들게 된 것이었습니다. 이는 1800년대 중반에 시작되어 1900년대 초까지 계속되었습니다.

Listening Skills

1 Most experts agree that the Romans did that more than 2,000 years ago.
2 Fortunately, in the 1790s, nail-making machines were invented.
3 This started in the mid-1800s and continued throughout the early 1900s.

Vocabulary Review p.136

A 1 invention
   2 craft
   3 sailors
   4 Gunpowder
   5 interlock

B 1 Ⓐ 2 Ⓑ 3 Ⓒ 4 Ⓐ 5 Ⓒ
C 1 Ⓒ 2 Ⓑ 3 Ⓐ 4 Ⓓ 5 Ⓐ
D 1 pinpoint
   2 patent
   3 magnetic
   4 direction
   5 wingspan

Practice Test p.138

1 Ⓒ 2 Ⓐ 3 Ⓒ 4 Ⓑ

스크립트 🎧 08-19

M Professor: All around the world, people use concrete for construction. What is concrete? It's a combination of cement, small stones, sand, and water. When it dries, it creates something very hard and long lasting. Ah, cement, by the way, is basically a mixture of clay and limestone.

So who invented concrete? More than 2,000 years ago, the Romans used concrete. They constructed the Colosseum with it. Most of their famous structures were made of concrete. Many are still standing today. Roman concrete was incredibly long lasting. But the Romans didn't invent it. The Egyptians used a type of concrete as far back as 3000 B.C. In fact, it's believed that they used concrete when they made some of their pyramids. Yet the Egyptians didn't invent concrete either. Right now, many experts say that Göbekli Tepe might be where concrete was invented.

Göbekli Tepe is believed to be the first permanent human settlement ever made. It's located in modern-day Turkey. It was built around 9500 B.C. The people there used terrazzo, which is a primitive type of concrete. Of course, the Egyptians, the Romans, and other people improved upon this invention over the years. But it looks like people have been working with concrete for more than 10,000 years now. Isn't that amazing?

해석

M Professor: 전 세계적으로, 사람들은 건설 작업에 콘크리트를 사용합니다. 콘크리트란 무엇일까요? 바로 시멘트, 자갈, 모래, 그리고 물의 조합입니다. 마르면 매우 단단하고 오래 지속되는 것을 만들어냅니다. 아, 그건 그렇고 시멘트는 기본적으로 진흙과 석회석의 혼합물입니다.

그러면 누가 콘크리트를 발명했을까요? 2,000년도 더 전에, 로마인들은 콘크리트를 사용했습니다. 그들은 콘크리트를 사용해서 콜로세움을 건설했습니다. 로마의 유명한 구조물 중 대부분이 콘크리트로 만들어졌어요. 많은 것들이 오늘날에도 여전히 남아 있습니다. 로마의 콘크리트는 놀라울 정도로 오래 지속되었습니다. 하지만 로마인들이 콘크리트를 발명한 것은 아니었습니다. 기원전 3000년으로 거슬러 올라가면 이집트인들이 일종의 콘크리트를 사용했습니다. 실제로 어떤 피라미드를 만들 때는 그들이 콘크리트를 사용했다고 여겨지고 있죠. 하지만 이집트인들 역시 콘크리트를 발명하지는 않았습니다. 현재 많은 전문가들은 콘크리트가 발명된 곳이 괴베클리 테페일지도 모른다고 말합니다.

괴베클리 테페는 인류 최초의 영구적인 정착이 이루어진 곳이라고 여겨집니다. 그곳은 현재의 튀르키예에 위치해 있죠. 그곳은 기원전 9500년 무렵에 건설되었습니다. 그곳 사람들은 원시적인 형태의 콘크리트인 테라초를 사용했습니다. 물론 이집트인들과 로마인들은 물론 다른 사람들이 오랜 시간에 걸쳐 이 발명품을 개선시켰습니다. 하지만 사람들은 이제 10,000년 이상의 시간 동안 콘크리트로 작업을 해 온 것 같습니다. 놀랍지 않나요?

Actual Test

Actual Test 1
p.142

1 Ⓓ   2 Ⓒ   3 Ⓑ   4 Ⓑ   5 Ⓑ   6 Ⓐ   7 Ⓐ
8 Ⓓ   9 Ⓑ

스크립트 09-01

W Student: Professor Morris, could I have a quick word with you? You don't have class now, do you?
M Professor: Hello, Amy. Sure, I can talk to you for a bit. What's going on?
W: I'm curious about the homework you assigned yesterday.
M: What about it?
W: Well . . . I don't know exactly what to do. I mean, uh, you said we should write a paper. But, um, a paper about what?
M: The easiest thing to do is to choose a topic we have covered in class. Then, write about it.
W: So you mean I should just write about, er . . . one of the Roman emperors we have covered? I just need to write about his life?
M: No, not exactly.
W: Then what should I do?
M: Your paper should have a theme. You know, decide what exactly you're going to write about and give your opinion on it.
W: Oh, I see.
M: Make sure your introduction has a thesis statement. That means you explain what your opinion is.
W: Ah, sure. I remember doing that in high school.
M: Great. Is there anything else?
W: One more thing. How much research do I need to do?
M: It's a five-page paper, so you don't need to do much. But you should still check out a book or two from the library once you determine your topic.
W: Okay. I guess I'll head there right now since I have some free time. Thanks.
M: Good luck. Come back here if you have any more questions.

해석

W Student: 모리스 교수님, 잠깐 저와 이야기하실 수 있나요? 지금은 수업이 없으시죠, 그렇죠?
M Professor: 반가워요, 에이미. 물론이죠. 잠깐 이야기를 할 수 있어요. 무슨 일인가요?
W: 어제 내 주신 과제에 대해 궁금한 점이 있어요.
M: 어떤 점이죠?
W: 음… 제가 정확히 무엇을 해야 하는지 모르겠어요. 제 말은, 어, 저희가 논문을 써야 한다고 말씀하셨잖아요. 그런데, 음, 무엇에 관한 논문이죠?
M: 가장 쉽게 할 수 있는 것은 우리가 수업에서 다룬 주제를 하나 고르는 거예요. 그런 다음 그에 대한 글을 쓰세요.
W: 그러면 제가 그냥 어… 우리가 다루었던 로마의 황제 중 한 명에 대해 쓰면 된다는 말씀이신가요? 그냥 그의 생애에 대해 쓰면 될까요?
M: 아니요, 정확히는 아니에요.
W: 그러면 어떻게 하는 게 좋을까요?
M: 논문에는 주제가 있어야 해요. 알겠지만, 정확히 무엇에 관해 쓸 것인지 정하고 그에 대한 자신의 의견을 넣으세요.
W: 아, 알겠어요.
M: 서론에 주제문을 꼭 넣도록 하세요. 그것은 자네의 의견이 무엇인지 자네가 설명한다는 걸 의미해요.
W: 아, 그렇게요. 고등학교 때 그렇게 했던 것이 기억나네요.
M: 좋네요. 다른 것이 또 있나요?
W: 한 가지 더 있어요. 제가 조사를 얼마나 많이 해야 하나요?
M: 5쪽 분량의 논문이기 때문에 많이 할 필요는 없어요. 하지만 그렇더라도 일단 주제를 정하면 도서관에서 한두 권의 책은 살펴 보는 게 좋아요.
W: 알겠습니다. 남는 시간이 좀 있으니 지금 바로 도서관에 가야겠어요. 감사합니다.
M: 행운을 빌어요. 질문이 조금이라도 더 생기면 다시 오도록 해요.

스크립트 09-02

M Professor: The Himalaya Mountains are located in Asia in parts of India, Pakistan, China, Bhutan, Tibet, and Nepal. The world's highest mountain, Mount Everest, is there. There are numerous other high peaks. In fact, more than 100 mountains in the Himalayas are higher than 7,200 meters above sea level.
The environment in the Himalayas is one of the harshest in the world. The mountains rise high above the ground. There are steep cliffs that can drop a thousand meters or more into deep valleys. Sudden snowstorms with powerful winds come at any time. Avalanches speed down slopes as well and bury anything within their paths.
In addition, climbing many mountains in the Himalayas can be a difficult task. For instance, each year, a large number of people attempt to climb Mount Everest. Base Camp on the mountain is about 5,300 meters above sea level. There, the oxygen level is approximately half of what it is at sea level. That can make people light headed. As they climb higher, the amount of oxygen in the air continues to decline. Climbers need to use bottled oxygen just to breathe. Most cannot finish the climb because they become too weak.
Sudden gusts of wind can push people off the mountain. Each year, climbers die. Their bodies remain on the mountain, forever frozen in snow and ice. Okay, uh, let's take a short break now. When we come back, we'll watch a video about climbing Mount Everest.

해석

M Professor: 히말라야 산맥은 아시아의 인도, 파키스탄, 중국, 부탄, 티베트, 그리고 네팔의 일부 지역에 위치해 있습니다. 세계에서 가장 높은 산인 에베레스트산이 이곳에 있죠. 다른 높은 산봉우리들도 많이 있습니다. 실제로 히말라야 산맥에 있는 100개 이상의 산들이 높이가 해발 7,200미터 이상입니다.
히말라야 산맥의 환경은 세계에서 가장 혹독한 곳 중 하나입니다. 산들은 땅 위로 높이 솟아 있습니다. 천 미터 이상 깊은 계곡으로 떨어질 수 있는 가파른 절벽들이 있죠. 강력한 바람을 동반한 갑작스러운 눈보라가 아무 때나 불어옵니다. 또한 눈사태가 일어나 경사면을 빠르게 내려가면서 가는 길목에 있는 모든 것을 묻어 버립니다.
게다가 히말라야 산맥의 여러 산을 오르는 것은 위험한 일일 수 있습니다. 예를 들어 매년 많은 수의 사람들이 에베레스트산 등반을 시도합니다. 그 산의 베이스캠프는 해발 약 5,300미터 정도에 있어요. 그곳의 산소량은 해수면 산소량의 절반 정도입니다. 그 때문에 사람들은 약간의 어지럼증을 느낄 수 있습니다. 더 높이 올라갈수록 공기 중의 산소량이 계속해서 감소합니다. 등반가들은 단지 호흡하기 위해 산소통을 사용해야 하죠. 대부분은 몸이 너무 약해져서 등반을 마치지 못합니다.

갑작스러운 돌풍 때문에 사람들이 산에서 떨어질 수도 있습니다. 매년 등반가들이 목숨을 잃고 있죠. 그들의 시신은 눈과 얼음 속에 영원히 얼어붙은 채 산에 남겨집니다. 좋아요, 아, 이제 잠깐 쉬도록 하죠. 돌아오면, 에베레스트산 등반에 관한 동영상을 한 편 볼 거예요.

Actual Test 2   p.146

1 Ⓑ   2 Ⓒ   3 Ⓓ   4 Ⓓ   5 Ⓒ   6 Ⓑ   7 Ⓓ
8 Ⓑ   9 Ⓐ

스크립트 🎧 09-03

M Student: Good morning. Could you tell me how many books I have checked out?

W Librarian: Sure. May I have your student ID card, please? I need to see it.

M: Of course. Uh . . . Here you are.

W: Thank you. Okay . . . Brian Robinson . . . It looks like you have six books checked out.

M: Six? Hmm . . . I thought I only had five.

W: Here. Take a look at the screen. You can see all of the titles.

M: Thanks. Ah, the book by Matthias Dunston. I had forgotten about it. I need to bring it back soon.

W: According to this, all six books are due tomorrow. If you don't renew them by then, you'll have to pay a fine. It's twenty-five cents a day for each overdue book.

M: I definitely don't want that to happen.

W: Shall I renew them for you now?

M: You don't need me to bring the books in?

W: Not at all. I can do it from here.

M: Great. Please go ahead and renew them.

W: All right . . . Your books are now due on December 14. Please remember that date since it isn't stamped in the back of the books.

M: I will. Thanks. Oh, since I'm here, can I check this book out, please?

W: Sorry, but that's a reference book.

M: Right. I got it from the reference section right over there. This book is invaluable for the work I'm doing for my economics class.

W: Sure, but books in the reference section are not permitted to be checked out from the library. You can only use them inside the library.

M: So I should just make copies of the pages I need?

W: Sure. Or you could take pictures of them with your phone. That would also work.

해석

M Student: 안녕하세요. 제가 책을 몇 권 대출했는지 알려주실 수 있나요?

W Librarian: 물론이죠. 학생증을 보여주시겠어요? 확인을 해야 해서요.

M: 그럼요. 어… 여기 있어요.

W: 고마워요. 좋아요… 브라이언 로빈슨… 6권을 대출한 것으로 보이는군요.

M: 6권이요? 흠… 5권만 대출했다고 생각했는데요.

W: 여기요. 화면을 보세요. 책 제목들이 모두 보이죠.

M: 고맙습니다. 아, 마티아스 던스턴의 책이군요. 그것에 대해서는 잊고 있었어요. 곧 반납해야겠네요.

W: 여기를 보시면 6권 전부 반납일이 내일이에요. 그때까지 대출 연장을 신청하지 않으면 연체료를 내야 해요. 연체료는 기한이 넘은 각 권당 하루에 25센트예요.

M: 그런 일이 생기는 건 정말 바라지 않아요.

W: 지금 연장을 해드릴까요?

M: 제가 책을 가지고 오지 않아도 되는 건가요?

W: 전혀요. 여기에서 그렇게 해드릴 수 있어요.

M: 좋아요. 어서 연장해 주세요.

W: 알겠어요… 이 책들은 이제 반납일이 12월 14일이에요. 책 뒤에 도장이 찍혀 있지 않기 때문에 그 날짜를 기억해두세요.

M: 그럴게요. 고맙습니다. 아, 여기에 온 김에 이 책을 대출할 수 있을까요?

W: 미안하지만 그건 참고 도서예요.

M: 맞아요. 바로 저쪽에 있는 참고 도서 구역에서 가지고 왔어요. 이 책은 경제학 수업에서 제가 하고 있는 공부에 매우 중요해요.

W: 그렇군요. 하지만 참고 도서 구역의 책들은 도서관 밖으로 대출이 허용되지 않아요. 도서관 안에서만 이용할 수 있어요.

M: 그러면 제가 필요한 페이지를 그냥 복사해야겠네요?

W: 그렇죠. 아니면 전화기로 사진을 찍어도 돼요. 그것도 가능합니다.

스크립트 🎧 09-04

W Professor: We all know about cave paintings in Europe. We studied them in our last class. They're really quite impressive. But you should know that there are cave paintings in other places, too. In fact, you can find cave paintings all around the world. Right now, I'd like to talk about Mayan cave paintings.

The Maya lived in rainforests in Central America. They had an advanced culture, but they died out before Columbus arrived in the Americas. They left lots of temples and other buildings in the jungle. They also left some amazing cave art.

Recently, some new cave art was discovered in the Yucatan. Here's a picture of some of the art . . . Notice the different figures . . . You can see some handprints here . . . There are also some birds . . . as well as some mammals . . . Here is a warrior . . . And check out these geometric figures . . .

As you can see, the Mayas created a wide variety of paintings. Many of the paintings are similar to those in Europe that we studied. Of course, the styles are different. The colors are different, too. And like cave art in Europe, Mayan cave art is in danger. People often loot caves containing Mayan treasure. They don't care about preserving cave art. So archaeologists are doing their best to find Mayan cave art before it gets ruined. Let's check out some art from another cave now.

해석

W Professor: 우리 모두 유럽의 동굴 벽화에 대해 알고 있습니다. 우리는 지

난 수업에서 그것에 대해 공부했죠. 그것들은 정말이지 꽤 인상적입니다. 하지만 다른 곳에도 동굴 벽화가 존재한다는 점을 아셔야 해요. 실제로 전 세계 각지에서 동굴 벽화를 찾아볼 수 있습니다. 지금은 마야의 동굴 벽화에 대해 이야기할까 합니다.

마야인들은 중앙아메리카의 우림 지대에서 살았습니다. 그들은 발전된 문화를 가지고 있었지만, 콜럼버스가 아메리카 대륙에 도착하기 전에 사라졌어요. 그들은 정글에 많은 사원과 기타 건축물들을 남겨 놓았습니다. 또한 몇몇 놀라운 동굴 벽화들도 남겼죠.

최근에 유카탄 지역에서 새로운 동굴 벽화 몇 점이 발견되었습니다. 몇몇 벽화의 사진을 보여드리면… 다양한 형태에 주목하시고…여기에서 손자국을 보실 수 있습니다… 또한 새들도 몇 마리 있고… 포유 동물들도 좀 있죠… 여기에 전사가 있고… 그리고 이 기하학적인 도형들을 살펴 보세요…

보다시피 마야인들은 정말 다양한 그림들을 그렸습니다. 많은 그림들이 우리가 공부한 유럽의 그림들과 유사해요. 물론 화풍은 서로 다릅니다. 색상 역시 다르고요. 그리고 유럽의 동굴 벽화와 마찬가지로 마야의 동굴 벽화는 위험에 처해 있어요. 사람들이 종종 마야의 보물이 있는 동굴들을 약탈합니다. 그들은 동굴 벽화를 보존하는 일에 관심이 없습니다. 그래서 고고학자들은 그것이 훼손되기 전에 마야의 동굴 벽화를 찾아내려고 최선을 다하고 있습니다. 이제 또 다른 몇 가지 동굴 벽화에 대해 살펴 보도록 할게요.

Actual Test 3

p.150

1 ⓒ 2 Ⓐ 3 Ⓓ 4 Ⓑ 5 Ⓓ 6 Ⓓ 7 Ⓑ
8 Carl von Linde: ①, ②, ④ Fred Wolf: ③ 9 Ⓑ

스크립트 🎧 09-05

M Professor: Good afternoon. Can I help you with something?
W Student: Yes, Professor Stabler. My name is Erika Jackson, and I'm in your biology class.
M: Which one?
W: The one that just finished a few minutes ago.
M: Ah, yes. I remember seeing you in class. Sorry, but I'm teaching three classes this semester. It's a bit hard to remember everyone.
W: Sure. I understand.
M: So what can I do for you today, Erika?
W: In today's class, you mentioned the possibility of doing an assignment for extra credit.
M: That's right.
W: Could you tell me what I can do? I'm a bit concerned about my grade, so I'd like to get a few extra points.
M: What was your grade on the midterm?
W: I got a ninety-five.
M: That's pretty good. You probably don't need to do any extra-credit work.
W: Well, I want to make sure I get an A in the class. I also enjoy learning, so this will be an opportunity to learn a bit more about biology.
M: Good attitude. I like that. Okay. Here's what you need to do.
W: Yes?
M: Go to the reserved materials section in the library. Ask to see the folder for Biology 62. Inside the folder, you will find a list of possible topics that you can research.
W: All right. Do I need to do a lab?
M: No, you don't. But you need to do a good amount of research on a topic and then write an eight-page paper.
W: That sounds fine to me. By when do you need it?
M: Make sure I have it before the last class of the semester. I won't accept any papers after the last class finishes.
W: No problem at all. Thank you for your time, sir.

해석

M Professor: 좋은 오후예요. 무슨 일을 도와줄까요?
W Student: 네, 스테이블러 교수님. 제 이름은 에리카 잭슨이고, 교수님의 생물학 수업을 듣고 있어요.
M: 어떤 수업이죠?
W: 몇 분 전에 방금 끝난 수업이요.
M: 아, 그렇군요. 수업에서 자네를 본 기억이 나요. 미안하지만 이번 학기에 세 개의 수업을 강의하고 있어요. 모두를 기억하는 일이 좀 어렵네요.
W: 그럼요. 이해합니다.
M: 그러면 내가 무엇을 오늘 도와주면 될까요, 에리카?
W: 오늘 수업에서 추가 점수를 위한 과제를 할 가능성이 있다고 말씀하셨잖아요.
M: 맞아요.
W: 제가 무엇을 하면 되는지 알려주실 수 있나요? 제 성적이 좀 걱정되어서 약간의 추가 점수를 받고 싶어요.
M: 중간고사 성적이 어땠나요?
W: 95점을 받았어요.
M: 상당히 높군요. 추가 점수 과제를 전혀 할 필요가 없을 것 같아요.
W: 음, 저는 그 수업에서 꼭 A를 받고 싶어요. 공부하는 것도 좋아해서, 이번이 생물학에 관해 좀 더 많이 배울 수 있는 기회가 될 거예요.
M: 자세가 좋군요. 마음에 들어요. 알겠어요. 자네가 해야 할 일을 알려주죠.
W: 네?
M: 도서관의 예비 자료 구역에 가세요. 생물학 62의 폴더를 요청해서 보세요. 폴더 안에서 자네가 조사할 수 있는 가능한 주제들의 목록을 찾을 수 있을 거예요.
W: 알겠습니다. 실험을 해야 하나요?
M: 아니, 그렇지 않아요. 하지만 주제에 대해 상당히 많은 양의 조사를 한 후에 8쪽 분량의 논문을 써야 해요.
W: 저에게는 괜찮을 것 같아요. 언제까지 필요하신가요?
M: 학기 마지막 수업 전까지는 내가 그것을 받도록 해주세요. 마지막 수업이 끝난 후에는 어떤 논문도 받지 않을 거예요.
W: 전혀 문제 없습니다. 시간을 내 주셔서 감사합니다, 교수님.

스크립트 🎧 09-06

M Professor: Today, almost every home has a refrigerator. I bet most of you have a small refrigerator in your dorm room. We take refrigerators for granted. But people in the past didn't have access to this technology.

Centuries ago, people had to use other means to keep their food cool. In cold places, people had access to ice. They could keep food in ice. In other places, they used cold water. Some people used underground storage areas to keep food cold. Of course, these were unreliable, so it was common for food to go bad.

Then, in the 1700s, the Industrial Revolution began. People began making a number of scientific advances. Some of them were related to cooling methods. Still, there were not any refrigerators for quite a while. Then, in 1876, Carl von Linde made a scientific discovery. He learned how to liquify gases in large amounts. This led to a breakthrough in refrigeration technology. Linde is considered the inventor of modern refrigeration.

A few decades later, Fred Wolf invented the first refrigerator for home usage. In the year 1927, refrigerators started to gain popularity. Demand for them increased. Improvements were made, which made refrigerators more efficient and cheaper. Today, as you know, refrigerators are everywhere and are extremely effective at keeping food cold.

해석

M Professor: 오늘날 거의 모든 가정에는 냉장고가 있습니다. 여러분 대부분이 기숙사 방에 작은 냉장고 하나쯤은 분명 가지고 있잖아요. 우리는 냉장고를 당연한 것으로 생각합니다. 하지만 과거의 사람들은 이러한 기술을 이용할 수 없었습니다.

수 세기 전에, 사람들은 음식을 차갑게 보관하기 위해 다른 방법을 이용해야 했습니다. 추운 지역에서는 얼음을 구할 수 있었죠. 얼음 안에 음식을 보관할 수 있었던 것입니다. 다른 지역에서는 차가운 물을 이용했습니다. 어떤 사람들은 음식을 차갑게 보관하기 위해 지하의 저장 공간을 이용했죠. 물론 이러한 방법들은 미덥지 않아서, 음식이 상하는 경우가 흔했습니다.

그러다가 1700년대에 산업 혁명이 시작되었습니다. 사람들은 많은 과학적인 발전들을 이루어내기 시작했죠. 그중 일부는 냉장 방법과 관련이 있었습니다. 하지만 꽤 오랫동안 냉장고는 존재하지 않았어요. 그러다가 1876년, 카를 폰 린드에 의해 과학적인 발견이 이루어졌습니다. 그는 가스를 다량으로 액화시키는 법을 알아냈어요. 이것은 냉장 기술의 획기적인 발전으로 이어졌습니다. 린드는 현대 냉장법의 창시자로 여겨집니다.

몇십 년 뒤 프레드 울프가 최초의 가정용 냉장고를 발명했습니다. 1927년에 냉장고는 인기를 얻기 시작했어요. 이에 대한 수요가 증가했습니다. 개선이 이루어지면서 냉장고는 보다 더 효율적이고 저렴해졌습니다. 오늘날에는 여러분도 알다시피 냉장고가 어디에나 존재하며 매우 효율적으로 음식을 차갑게 보관해 줍니다.